Decolonizing Politics and Theories from the Abya Yala

EDITED BY

FERNANDO DAVID MÁRQUEZ DUARTE
& VÍCTOR ALEJANDRO ESPINOZA VALLE

EDITORIAL ASSISTANTS

RENÉE PAULINA GARCÍA BOJÓRQUEZ
& AMAIRANI TAPIA ALVAREZ

E-INTERNATIONAL RELATIONS PUBLISHING

E-International Relations
Bristol, England
2022

ISBN 978-1-910814-62-8

This book is published under a Creative Commons CC BY-NC 4.0 license. You are free to:

- **Share** – copy and redistribute the material in any medium or format.

- **Adapt** – remix, transform, and build upon the material.

Under the following terms:

- **Attribution** – You must give appropriate credit to the author(s) and publisher, provide a link to the license and indicate if changes were made. You may do so in any reasonable manner, but not in any way that suggests the licensor endorses you or your use.

- **Non-Commercial** – You may not use the material for commercial purposes.

Any of the above conditions can be waived if you get permission. Please contact info@e-ir.info for any such enquiries, including for licensing and translation requests. Other than the terms noted above, there are no restrictions placed on the use and dissemination of this book for student learning materials or scholarly use.

Production: Michael Tang
Cover Image: namchetolukla/Shutterstock

A catalogue record for this book is available from the British Library.

E-International Relations

Editor-in-Chief and Publisher: Stephen McGlinchey
Books Editor: Bill Kakenmaster
Editorial Assistance: Rohan Chopra, Adeleke Olumide Ogunnoiki, Jinze Zhang, Vaishnavi Pallapothu, Yagnesh Sharma.

E-International Relations is the world's leading International Relations website. Our daily publications feature expert articles, reviews and interviews – as well as student learning resources. The website is run by a non-profit organisation based in Bristol, England and staffed by an all-volunteer team of students and academics. In addition to our website content, E-International Relations publishes a range of books. As E-International Relations is committed to open access in the fullest sense, free electronic versions of our books, including this one, are available on our website.

Find out more at https://www.e-ir.info/

Contents

INTRODUCTION
    Aura Cumes   1

PART ONE - THEORETICAL DISCUSSIONS

1. DECOLONIALITY AND CONTEMPORARY REGIONALISM IN ALIANZA BOLIVARIANA PARA LOS PUEBLOS DE NUESTRA AMÉRICA (ALBA)
   Alina Ribeiro & Marina Scotelaro   10

2. DECOLONIZING SOUTH-SOUTH COOPERATION: AN ANALYTICAL FRAMEWORK FOUNDED ON POST-DEVELOPMENT AND THE COMMON
   Marina Bolfarine Caixeta & Maria do Carmo Reboucas dos Santos   28

3. ARMED ACTORS IN THE COLOMBIAN CONFLICT: STATE VS ARMED GROUPS
   Deisy Milena Sorzano Rodriguez & Etienne Mulume Oderhwa   50

4. DECOLONIZING ENVIRONMENTAL POLITICS: *SUMAK KAWSAY* AS A POSSIBLE MORAL FOUNDATION FOR GREEN POLICIES
   Valeria Victoria Rodríguez Morales   65

5. LATIN AMERICAN CRITICAL ECONOMIC THINKING AND THE LABOR MARKET
   Rocio Arredondo & Javier Castellon   78

6. LATIN AMERICAN ANTIPHILOSOPHIES
   Christina Soto Van der Plas   95

PART TWO - PRAXIS ANALYSIS

7. THE CRIME OF DEFENDING A RIVER: DOMINATION, RACISM, AND STRUCTURAL VIOLENCE IN GUATEMALA
   Miguel Alejandro Saquimux Contreras   108

8. DECOLONISING SOCIAL MOVEMENTS IN LATIN AMERICA: AN APPROACH OVER THE INTERNATIONALIZATION OF THE LANDLESS WORKERS MOVEMENT (MST)
   Ellen Monielle do Vale Silva & Guilherme de Lima Souza   127

9. MESSAGES FROM THE MEEK: DYNAMIC RESISTANCES AT THE EDGE OF AMAZONIAN COLONIZATION AND CAPITALISM
   Christian Ferreira Crevels   141

10. DEVELOPMENT OR BEM VIVER? THE XUKURU DO ORORUBÁ PEOPLE'S VISION OF SACRED AGRICULTURE AS A COUNTER-HEGEMONIC PROPOSAL FOR THE RELATIONSHIP BETWEEN HUMAN BEINGS AND NATURE
    Iran Neves Ordonio, Carla Ladeira Pimentel Águas
    & Marcos Moraes Valença   155

11. 'EL PUEBLO MANDA Y EL GOBIERNO OBEDECE': DECOLONISING POLITICS AND CONSTRUCTING WORLDS IN THE EVERYDAY THROUGH ZAPATISTA AUTONOMY
    Sebastián Granda Henao   172

12. CULTURAL AND ARTISTIC EXPRESSIONS OF HAITIANS ON MEXICALI, BAJA CALIFORNIA: THE ROAD TOWARD INTERCULTURALISM.
    Kenia María Ramírez Meda & Adriana Teresa Moreno-Gutiérrez 192

NOTE ON INDEXING   208

Acknowledgements

There are several people that we would like to thank that were part of this project. First of all, we would like to thank the authors that accepted to be part of this project, especially the Black and Indigenous authors that participated in this book. We consider that this book is more than just an edited collection, but rather a decolonial proposal in itself, that seeks to let academia know that western authors are not the only ones that are important, and that western academia can learn a lot from decolonial authors from the Abya Yala. We also want to thank Stephen McGlinchey and the E-International Relations editorial team for receiving this project and for being open to different perspectives about sociopolitical studies. In addition, we want to thank Renée and Amairani, our editorial assistants, who helped to put this volume together. Finally, we would like to thank all the marginalized groups in the Abya Yala, especially Indigenous and Black groups: We support your struggle. No one is free until everyone is free.

Abstract

This work brings together twelve chapters that address, from a decolonial approach, various aspects of the original history of Abya Yala. Divided into two sections, Theoretical Discussions and Praxis Analyses, they provide a general and critical view of the colonization of Indigenous Peoples that not only explains social or economic subjugation of Latin American people, but also makes it clear that colonization is ontological and epistemological. It is a way of conceiving history and memory as subjugation imposed by those who set themselves up as lords and masters of the land and of the social and cultural heritage of Latin America. Thus, colonization must be conceived as a totality. Therefore, deconstructing the hegemonic vision of history is necessary in order to recognize the ancestral rights of Indigenous communities. The decolonial vision is radical in the sense that it goes beyond the European descendants or mestizo visions from which the explanation of Latin American development was constructed. The book's contents are developed by specialists committed to a contested vision of history. This book aims to investigate the roots of hegemonic thought and provide theoretical and empirical tools to imagine other readings of Abya Yala.

About the editors

Fernando David Márquez Duarte is a Mexican decolonial activist and thinker from the Abya Yala. He has a BA in International Relations with Honorific Mention from UABC, as well as a MSc in Regional Development from El Colegio de la Frontera Norte (COLEF) with a CONACYT scholarship. He is currently enrolled in the PhD Political Science program at the University of California Riverside (UCR) with a Fulbright García Robles scholarship and the Dean's Fellowship. He has more than 5 years of teaching experience in different universities in México and the USA, and is currently teaching at UCR. He has academic articles published in indexed journals of México, Brazil, Ecuador, Russia, Germany and the UK, as well as book chapters in México and Spain. He has worked advising and supporting Indigenous groups such as the *Triquis* and *Cucapáh* Indigenous communities in Baja California, México, regarding Indigenous rights and political participation. He has also worked with the Resistance in defense of water in Baja California with a participatory action-research project. He is proficient in Spanish, English, Portuguese and Náhuatl languages.

Victor Alejandro Espinoza is a tenured professor at El Colegio de la Frontera Norte. He has also taught at UABC and Universidad Autónoma Metropolitana (UAM). He is a member of the SNI (National Researchers System). He holds a Master's and PhD in Political Science from the National Autonomous University of Mexico (UNAM) and in Political Sociology from the Complutense University of Madrid. In 2019–2020 he was a visiting professor at the Center for U.S.-Mexican Studies at the University of California at San Diego, and in 2008 he was visiting fellow at the Mexico Institute, Woodrow Wilson International Center for Scholars. He has served as the director of journals *Frontera Norte* and the *Revista Mexicana de Estudios Electorales* and is the author of ten books and the editor of ten books. He has published 5 working papers, 65 book chapters and 40 articles in academic journals. He has made TV appearances on *Novedades, Diario 29, La Crónica, El Mexicano & Zeta*. He is a contributor for El Nacional, El Financiero and Excélsior – and since its founding in July 1999, a weekly contributor to *Frontera & La Crónica*.

Contributors

Rocio Arredondo Botello has a bachelor's and master's degree in economics from the Universidad Autónoma de Baja California (UABC), she also has a PhD in economics from UABC in Co-tutelle with the University of Castilla La Mancha, Spain obtaining the distinction *cum laude* with her thesis entitled "Measuring Decent Work in Mexico". She has collaborated with several civil society organizations and has participated in research projects and currently works as a professor in the School of Social and Political Sciences at UABC.

Marina Bolfarine Caixeta is a PhD candidate in Latin-American Studies from Universidade de Brasília (UnB) and a research fellow and member of the management board of 'Articulação Sul' (Center for Studies and Articulation of South-South Cooperation). Her academic work and professional career are dedicated to South-South Cooperation through a Southern perspective. She is a member of the Brazilian International Relations Association (ABRI) and of two research groups on decolonizing the International.

Francisco Javier Castellón Najar has a Bachelor's degree in economics from the Universidad de Guadalajara (UdeG) and a Master's degree in economics from the Universidad Nacional Autónoma de México (UNAM). He also holds a PhD in economics from UABC in Co-tutelle with the Universidad Castilla La Mancha, Spain. He has collaborated in research projects at UdeG and UNAM on diverse topics such as Mexican macroeconomics, labor markets and economic growth, and has worked as a professor at universities such as Autonomous University of Baja California (UABC), National Autonomous University of Mexico (UNAM), and Universidad Autónoma de Nayarit (UAN).

Christian Crevels is a Brazilian anthropologist. He has been engaged in Indigenous causes and issues since 2010, especially regarding land and territory regulation and rights; interactions, prejudice and conflict among Indigenous Peoples and national society; and colonial, economic and social history of Indigenous Peoples and settlers of the Amazon. Up to 2017, he worked with the Madihadeni – an Indigenous group. He earned his Master's thesis at the Universidade Federal do Amazonas, where he studied the history of Indigenous People from contrasting perspectives.

Aura Cumes is an Indigenous Mayan Kaqchiquel woman from Guatemala. She has a PhD in Anthropology from CIESAS (Center for Research and Higher Studies in Social Anthropology) Mexico, a Master's in Social Sciences from FLACSO Guatemala, a degree in Social Work from the Rafael Landivar

University and is a member of the Autonomous Collective of Saberes Mayas Ixb'alamkyej Junajpu Wunaq.

Guilherme de Lima Souza has a Bachelor's degree in International Relations from Federal University of Paraíba (UFPB). He is a member of the Decentralized Cooperation Observatory (IDeF), researcher for the Institutional Programme of Scientific Initiation (PIVIC), and coordinator of the Environment and International Relations Group of Studies. Currently he's in an international mobility programme at the Instituto Politécnico de Bragança (Portugal). His research studies focus on the areas of paradiplomacy, decentralized internationalization and political ecology.

Ellen Monielle do Vale Silva is a Brazilian researcher with an emphasis on Amazonian studies, sustainable development, and ecological and food issues. She was Vice Secretary-General of Potiguar Model United Nations (POTIMUN) and was a research assistant for the Research Group and Contemporary Studies in International Relations (GPECRI). She is a writer for the news site La Proleta, a Master's student in the Public Management and International Cooperation Program at the Federal University of Paraíba, and holds a scholarship from the Research Support Foundation of the State of Paraíba (FAPESQ).

Sebastián Granda Henao is a Colombian queer migrant in Brazil. He holds a PhD in International Relations from Pontifical Catholic University of Rio de Janeiro, Brazil and a Master's degree in International Relations from the Universidade de Brasília. He is currently an independent researcher dealing with decolonial perspectives in the field of International Security, relational onto-epistemologies, and the role of sexual and gender diversity in the struggles for rights and territorial defence of Indigenous and peasants' movements in Latin America. He is a member of the Bodies, Territories and Resistance Working Group at the Latin American Council of Social Sciences (GT-CUTER, CLACSO).

Carla Ladeira Pimentel Águas is a post-doctoral research fellow (PNPD/Capes) at the Department of Scientific and Technological Policy/Institute of Geosciences, University of Campinas (DPCT/IG/Unicamp, Brazil), with a PhD in Post-Colonialisms and Global Citizenship (University of Coimbra, Portugal).

Marcos Moraes Valença is a professor, researcher and extension worker at the Federal Institute of Education, Science and Technology of Pernambuco (IFPE, Brazil), with a PhD in Post-Colonialisms and Global Citizenship (University of Coimbra, Portugal).

Adriana Teresa Moreno-Gutiérrez is a doctoral student in Government and Public Policy at the Autonomous University of Baja California. She earned a Master's of Public Administration at UABC and a Master's in Education at Universidad del Valle de México. She teaches public administration of Baja California at the Autonomous University of Baja California (UABC). Her research areas are migration, vulnerability, and public policies.

Etienne Mulume Oderhwa has a PhD in global development studies from Autonomous University of Baja California. She is specialist in the history of sociopolitical ideas.

Iran Neves Ordonio is a member of Xukuru do Ororubá ethnic group (Pesqueira, Pernambuco, Brazil) and a member of the Xukuru Indigenous Agriculture Group Ororubá Jupago Kreká. He is an agronomist with a Master's degree in Soil Sciences from the Federal Rural University of Pernambuco (UFRPE) and a religious leader of the Sacred Lands of Boa Vista and leader of the Centro de Agricultura Xukuru do Ororubá-CAXO da Boa Vista religious complex.

Kenia María Ramirez Meda is a professor at the Autonomous University of Baja California (UABC). She received her doctorate in Trans-Pacific Relations from the University of Colima. She is a member of the National System of Researchers (SNI-Conacyt, Level 1), a member of the Mexican Network for International Development Cooperation (REMECID) and a member of the Academic Network of Latin America and the Caribbean on China. She serves as vice president of PECC-Mexico for the academic sector.

Maria do Carmo Rebouças dos Santos is a professor at Universidade Federal do Sul da Bahia, Brazil. She has a PhD in Development, Society, and International Cooperation from the University of Brasilia. She is a researcher and member of the Management Board of the Center for Studies and Articulation of South-South Cooperation, Associate Researcher of the National Institute of Studies and Research of Guinea-Bissau and member of the Latin-American Studies Association (LASA). She is the author of the book *Guinea-Bissau: from colonial independence to dependence on international development cooperation* (2019).

Alina Ribeiro has a Bachelor's degree in International Relations from the Institute of Higher Education of Brasília (IESB-Brazil). She is currently a Master's student in Social Sciences at the Department of Latin American Studies at the University of Brasília (ELA-UnB), Brazil, a collaborator at the Center for International Policy Studies (CEPI – University of Buenos Aires) and a student researcher at the Research Group on Latin America (NEL/

UnB). Her main research interests include democracy, decolonial thinking, epistemologies of the South and the formation of the Bolivian plurinational state.

Valeria Victoria Rodríguez Morales graduated with academic excellence from the Bolivian Catholic University (UCB), with a BA in Philosophy and Letters. She is currently a professor at UCB university and a columnist in the cultural supplement 'La Ramona' of the newspaper *Opinion*. In 2020 she won the first prize in an essay contest organized by the delegation of the European Union in Bolivia, and in 2021 she was elected president of the Bolivian Association of Philosophy.

Miguel Alejandro Saquimux Contreras is a Guatemalan sociologist at the Universidad de San Carlos de Guatemala and holds a Master's degree in Governance and Development from the Universiteit Antwerpen. He has researched gender-based, symbolic and institutional violence.

Marina Scotelardo holds Bachelor's and PhD degrees in International Relations from the Pontifical University of Minas Gerais (PUCMG-Brazil) and a Master's in Social Policy from the Federal University of Espírito Santo (UFES-Brazil). She is currently a post-doctoral fellow in International Relations at the Federal University of Brasília (UnB-Brasil). Her research interests include international political economy, regionalism, sociology of knowledge, and postcolonialism.

Deisy Milena Sorzano Rodriguez is a PhD student in global development studies at the Autonomous University of Baja California. She holds a Master's degree in social sciences with a specialty in regional studies from the University of Baja California and has taught a range of post and undergraduate courses.

Christina Soto van der Plas received her PhD in Spanish Literature from Cornell University in 2016. She currently teaches at Santa Clara University, California. She has published several articles and essays on Latin American literature in national and international journals. Her non-fiction book, *Curaçao, costa de cemento pueblo de prisión* (FETA, 2019) won the National Prize for Young Chronicle in Mexico. She has translated three books by Alenka Zupančič into Spanish and writes pieces regularly for magazines and websites in Mexico such as *Tierra Adentro*. She is also a student of counseling psychology.

Introduction

AURA CUMES

This chapter has been translated from Spanish. You can read the original at: https://www.e-ir.info/wp-content/uploads/2022/01/Prefacio.pdf

The colonizers in the sixteenth century brought with them epistemologies of domination, imposing capitalism, patriarchy, and colonialism, which operated with similar and intertwined logics, like three harmful poisons that, when combined, turned much more lethal. The supremacy of class, sex, and race, operated as power resources to legitimize the domination of the strongest over the weakest, the rich over the poor, the urban over the rural, men over women, 'Man' over nature, Christians over the 'witches', Jews, Moors, 'heretics', then 'Blacks' and 'Indians'. In the sixteenth century, the territories that today make up Spain were places of war, persecution, death, famine, and pestilence. It is from this context that the invaders and colonizers of the territories now known as Latin America and the Caribbean surged.

The system of colonial domination has had a pretension of totality, which means that it has sought to colonize the entire life of these territories and their inhabitants. For this reason, colonization is at the same time ontological, epistemic, spiritual, political, economic, cultural, moral, etc. From a certain Marxist vision from the 1970s, recognizing the colonial oppression was an insult to the dominant left-wing ideology (Martínez, 1990), thus, coloniality was considered as an almost exclusively economic problem linked to the feudal heritage imposed by the colonizers. However, at that time and since the beginning of the colonial process, Indigenous Peoples understood it as an artifact that sought the integral destruction of their lives. Thus, when they observed the destruction of their history and their memory, with the murder of their wise men and women, the burning of their handwriting, the destruction of their temples, and the rape of their women, they rushed to leave records about their world, origin, wisdom, conflicts and how they were experiencing colonial violence. It is for this reason that we are fortunate to have writings by members of the Native Peoples, which should not be treated as museum pieces, but as places for the safeguarding of an ancient memory that still inhabits us and with which we can dialogue.

This book contains a range of chapters written by different authors from Abya Yala who each analyze colonial domination from different perspectives. It is an example that shows how coloniality has had the pretension of totality and, therefore, must be challenged via multiple pathways. Some insist on saying that colonizers never cared how the inhabitants of Indigenous Peoples thought about life and death, what languages they spoke, what deities they worshiped or how they dressed; what those pragmatic men cared about was how to find riches in the lands and bodies they invaded. But colonization ontologically reinvented the colonized when it provoked the destruction of memory via the annihilation of knowledge, and when it sought to impose identities of orphanhood and servitude. The ontological and epistemological colonization seeks to destroy those peoples of ancient pasts and leave 'masses' of 'miserable' 'Indians without past', 'demon worshipers', 'barbarians', who shouldn't rebel against the colonial servitude and looting, but rather be grateful for been rescued by 'those good Christians'. This way, the bodies whose memories have been erased would be more useful for forced labor, for those who do not remember that they were once free did not seek their freedom. For this reason, the annihilation of memory is crucial to the perpetuation of colonial domination.

Despite the fact that colonization has had an aspiration to totality, it has not been able to be total, since the dignity and permanent resistance of the enslaved Native and African Peoples has set limits to its voracity. These resistances should not present themselves as recent, or as a product that foreign individuals came to awake. On the contrary, they began when Cristobal Colón and his followers set foot in these territories. The forms of resistance were different. Some preferred death in the face of slavery, others sought strategies to confuse the colonial power while trying to live and defend life for the peoples – just as the Kaqchikeles Mayans wrote in the first decades of the colonization, in the *Memorial de Sololá* or *Crónica Xajil*:

> Then Tunatiuh [colonizer Pedro de Alvarado] came out of Xepau and began to harass us because the people would not humble themselves before him. Six months had passed in the second year of our escape from the city ... when Tunatiuh arrived there and burned it ... We did not submit to the Castilians and we were living in Holom Balam. Oh my children! (Memorial de Sololá, translation by Adrián Recinos, 1999: 105)

> On the 1st Coak day [27 March 1527] our slaughter by the Castilians began. They were fought by the people and continued to wage a prolonged war. The death harmed us again, but none of the people paid the tribute (Memorial de Sololá, translation by Adrián Recinos, 1999: 105).

Africans brought as slaves also resisted in multiple ways, such as through Quilombismo, as Maria do Carmo Reboucas dos Santos and Marina Bolfarine Caixeta show in this book. In Quilombos they protected and re-signified food, collective care, languages, knowledge, spiritualities, rebelliousness and the meaning of life. It is due to the resistance of the Native Peoples and enslaved African Peoples that today it is possible to speak of the permanence of the wisdom contained in each of their languages and ways of living.

In Latin America and the Caribbean, we cannot talk about the postcolonial, because the colonizers did not leave. They stayed and built states responding to their interests. The state is the apparatus that has allowed them to manage the accumulated wealth obtained through dispossession for more than 300 years. Furthermore, such states were configured in such a way that the perpetuation of the colonial dispossession upon a racist order would be possible. Thus, they institutionalized the colonial domination through racism rather than break with it. The independence movements of the nineteenth century, similar to what happened in the United States, allowed European colonizers and their descendants to use and possess the riches that allowed them to perpetuate the 'new' colonial and racist order.

After those independence movements, the European colonizers and their descendants throughout Latin America and the Caribbean brought in more white Europeans to whom they offered land in abundance, 'Indians of service' and tax benefits. As long as they did not feel themselves natives from these territories, because they were not, they created nationalisms based on symbols such as national anthems that later spread throughout each of the states they invented. The nineteenth century was also a time in which the mestizos emerged (a classification used to describe a person of combined European and Indigenous American ancestry). They entered local government and took on leadership positions, expanding the cruelty of the colonial racist power over the original inhabitants. Many states also attempted to hide the problem of racism by imposing ethnocide and genocidal miscegenation. This is a topic that is often not problematized in decolonial studies, when the analysis is posed as bipolar, Europe versus Latin America. An example is when the president of Mexico, Andrés Manuel López Obrador, demanded that the Pope and the King of Spain ask Mexico for forgiveness for the events committed during the 'conquest'. However, as mestizo, he does not seem to identify himself as part of the problem and therefore does not try to stop it. Countless other examples can be given here, such as the case of the Tren Maya, an intercity railway project that affects many Indigenous communities.

Colonial continuity is a global reality in all fields of life. Just as in its beginning there could be no capitalist accumulation without the enslavement of African inhabitants, genocide and the plundering of the territories of Mother Earth and the lives of the Indigenous Peoples. The current capitalist expansion continues to use racism as the basis of its accumulation, as it is clearly expressed in the chapter by Miguel Alejandro Saquimux Contreras. Indigenous Peoples' territories are invaded by mining, hydroelectricity projects and logging projects. Similarly, the forests are sought after by pharmaceutical and cosmetics industries and the villages folklorized for tourism. The Indigenous Peoples also continue their resistance processes, which is why they are the ones who often face state persecution and death. However, it is still difficult for academics, intellectuals and politicians to recognize that racism as a colonial power device legitimizes looting against the Indigenous Peoples.

The works gathered in this book problematize the colonial and suggest ways of decolonization from different fields. Valeria Victoria Rodriguez Morales discusses Sumak Kawsay, translated as Buen Vivir, as a possible moral base for green policies – criticizing the concept of development. Iran Neves Ordonio, Carla Ladeira Pimentel Águas and Marcos Moraes Valenca also address the notion of development as modern and anthropocentric as opposed to the practice and thought of Buen Vivir of the Xukuru do Ororubá People (located in Brazil) who understand agriculture as sacred. The authors argue that this is a counter-hegemonic proposition to the western relationship of the human being with nature. Thus, to understand the meaning of life for Indigenous Peoples and their relationship with Mother Earth and everything that creates life, it is vital to understand its semantic content. This content is expressed in different languages, in the relationships established between people, between communities and with everything that generates life. This would prevent similar concepts of Buen Vivir from becoming standardized, reduced to intellectual creations or kidnapped by state power and losing their complex and transformative meaning.

Christina Soto's chapter proposes an innovative topic. According to the author, the form of thought that emerges from the Latin American region, due to its political and epistemological circumstances, can be characterized as anti-philosophical nature. In my opinion, this analysis could dialogue with those who claim a Latin American philosophy, partially as a response to the denial of the existence of a philosophy of its own or one that was created in this region. A consideration from Indigenous Peoples thinkers could also be added to the problematization of the 'Latin American' generalization, since it generalizes an experience that is not common. Those who insist on claiming a Latin American thought, science or philosophy are often those thinkers subalternated by academia and by European and North American intellectuals. Even being white or mestizo, they are treated as inhabitants of the 'Third World', a space seen from eurocentrism as a consumer of their theories – a situation that to a great extent has been the case. However, Indigenous Peoples do not begin from European knowledge to create life. That is to say, by the mere fact of being Latin American, Indigenous Peoples do not necessarily agree with white or mestizo intellectuals, especially if they have a colonial, denialist or extractivist positions of indigenous knowledge.

In the region so-called Latin America, and vindicated as Abya Yala by Indigenous Peoples, there is no single way of thinking. Quite the opposite. There exists a plurality of thoughts, experiences and creations that have been, and can continue to be, denied under the umbrella of 'Latin American thought' as protected by politicians, academics and intellectuals, whose racial, gender and class privileges do not allow them to recognize their powerful positions. Thus, it exists as an immense area within which to understand the framework of colonial power, giving shape to a thought that arises in these territories, local and at the same time universal, that seeks to be decolonized.

Latin America, as a region, has been a space of contestation due to its origin, structure and colonial organization. As said before, the Latin American states were built by Europeans, their descendants and mestizos to manage the accumulation of colonial wealth and guarantee the perpetuation of dispossession against Indigenous Peoples and peasants. Deisy Sorzano and Etienne Oderhwa, explain that the armed conflicts, such as those that happened in Colombia for fifty years, show the state functioning as the machinery of powerful economic, political and military groups. As the guardian of capitalist interests against the threat of armed groups like the Fuerzas Armadas Revolucionarias Colombianas (FARC), inspired in the socialist narrative, the Colombian state was incapable of understanding other actors such as natives, Afro-descendents, peasants and women who were all involved and affected by the conflict. Far from admitting the conditions that pushed these armed and unarmed actors to get involved in the conflict, the Colombian state named and treated all as insurgents. Thus, the colonial state was sectarian, and it was an agent of the capitalist system – showing ignorance of the conflict.

The resistance and political action of the different movements and communities face the colonial problem that is nested in everything – but so often denied by academia, non-governmental organizations (NGOs) and certain international organizations that have placed its precepts as dominant. Brazil's Landless Movement is explored by Ellen Monielle do Vale Silva and Guilherme de Limo Sousa. A movement that had class solidarity and internationalism as central elements today discusses its actions focusing on the colonial as a unifying element of struggles to challenge extractivism and decomposition of peasant economies. As Christian Ferreira Crevels discusses in his chapter the colonial labels imposed on the Madihadeni People, which range between 'meek' or 'brave'. This lexicon, in addition to being animalistic, takes away their condition as complex societies that have used multiple and sinuous strategies of resistance in the midst of colonial enclosure.

The Zapatista Movement located in Chiapas, Mexico, gives us many epistemic inspirations of political practice and of autonomy – as Sebastián Granda Henao's chapter details. A large resistance and collective rebelliousness have made other societies possible, where autonomy is central, where there has been the conviction of not being subordinate to the state apparatus. To say 'the people order and the government obeys' is a principle opposite to colonial democracy. Zapatismo is one of the movements with more integrity that challenges capitalism, patriarchy and colonialism.

Alina Ribeiro and Marina Scotelaro's chapter proposes that the Bolivarian Alliance for the Peoples of Our America (ALBA) can be understood as a project against hegemonic and colonial thinking since it not only admitted the existence of the colonial problem, but also sought ways to break with it by including historically excluded perspectives. ALBA was counter-hegemonic with a clearly anti-imperialist discourse that understands the colonial as the relationship of dependency created between countries. However, it is necessary to reflect on how the different states that made up ALBA problematized the colonial within their societies. You can see here two ways of understanding the colonial – one based on the relationship between 'First World' and 'Third World' as the geopolitics of power, and the other understood as a racial order where Indigenous and Black Peoples continue to be the dispossessed subjects. How the governments of the states that make up ALBA related to Indigenous Peoples and Afro-descendants is crucial for understanding how ALBA pursued an anti-colonial and decolonial project.

María do Carmo Reboucas dos Santos and Marina Bolfarine Caixeta's chapter proposes the decolonization of South-South Cooperation (SSC) from an analytical framework based on post-development. They understand SSC as a social and political opportunity to practice cooperation in a new and more coherent way – in solidary, horizontal and collective relations based in social groups and not in states, neither in the logic of the North-South. It can even be seen as cooperation between those doing their own anti-capitalist, anti-patriarchal and anti-colonial struggles around the planet. It is essential to reflect on how solidarity is understood in the decolonization of South-South Cooperation. Many impoverished peoples are not in such a situation because they are incapable of building 'development', but rather because they have been constantly looted and exploited. Hence, cooperation with these peoples cannot be understood as charity but rather as the possibility of returning to them something that has been taken from them. Thinking about reciprocity seems to be crucial because it could work as a way for people to contain and sustain each other and hence sustain the importance of the commons.

Francisco Javier Castellón and Rocío Nirari Arredondo Botello's chapter discusses labor from the perspectives of Latin American critical thinking and decolonial theory. They expect to make a call toward the formulation of a theory to contribute to the design of policies able to attack these problems. The regions and countries that surge from colonial history carry a reality rooted in the racial division of labor that is intertwined with the social and sexual division of labor. Thus, being born 'Indigenous', 'Black' or a woman implies being forced into a form of servitude. Jobs considered prestigious – such as those conducted with intellect, with weapons or with words – were well-paid and destined for racialized individuals considered as 'superior'. On the other hand, those jobs done with manual labor were imposed on racialized individuals considered 'inferior'. The latter were unpaid or underpaid and undervalued in the colonial world. Racism steals human vitality and capacities when it violently conditions large groups to exclusively carry out a certain activity in conditions of slavery and servitude. Given this, 'thinking about informal work' in terms of backwardness, compared to industrialization, is deeply problematic. Such an approach deserves to be analyzed in greater detail as proposed by the authors.

This book has important contributions due to the studies presented and the analyses that accompany them. But it has a greater virtue, which is to generate concerns of various topics from decolonial thought of great relevance at this time for the social sciences and for the political intelligentsia that has embraced it. She, who writes this preface, does not consider herself to be part of decolonial thought, which, as can be seen in the writings, marks its beginnings in the 1990s. Undoubtedly, having been asked to write this introduction is due to the fact that there is a coincidence between my thinking and decolonial thinking, but I must emphasize that my analytical trajectory goes back to the vindication of this old problematization of the colonial, and the struggle to rebel against this system has been unstoppable. Those who did so left their mark in writings where they denounced the atrocities that they were objects 'for being Indians', 'for being natural', 'for being Black'. Others did not leave their mark in writing, but they inherited the possibility to detect this problem even though it was preached that such a problem no longer existed.

It is healthy to reflect on the racialization of knowledge consumption that is occurring in the problematization of the colonial issue. It is curious how the analysis of the colonial was, with exceptions, rejected by the social sciences for almost five centuries. Analysts of Indigenous Peoples, Afro-descendants or Blacks were often ridiculed. However, when Latin Americans from European descent or mestizos, privileged as whites in their countries, settled in the US and Europe and were treated as inferior, they opened up to an understanding of racism and the colonial problem that they once rejected or of which they were sceptical. Ironically, when they return their theories from the North to the Latin American territories, they have greater possibilities of being heard due to the fact that in racialized societies, their words achieve greater legitimacy than that of Indigenous and Black Peoples. This process reaches its most serious implications when it begins to generate a monoculture of decolonial thinking, where the multiple paths and understandings are no longer recognized.

In these lines, I have made an effort to recognize the multiple trajectories of the analysis of the colonial, thus rejecting the racialization of knowledge from the social sciences. This book constitutes a sample of pluralities that opens up a horizon of possibilities.

PART ONE

Theoretical Discussions

1

Decoloniality and Contemporary Regionalism in Alianza Bolivariana para los Pueblos de Nuestra América (ALBA)

ALINA RIBEIRO & MARINA SCOTELARO

Colonial domination, which spread globally from the 15th century onwards, was ubiquitous, reaching the most diverse spaces of human experience. The imposition of the ideal of modernity in the 'New World' limited in great measure the epistemological and practical possibilities of social liberation. In Latin America, the independence processes carried out throughout the 19th century put a formal end to the colonization exercised by European states.

However, even with the end of political colonialism, coloniality has not been exhausted and still functions as the ordering axis not only of diverse aspects of the economic, political, and social areas of societies but also of the intersubjective relations between the citizens that compose them (Quijano 2005; Mignolo 2011). Broadening this perspective, international relations is also shaped by the logic of coloniality. From this, it becomes important to understand the configuration of this coloniality and how the struggle for the inclusion of other *saberes* (worldviews) in knowledge production at the global, regional, and sub-regional levels is constituted. Due to the epistemic silencing historically imposed by Western knowledge and science, it is important to differentiate *saberes* – the set of conceptions of different historically subordinate groups, which understand reality in a more inclusive way, constantly evoking an ideal of justice (Márquez Duarte 2021) – from Western knowledge.

From the 1950s onwards, the materialization of regional integration initiatives in Latin America were referenced in the European model, whose liberal capitalist prescription resulted in even deeper levels of dependency in the international insertion of Latin American states. In the first regionalist movement that began with the Economic Commission for Latin America and the Caribbean (ECLAC) structuralist approach, states promoted integrationist initiatives with the intention of creating a protected regional market (Dos Santos 1968, Cardoso and Faletto 1979). From the late 1970s onwards, when Latin American countries implemented a set of structural adjustments in the macroeconomic field in response to the conditionalities imposed by the consolidating financial system, there was a redirection of the countries' strategies towards a regionalism focused on the liberalized global economy. It was in this political context that, in 1991, the United States formulated the Free Trade Area of the Americas (FTAA) as a strategy to expand state economic influence on the continent. This period marked the consolidation of neoliberalism in the region, presenting little growth, but still achieving some economic stability (ECLAC 1999).

In the early 2000s, Latin America experienced the so-called progressive cycle, with the rise of left-wing governments that were generally opposed to the FTAA proposal (de La Rosa 2011; Nieto Roa et al 2017). The third wave of regionalism was marked by criticism of US practices in Latin America, coupled with economic gains from the commodities boom that provided the conditions for Latin American states to obtain a greater degree of political autonomy from their traditional influence (Riggirozzi and Tussie 2012). In this context, an alternative project of regional integration was structured, based on ideals of cooperativism and solidarity that aimed, above all, at human development. The Bolivarian Alliance for the Peoples of Our America (ALBA) sought to promote the unification of the Latin American region and simultaneously break away from colonial, capitalist, and neoliberal ties.

Based on the notion of a plurality of *saberes*, the zenith of decolonial thought developed by scholars since the late 1990s, this chapter analyzes the extent to which the ALBA project can be understood as a counter-hegemonic and decolonial movement in Latin America (Al-Kassimi 2018; Seabra and Gimenez 2015). For this, it seeks to point out its challenges and contributions to the process of regional integration, and its contributions to regionalism studies. ALBA does represent a decolonial project of regional integration, as it has not only admitted the existence of coloniality but has also sought ways to break with it through the inclusion of perspectives historically excluded from the mainstream. However, decoloniality is a project under constant construction; and the regional integration in the molds proposed by ALBA should overcome not only the existing asymmetries between the different countries that make up the region, but the current relationship between individuals, nature, and capital.

Decoloniality and Regional Integration

The origin of the term decolonial thought dates back to the creation of the modernity/coloniality group, a transdisciplinary space that was formed at the end of the 1990s from meetings, conferences and publications among different Latin American thinkers. From the perspective of decolonial thought developed in the academic field, modernity was born in 1492, the year in which Europe *discovered* the Caribbean and confronted the Other. This encounter occurred through the exclusion and silencing of this non-European Other who, according to modern logic, found themselves in a backward stage of evolution *vis-à-vis* cultural progress, until then achieved by Europeans. The suffering of this conquered, colonized, or underdeveloped Other was held as a necessary stage for them to reach the modern and developed stage. Modernity, therefore, 'appears when Europe asserts itself as the "center" of a World History that it inaugurates, and therefore the "periphery" is part of its own definition' (Dussel 2004, 65).

Modernity presents only one of its faces: that of salvation, through the rhetoric of development and progress. However, coloniality is intrinsic to it. While colonialism is the definition of one nation's sovereignty grounded in the power of another nation, coloniality refers to patterns of power that were established during colonialism and that currently define culture, intersubjective relations, and conceptual production at the world level. Coloniality does not end with the end of colonialism, but 'endures throughout history rooted in cultural schemas and social power relations, shaping the socio-spatial organization of countries and regions' (Porto-Gonçalves and Quental 2012, 15).

Decoloniality can be understood as the energy that has existed since the early colonial era that seeks to break with the logic of coloniality, not necessarily expressed in the form of books, articles and texts. Decolonial thinking takes the form of epistemic disobedience and demands an openness to other ways of thinking and knowing that are not circumscribed to Eurocentric/Western-centric epistemology. Although the genealogy of decolonial thinking is unknown to the genealogy of European thinking, 'the force and energy of decolonial thinking has always been there, in the exteriority, in the negated by imperial/colonial thinking' (Mignolo 2011, 62).

Border thinking represents an instrument of intellectual, political, and economic decoloniality. It is a reflexive exercise carried out within colonial subalternity that, although it cannot ignore modern epistemology, does not subjugate itself to it. Decolonial thinking, through this border approach, does not reject but rather seeks to redefine concepts such as human rights, humanity, citizenship, democracy, and development. These other perspectives redefine the progressive and developmental rhetoric of modernity, fostering the decolonial liberation struggle 'for a world beyond Euro-centered modernity' (Grosfoguel 2011, 26).

To bring the decolonial perspective to regionalism studies is to understand that the theoretical tools developed for the study of regional integration in Europe, although constructive and important, are limited when the challenge is to outline the necessary paths for a regional integration that is congruent with the Latin American reality. The region, despite presenting heterogeneous and multiple realities, shares an idiosyncratic historical, political, and social structure. Therefore, specific analytical instruments and regional integration mechanisms designed for the Latin American context are necessary.

The region now called Latin America was known by the original peoples by other names such as Abya-Yala (Guna people), Tawantinsuyu (Inca Empire) and Cem Anahuac (Mexica Empire). The attribution of the name *America* to the region was one of the first acts of power of the Europeans in the confrontation with the Other. According to Porto-Gonçalves and Quental (2012, 3), 'the concept of America – and, later, Latin America – is a semantic construction with political, economic, epistemic, and ethical implications that emerged and imposed itself at the expense of conceptualizations and denominations originating from this same continent.'

For the entire Latin American region, making use of the region as an object of study has been one of the most determinant characteristics for the evolution of its thinking about the international. That is, the region can only be understood when incorporated into the world processes initiated with modernity. The colonial formation of the region – later named Latin America – from the 15th century to the end of the 19th century was essential to the concerns of the nation-states that were experiencing moments of independence in the region. Although political practices have been different since then, there is a nascent political intelligentsia that shares an identity about forms of resistance for the newly formed Latin American states against the colonial yoke. In this sense, it is argued here that thinking about the region has been akin to thinking about the autonomy necessary for them to prosper (Deciancio 2016, 95–96). The regionalist ideas produced in the continent are, therefore, an inseparable part of the states' understanding of the world and their form of international insertion that constitutes the capitalist, modern, colonial global order.

The colonial condition and formation shared within the region was the impetus for a first rapprochement between the newly independent nation-states being formed throughout the 19th century. From the moment they became integrated into the system in the formal condition of sovereignty, it became evident that their capacities for progress were circumscribed *a priori* to their positions in the expanding capitalist system. Since they operated in analogous positions in the global relations of production and circulation (as a bloc), Latin American states would enhance their possibilities of empirically achieving their independence if they acted collectively. Achieving autonomy from the condition of coloniality has, since then, been linked to the idea of obtaining better conditions to develop their domestic structures via regional projection. In practice, it was only in the post-World War II period that a series of regional integration initiatives became experiments towards improving the models of international insertion for the countries in the region.

Since the first independence movements in the Latin American region, the idea of regional unity has been raised by figures such as Simón Bolívar and has been present throughout the 19th and early 20th centuries through thinkers like José Martí, Manuel Ugarte, Salvador Mendieta, among others. Bolívar, a Latin American icon of the struggle against colonization, wrote, in 1815, his Letter from Jamaica. In it, he declared the goal of creating a Hispanic-American confederation that would stand up to the centers of power, represented at the time by the European states and the United States. The leader pointed out that the regions previously colonized by the Spanish Empire had a common past, with similar institutions, religion, and language. However, as Ruiz and Lombaerde (2018) state, these thinkers did not develop explanatory theories, 'but contributed with a "knowledge"' that still reverberates in contemporary Latin America'.

Traditional Integration Processes in Latin America and their Limitations

In historiographical terms, Latin American regionalism can be described as occurring in four waves, depending on the role attributed to the region in the interests of the Latin American states and the practical consequences of these perceptions on the integration models. What can be extracted from the continuity of this process is the mix of elements specific to the region that makes it a research unit. There is also a dimension that refers to a level of analysis capable of elucidating the paths of agency and models of international insertion of Latin American countries in favor of both national and regional development.

The foundation of thought on Latin American regionalism emerged from the structuralist ideas of Raul Prebisch, within the ECLAC. In this context, the continental space was understood as a fundamental level for a more efficient economic development process, which would meet the demands of industrialization. This model of regionalism is linked to the promotion of an integrationist policy for the development of economic capacity and the creation of a regional market for the production and circulation of goods. In this way, the idea of altering the most appropriate international insertion in the face of the diagnosis of an unequal economic structure in the global economy was constituted as the center of the argument: the region became the economic unit through which the 'closed regionalism' that emerged as a proposal from the 1950s onwards was understood and justified (Briceño and Lombaerde 2018, 263–268; Deciancio 2016). This phase, understood as the first wave of Latin American regionalism, marks the beginning of a tradition of knowledge specifically from the region, for the region. The realization of the center/periphery configuration marked this first phase.

The limits of this political-economic conception, anchored in an instrumental interpretation of the region, became evident in the 1960s, given the infeasibility of sustaining national industrialist processes and their pretensions of market complementarity. With the weakening of the nationalist projects in the 1970s and the indebtedness of many countries in the region stemming from the need to maintain their development plans, little room was left for strategies that privileged regional dynamics. It is in the context of these obstacles that the Washington Consensus marked a fundamental turning point in relation to what was understood, until then, as the role of the region for the political economy of Latin America. As a result, integration projects were anchored in a 'New Regionalism', of open characteristics in economic terms, which became the primary conception of the notion of regional space for the formulation of foreign policy by Latin American states.

Thus, the moment characterized as the second wave of regionalism was marked by the inextricable incorporation of Latin America into an increasingly flexible and deregulated global market (Riggirozzi and Tussie 2012). This was the apex of foreign neoliberal influence on the countries of the region – even if its absorption did not proceed in an analogous way in all countries. Based on the new integrationist trends, a new regionalism was taking shape – including in academic trends – as a pragmatic option given the need for financial and trade liberalization imposed by the emergence of the post-Cold War order.

The limits of the legitimacy of this new configuration under a supposed US liberal-democratic hegemony presented themselves concomitantly with the emergence of progressive projects in the countries of the region at the end of the 1990s. The post-Cold War development models and their economic and political effects in the Global South continued developing underdevelopment (Al-Kassimi 2018). On one hand, the turning point stemming from the economic crises at the turn of the millennium in Latin America was marked by the rise of center-left governments in the region. From this, national political strategies revalued the dimensions of collective social welfare, based on the questioning of the ills resulting from market and labor flexibilization. On the other hand, the reorientation of the United States in the international scene, due to transnational security agendas, added to its regional weakening, opened space for the emergence of a new balance of regional power, which was redistributed among diverse regional integration initiatives.

The end of the 20th century imposed on the states of the region a context of economic crises as a result of state deregulation, as well as the social consequences resulting from the precarization of labor. Starting in the early 2000s, the upward movement of progressive governments, from a more left-oriented political spectrum, known as the 'Pink Tide', was considered fundamental to the counter-hegemonic ascent in recent Latin American history (Nieto Roa et al 2017). The proposal to create a continental economic space that would operationalize the dominance and consolidation of a regional balance favorable to global power was supplanted by the initiative of several Latin American countries.

This moment marks the emergence of the third wave of regionalism in Latin America as a proposal to deconstruct the classical notion of the region as a strategic space into an idea of an independent political arena. What Latin American academics have called *post-regionalisms* is part of a research agenda that sought to reconstruct developmentalist ideas. Now, as active subjects in the processes of building a regional identity, the region's states outline a strategy of autonomation that shields them from foreign influences within spaces of cooperation that reach beyond traditional economic dynamics (Deciancio 2016, 103–105).

The new adjectivizations elaborated by this school of thought had the purpose of elucidating the moment of rediscovery of the region as a space for those who demarcated a supposed collective counter-hegemony in face of the old patterns of Anglo-Saxon politics that prevailed until the end of the 20th century. More than seeking a more advantageous international insertion, Latin American states – through movements of re-signification and innovation in integration structures – sought to assume roles in global decision-making by strengthening and renewing their perspectives on the meaning of the region. The complementarity between the so-called post-hegemonic regionalism and post-liberal regionalism represented a moment of optimism in regional politics, in a world context that was economically and politically favorable to the rise of the periphery, but which soon presented a series of empirical weaknesses.

The Community of Latin American and Caribbean States (CELAC) and the ALBA-TCP (Peoples' Trade Treaty) are the main examples of manifestation of the importance of Latin American countries assuming not only the management of macroeconomic issues concerning the states in the subcontinent, but also in the new roles developed by the region's social agents – both state and non-state (Mariano, Romero and Ribeiro 2015; Nieto Roa et al 2017). This group of countries represents an opposition to traditional US neoliberal hegemony as applied to this region; a 'post-hegemonic' moment (Tussie and Riggirozzi 2015), which has resulted in a regional optimism with the goal of reaching a new stage of development from the renewal or creation of new regional blocs.

The so-called post-regionalisms (post-hegemonic or post-liberal) complement each other since their perspectives comprise the overcoming of a long period that includes the liberal hegemony of the United States in Latin America, which began in the 19th century and was consolidated during the 20th century. This new perspective also points to the transformation of the role played by the state in regional processes. As active subjects in the process of building regional identity – something considered feasible given the proximity of policy projects among some states in the region – Latin American states can seek their autonomy by curbing some foreign influences by creating rules and cooperative practices in spaces beyond the economic and/or the security sphere (Deciancio 2016, 103–105).

This movement of constant resignification and geolocalized understanding of Latin and South American politics have motivated the existence of theories coming from below since the early days of Latin American IR fields. As Acharya highlights, 'regionalism is an important form of agency for non-Western actors' (Acharya 2016, 7). These approaches position themselves critically in relation to the asymmetries between states in world politics and, to some extent, propose alternatives to mitigate the peripheral situation within the system (Bologna 1987).

Late 1990s: FTAA vs. Latin America

For a long time, the United States was opposed to free trade agreements and customs unions since both hinder the construction of a free and extensive multilateral system. As a result of the Cold War and the consequent need to contain the Soviets in various parts of the globe, the United States accepted the 1957 Treaty of Rome, constituting the European Common Market, which by then had six members (West Germany, France, Italy, Belgium, the Netherlands, and Luxembourg).

Throughout the Uruguay Round, launched in 1986 within the framework of the GATT (General Agreement on Tariffs and Trade), the United States distanced itself from the idea of unconditional defense of multilateralism when they realized that, in certain cases, progress is faster when there is a smaller number of participants who share affinities and interests (Ramina 2010). In

1988, the U.S. and Canada signed a free trade agreement. In 1994, the U.S., Canada, and Mexico signed the NAFTA (North American Free Trade Agreement). The new bloc went on to sign other bilateral agreements, culminating in the launch of the Free Trade Area of the Americas (FTAA) in December 1994.

The idea of a free trade area in the Americas was born through the Enterprise for the Americas Initiative (EAI) proposal in 1990 by former U.S. President George Bush. The central objective was to create a free trade area that would stretch from Canada to Tierra del Fuego, Argentina. According to The United States Agency for International Development (USAID), the initiative had three components: the development of free trade agreements (including NAFTA), a $1.5 billion endowment fund for the implementation of investment reform programs, and an official debt relief program (USAID 2014).

It fell to the next president, Bill Clinton, to revitalize the EAI at the first Summit of the Americas, held in Miami in December 1994. Clinton called on the heads of government of the American republics to unite behind the formation of the free trade area. The heads of state and government of 34 countries of the Americas opted to conclude the FTAA negotiations by 2005. According to ECLAC, 'the FTAA [represented] the most important regional integration agreement signed between developed and undeveloped countries that aims to establish the free flow of trade between their economies' (ECLAC 1999, online).

It is important to point out that the 1980s were marked by the failure of neoliberalism in Latin American countries and that, since then, an environment critical of neoliberalism has emerged in the region. The proposal of neoliberal measures as a solution to structural problems related to underdevelopment in Latin America, especially at the time of the Washington Consensus, began to be viewed with great suspicion. In this sense, the FTAA has been understood as having more complex objectives than simple economic integration: it was also one of the United States' strategies to amplify its economic dominance over Latin American countries.

In light of global changes – especially the transformations in the perspective of international security caused by the redirection of international focus toward transnational terrorism – the United States lost strength with the failure of the FTAA project at the Mar del Plata Summit (2005) (de La Rosa 2011). This opened up space for the emergence of a new regional balance of power, which was distributed among the various integration initiatives. Processes such as UNASUR (Union of Southern Nations), ALBA and a new MERCOSUR (Southern Common Market) have posed new challenges for regional rapprochement.

ALBA as a Project of Resistance to Traditional Models

The idea of the Bolivarian Alliance for the Peoples of Our America (ALBA) was conceived in an environment critical of the economic neoliberalism that had been taking shape since the late 1980s in the Latin American region. It is in the context of the progressive cycle of the early 2000s that the ALBA emerges as a counterforce not only to the FTAA project, but also to previous initiatives of regional integration in Latin America and to US plans for the region. In addition to standing up to the FTAA, the main motivations for the creation of the ALBA-TCP were, according to Hernández and Chaudary (2015): (i) the negative impact that liberal and neoliberal policies had on Latin America; (ii) the threat of the market's globalizing transculturation to Latin American identity, devaluing and silencing traditional and original knowledge and cultures; (iii) South-South cooperation, which broke with the paradigms of North-South cooperation; (iv) the so-called *ola rosada* (pink tide), that is, the rise of leftist leaders in the region; v) the assured possibility of using Venezuelan oil as an instrument to promote a regional integration that was not market-oriented; and vi) the need to build a space for dialogue and consensus aimed at proposing solutions to the problems historically faced by the region, without foreign interference from continental hegemonic powers.

The Bolivarian ideal of the 19th century was recovered during the government of Venezuelan President Hugo Chávez (1999–2013), who had, since 1999, defended the idea that Latin American integration should go beyond the economic and social stages. Chávez included in his speeches the idea of a Confederation of Latin American and Caribbean States and delivered them in successive international forums. According to Manzur and García (2007), the presentation of this idea was not included in the final conclusions of these forums during 1999, 2000, 2001, and early 2002, and, therefore, was not recognized within the regional scene. However, it gained strength between 2004–2006.

The 2002 coup against Chávez was a fundamental precedent in the conformation of the ALBA. From this moment on, the Bolivarian proposal emerged with even more force as an anti-capitalist, anti-imperialist, and anti-U.S. project. Concomitant with the gradual rejection of US regionalism through the FTAA and the Free Trade Agreements, Venezuela moved closer and closer to Cuba. On 14 December 2004, the presidents of both countries, Hugo Chávez and Fidel Castro, signed the 'Agreement between the president of the Bolivarian Republic of Venezuela and the President of the Council of State of the Republic of Cuba for the implementation of the Bolivarian Alternative for the Americas'. At the same time, the presidents presented some of the problems involved in the FTAA project and the premises of the liberal regionalism applied until then in the region:

We wish to draw attention to the fact that the Free Trade Area of the Americas (FTAA) is the most blatant expression yet of a hunger to dominate the region and, were it to come into effect, it would mark an intensification of neoliberalism and create unprecedented levels of dependence and subordination. We have made an historical analysis of the integration process in Latin America and the Caribbean, and we find that – far from responding to aspirations of independent development and regional economic complementarity – it has acted as a mechanism to increase dependence and foreign domination (Cuban Government 2004).

In 2005, Venezuela and Cuba signed the Strategic Plan, creating the ALBA. The alliance was born, therefore, as a proposal to rethink regional integration agreements in order to achieve an 'endogenous national and regional development that eradicates poverty, corrects inequalities and ensures the quality of life of its peoples' (Hernández and Chaudary 2015, 7). A second agreement was signed in 2006, in the same format as the 2004 agreement, but now including Bolivia. From 2007 onwards, the ALBA-TCP went into expansion: starting in 2007, the countries Nicaragua (2007), Dominica (2008), Antigua and Barbuda (2009), Ecuador (2009), Saint Vincent and the Grenadines (2009) and Saint Lucia (2013) were incorporated into the agreement. In the position of Special Guest Countries, Syria (2010), Haiti (2012), and Suriname (2012) were included.

In 2005, Bolivian President Evo Morales, Venezuelan President Hugo Chávez, and Cuban Vice President Carlos Lage met in Bolivia. On that occasion, the leaders ratified the Bolivarian Alternative for the Americas (ALBA) and the Peoples Trade Treaty (TCP), the latter proposed by Morales. In this way, the acronym TCP (People's Trade Treaty) was added to the acronym ALBA, forming an alternative to the FTAs (Free Trade Agreements). The TCP sought to establish fair commercial relations through the principles of South-South cooperation, economic complementarity, and solidarity. It is important to point out that ALBA began as the *Alternativa Bolivariana para los Pueblos de Nuestra América*, but in 2009 the word *Alternativa* was changed to *Alianza*, which in the language of international diplomacy suggests a political – and even military – pact, rather than a trading organization (Adams and Gunsan 2015, 34).

There are 12 principles that underpin the ALBA-TCP: trade and investment should not be ends in themselves; special and differentiated treatment according to the level of development of the countries; economic complementarity and cooperation; cooperation and solidarity; creation of a Social Emergency Fund; integral development of communications and transportation; sustainability of development; energy integration; promotion of investments of Latin American capital in the region; defense of Latin American and Caribbean identity and culture; respect for intellectual property; and agreement on multilateral positions and in negotiations with countries and blocs in other regions.

The ALBA-TCP rejects strictly commercial regional integration and prioritizes its political and social aspects, rescaling the state's role in economic activity (Hernández and Chaudary 2015). Therefore, it developed its project based on an anti-capitalist, anti-imperialist, and counter-hegemonic model of integration, underpinned by the principles of complementarity, cooperation, collaboration, solidarity, improvement of the quality of life of citizens, and direct participation of social movements. This model is reflected in the deliberative structure of the alliance, currently made up of the Presidential Council (the highest instance of deliberation, decision, and political orientation) and by the Political, Social, Economic, and Social Movements Councils. This last Council was created to expand the discourse between social movements in member and non-member countries. In this sense, social movements are key actors in the regional integration process developed by ALBA-TCP.

One of the central aspects of the mode of regional integration pursued within the ALBA-TCP framework is the approximation between its regional social policies and *Buen Vivir* (Spanish term for living well), or *Vivir Bien* – the latter being used more commonly in Bolivia (Ruiz 2018). The term is inspired by the expressions *sumak kawsay* and *sumaq qamaña*, of the Kichwa and Aymara Indigenous groups living in Ecuador and Bolivia (Arteaga-Cruz 2017). *Buen Vivir* represents a set of critical ideas, worldviews, and *saberes* that has been constructed by social movements, Indigenous groups, and academics who study the Indigenous issue. Given the plurality of Andean Indigenous Peoples, the understandings of this term are multiple.

Therefore, the potential of the ALBA-TCP is also related to the countless natural riches present in the Latin American region, not in terms of exporting and strengthening foreign trade, but in the sense of harnessing these riches – which belong to the Latin American peoples, but are not enjoyed by them – in favor of the quality of life, of *Buen Vivir*, of the peoples who reside in the territory. According to Seabra and Gimenez (2015, 3), the ALBA-TCP not only rediscovers Latin American anti-imperialism and anti-capitalism, but 'builds an alternative based on the refusal of the pattern of capital accumulation on a regional scale'.

Regarding the developmental aspect of regional integration, ALBA-TCP is not limited to strictly following the rules of international law or traditional international trade, nor does it have trade liberalization as its overarching goal. It seeks to achieve the integral and collective development of the region through compensatory policies. Economic complementarity should be achieved through a balanced and symmetrical commercial exchange. Although regional integration, in this project, comprises extensive trade among member countries, it is not reduced to it.

One of the greatest challenges to be faced by the alliance is the need to overcome the profound asymmetries that exist between its member countries. In terms of economic activity, there is a significant disparity. For example, according to World Bank data, while Venezuela's Gross Domestic Product (GDP) is US$482.359 million, Bolivia's is US$40.895 million, and Dominica's is US$582 thousand. In this sense, the asymmetries between countries should be overcome through compensated trade modalities and/or mechanisms that favor the most vulnerable countries. Between Cuba and Venezuela, for instance, these mechanisms work through what is called cooperative advantage. Venezuelan oil is supplied to Cubans at special prices and payment modalities, and part of the payment is made through Cuban medical, educational, and agricultural services in Venezuelan social programs, or through scholarships provided to Venezuelans who wish to study in Cuba.

The Bank of Alba, created in January 2008, proposes a new financial architecture, seeking to overcome the dependence on foreign currency and international financial institutions. Its main function is to finance programs and projects in the areas of economic development (job creation, innovation, invention, development of production chains, etc.), social development (health, education, social security, social economy, promotion and strengthening of participatory democracy, etc.), expansion and connection of the infrastructure among countries, creation of bi-national or grand-national companies, development and promotion of fair trade practices for goods and services, among others.

The consolidation process of the ALBA-TCP regional integration model is still ongoing. It is under constant construction. Since its founding in 2004, the alliance has undergone several changes and is no longer just a counterpoint to the US model of regional integration, but represents a more concrete proposal structured by medical-hospital agreements, literacy programs, new financial and monetary systems, infrastructure development, and energy integration (Seabra and Gimenez 2015).

However, some authors point out that a greater theoretical foundation that specifies the model of integration that the ALBA-TCP project wishes to achieve is necessary. By this logic, precisely because it is proposed as an alternative to the current integration models, the alliance should not be based merely on the rejection of hegemonic models, but also on a theoretical orientation. It is possible that, in this way, the initiative could contribute to regionalism studies to a greater extent.

For Ruiz (2014), the ALBA-TCP project represents an anti-systemic axis of existing regional integration processes in Latin America. Its integration model does not adapt to the models traditionally known in the academic literature on regional integration, nor does it manifest this intent. This might be the reason behind the lack of consensus on the integration model advocated by the alliance.

Besides its characterization as anti-systemic and counter-hegemonic, the ALBA-TCP project can also be understood as decolonial. As mentioned above, decolonial thinking assumes a form of epistemic disobedience and openness to other forms of thinking and knowing that are not circumscribed to the Eurocentric/Western-centric epistemology. The ALBA-TCP was structured through a border dialogue that developed a project of regional integration and developed from the standpoint of global subalternity. Although it could not ignore the modern epistemology that concerns regionalism, global subalternity did not subjugate itself to it.

The decolonial and counter-hegemonic project set in motion by the alliance inscribed the legacies of decolonial thought (especially that cultivated by the Andean Indigenous population) in its organizational structure. It was, therefore, a moment of 'opening and the freedom from the thinking and the forms of living (economies-other, political theories-other)' (Mignolo 2011, 48). The ALBA-TCP – by understanding economy, politics, and society as intricate parts of the same reality – transcends the notion of regional integration as a strictly economic-commercial process.

Conclusion

The FTAA vs. the ALBA dilemma seems to be one more chapter in the history of political projects that are in constant dispute in the Latin American region. Within the post-Cold War neoliberal context, in which trade liberalization and separation between state and economy seemed to be a necessary phase for progress and development, the ALBA-TCP represents a decolonial project of regional development that has sought and continues to seek to re-signify the principles of regional integration.

In addition to being decolonial and counter-hegemonic, the project set forth in this study is also the representation of a democratic-participatory project. This is because regional integration, in the molds proposed by the ALBA-TCP, would not happen only through the action of states, but also through the participation of social movements. In this sense, the alliance represents a space of contestation of the political spaces produced and dominated by capitalism and modernity. The exercise of collectively thinking ways to manage common existence through a border dialogue that involves different social groups, especially the subaltern ones, expands the borders of democracy.

However, like all projects, the decolonial project of regional integration idealized by ALBA-TCP is currently under construction. Since decolonial movements tend to go against state-centrism, there is some controversy in ALBA-TCP, which is a state-centric initiative. Furthermore, as we have seen, for the alliance to effectively put into practice an integration process that transforms the lives of millions of Latin American citizens, it is necessary to overcome the existing social, political, economic, and cultural divisions between member countries. This becomes even more important at a moment in which Latin American governments present significant ideological divergences, quite different from the context existing at the beginning of the 2000s. It seems that the neoliberal project once again prevails in Latin America, and this affects the regional integration processes.

The purpose of this chapter was to analyze the idea proposed by the ALBA-TCP and to what extent it represents a decolonial project. Neoliberalism did not provide sufficient solutions to the crises of the integration model throughout the 1980s and does not seem to do so at the present time. Although there is a weakening of the alliance in the region, it is possible and urgent to reflect on new ways to promote regional integration in Latin America. As a result, emancipatory approaches are gradually gaining space in knowledge production.

The process of conformation and development of the ALBA-TCP contributes in great measure to the discussion on regionalism, in the sense that it highlights the need for an opening to other forms of knowledge that can contribute to the formulation of a method of regional integration that corresponds to Latin American reality – including community and collective perspectives, born and cultivated by original peoples and social movements. In this way, it becomes ever more possible to overcome the coloniality that persists.

References

Acharya, Amitav. "Advancing Global IR: Challenges, Contentions, and Contributions." *International Studies Review* 18 no. 1 (March 2016): 4–15, https://doi.org/10.1093/isr/viv016.

Al-Kassimi, Khaled. "ALBA: A decolonial delinking performance towards (western) modernity – An alternative to development project." *Cogent Social Sciences* 4, no. 1 (November 2018): 1–35, https://doi.org/10.1080/23311886.2018.1546418.

Arteaga-Cruz, Erika. "Buen Vivir (*Sumak Kawsay*): definiciones, crítica e implicaciones en la planificación del desarrollo en Ecuador." *Saúde Debate* 41, no. 114 (July-September 2017): 907–919, https://doi.org/10.1590/0103-1104201711419.

Briceño-Ruiz, J. and Lombaerde, P. "Regionalismo latino-americano: produção de saber e criação e importação de teoria." *Civitas* 18, no. 2 (March-August 2018): 262–284, https://doi.org/10.15448/1984-7289.2018.2.29593.

Bologna, Alfredo. "Teorías y propuesta de Relaciones Internacionales para los países sur." In *Cuadernos de Política Exterior Argentina*, edited by Promopea. Rosario: Centro de Estudios en Relaciones Internacionales de Rosario, 1987.

Cardoso, Fernando and Faletto, Enzo. *Dependency and Development in Latin America.* California: University of California Press, 1979.

Cuban government. Agreement between the president of the Bolivarian Republic of Venezuela and the President of the Council of State of the Republic of Cuba for the implementation of the Bolivarian Alternative for the Americas (2004), http://www.cuba.cu/gobierno/discursos/2004/ing/a141204i.html.

Deciancio, Melisa. 2016. "El regionalismo latinoamericano en la agenda de la teoría de las Relaciones Internacionales." *Iberoamericana* 16, no. 63 (November 2016): 91–110, https://doi.org/10.18441/ibam.16.2016.63.91-110.

Dos Santos, Theotonio. "El nuevo caracter de la dependencia." *Instituto de Estudios Peruanos.* (October 1968): 1–22.

Dussel, Enrique. "Eurocentrism and Modernity (Introduction to the Frankfurt Lectures)," *Boundary* 20, no. 3 (November 2004): 65–76.

Economic Commission for Latin America and the Caribbean. La conformación del Área del Libre Comercio de las Américas (ALCA). México: Naciones Unidas (1999).

Grosfoguel, Ramón. "Decolonizing Post-Colonial Studies and Paradigms of Political-Economy: Transmodernity, Decolonial Thinking, and Global Coloniality." *Journal of Peripheral Cultural Production of the Luso-Hispanic World* 1, no. 1 (May 2011). https://dialogoglobal.com/texts/grosfoguel/Grosfoguel-Decolonizing-Pol-Econ-and-Postcolonial.pdf.

Hernández, Dilio, and Chaudary, Yudi. 2015. "La Alianza Bolivariana para los Pueblos de Nuestra América - Tratado de Comercio de los Pueblos (ALBA-TCP) - Vigencia y viabilidad en el actual contexto venezolano y regional" *Friedrich Ebert Stifung* (2015). http://library.fes.de/pdf-files/bueros/caracas/11379.pdf.

Manzur, Juan, and García, Lucrecia. "Origen y naturaleza de la Alternativa Bolivariana para las Américas." *Polis* 3, no. 1 (2007): 55–85. http://www.scielo.org.mx/pdf/polis/v3n1/v3n1a4.pdf.

Mariano, Karina, Romero, Ana, and Ribeiro, Clarissa. "Percepções governamentais sobre a integração regional na América do Sul." *Boletim de Economia e Política Internacional (BEPI)* no. 21 (September/December 2015): 33–43. http://repositorio.ipea.gov.br/bitstream/11058/6474/1/BEPI_n21_Percep%C3%A7%C3%B5es.pdf.

Márquez Duarte, Fernando. "Rethinking development with Nahuas saberes" *Alternautas* 8, no.1 (October 2021): 9-25. http://www.alternautas.net/blog/2021/3/17/rethinking-development-with-nahuas-saberes.

Mignolo, Walter. "Epistemic Disobedience and the Decolonial Option: A Manifesto." *Duke University* 1, no. 2 (2011): 44–66. https://doi.org/10.5070/T412011807

Nieto Roa, A. et. al. "La integración regional como proceso contrahegemónico: aportes teóricos acerca de la Unasur como integrador." *Ánfora* 24, no. 42 (June 2017): 95–115. https://publicaciones.autonoma.edu.co/index.php/anfora/article/view/166/136.

Porto-Gonçalves, Carlos, and Quental, Pedro. "Colonialidade do poder e os desafios da integração regional na América Latina." *Polis* 31 (December 2012). https://scielo.conicyt.cl/pdf/polis/v11n31/art17.pdf.

Quijano, Aníbal. 2005. "Colonialidade do Poder, Eurocentrismo e América Latina." In *A colonialidade do saber: eurocentrismo e ciências sociais*, 117-142. Buenos Aires: CLACSO. http://biblioteca.clacso.edu.ar/clacso/sur-sur/20100624103322/12_Quijano.pdf.

Ramina, Larissa. "Área de Livre Comércio das Américas." *Jus*. Last modified October, 2010. https://jus.com.br/artigos/17626/area-de-livre-comercio-das-americas-alca.

Riggirozzi, Pía. "Reconstructing Regionalism: What does Development have to do with It?" in *The Rise of Post-hegemonic Regionalism: The Case of Latin America*, edited by Pía Riggirozzi and Diana Tussie, 17–40. Dordrecht/Heidelberg/London/New York: Springer, 2012.

Riggirozzi, Pía, and Tussie, Diana. "The Rise of Post-Hegemonic Regionalism in Latin America," in *The Rise of Post-hegemonic Regionalism: The Case of Latin America*, edited by Pía Riggirozzi and Diana Tussie, 1–16. Dordrecht/Heidelberg/London/New York: Springer, 2012.

Rosero, Luis, and Blandón, Melissa. "Alianza Bolivariana para los Pueblos de Nuestra América - Tratado de Comercio de los Pueblos (ALBA-TCP) un nuevo modelo de integración regional." *Justicia* no. 26 (December 2014): 26–43. http://www.scielo.org.co/pdf/just/n26/n26a03.pdf.

Seabra, Raphael and Gimenez, Heloisa. "Contra o 'vazio teórico' da ALBA, uma análise propositiva a partir da lei do valor."' *Revista de Estudos e Pesquisas sobre as Américas* 9, no. 1 (June 2015). https://periodicos.unb.br/index.php/repam/article/view/16048/14337.

The United States Agency for International Development - USAID. 2014. Enterprise for the Americas Initiative. Last modified July 12, 2021. https://www.usaid.gov/biodiversity/TFCA/enterprise-for-the-americas-initiative.

2

Decolonizing South-South Cooperation: An Analytical Framework Founded on Post-development and the Common

MARINA BOLFARINE CAIXETA
& MARIA DO CARMO REBOUCAS DOS SANTOS

To think South-South Cooperation (SSC) from a decolonial perspective, we intend to introduce some critical studies that originated in the Global South to question the notions of development and international cooperation. As formulated by the Modernity/Coloniality Group (a working group that led to the surge of decoloniality as a research area, composed by prestigious decolonial authors like Aníbal Quijano, Enrique Dussel, María Lugones, Arturo Escobar, etc.), the Latin American version of postcolonialism, there are political and epistemological proposals in our discussion. We have identified two main debates that emerge from decolonial studies: post-development and the common. We start from the assumption that Latin America and the Caribbean make important contributions in the field of SSC, which is the case in terms of technical cooperation initiatives through which countries share know-how and relevant experiences for the implementation of public policies – and of a Southern identity that allows critical reactions to the status quo of the world order. In this chapter, we intend to address epistemological contributions and practices of different social groups to highlight some important aspects of SSC to be based on a new analytical criterion.

South-South Cooperation as a decolonial tool

South-South Cooperation is understood as an opportunity for the Global South to change the global order and innovate the International Development

Cooperation (IDC) system. It represents a new trend in the twenty-first century. Since the Second World War marked a parameter of hegemonic development (Santos 2017), the Global South has emerged as an identity in politics in reaction to inequalities in the international and domestic political plans of states (Menezes and Caixeta 2021). Forged in a diverse group of countries, SSC has consolidated itself as an expression of solidarity between the peoples and governments of the South and as a strategy of economic and political autonomy, through horizontal relations and mutual strengthening.

This alliance meant the convergence of the national interests of the countries of the South in international politics and, also, the introduction of new worldviews from the periphery concerning development policies. In the present 21st century, the rise of the South was a phenomenon that manifested itself both at the political level, through SSC, and at the academic level, through the Epistemologies of the South (Caixeta 2015).

In the context of Southern Epistemologies, in Latin America, we had the decolonial turn – which promoted a liberating praxis. South-South Cooperation, according to this perspective, should be able to value different worldviews, especially those that have been silenced for a long time. Through social theories and concepts proposed from elsewhere (the Global South), an engaged knowledge is sought to update the critical tradition of Latin American thinking – offering historical reinterpretations and problematizing the issues of the continent.

> It defends the epistemological, theoretical and political "decolonial option" to understand and act in a world marked by the persistence of global coloniality [overcoming the coloniality of power, knowledge and being] at different levels of personal and collective life' (Ballestrín 2013, 89–90).

However, the heterogeneity of what is conceived by the Global South, the crises of capitalism, and the search for the realization of national geostrategic interest places SSC under several and serious criticisms. Therefore, the principles agreed at the Bandung Conference (1955), as well as in the Buenos Aires Plan of Action (PABA, 1978) – and reaffirmed in the Nairobi Declaration (2009) – are at risk of being discredited by a SSC that just replicates dominant practices. Note, for example, that SSC continues to be thought and carried out by the elites of the countries of the South, with a state-centric approach, mediated by economic interests and international political conditionality that disregards different worldviews in the initiatives proposed by new historical subjects from the Southern countries (Kabunda 2011; Chidaushe 2010; Santos and Caixeta 2018).

Conceiving SSC as an opportunity to decolonize development practices, according to Santos (2017, 272), implies,

> re-discussing the role of emerging countries in search of their strategic autonomy and the role of poor countries in the pursuit of their national interests, and more than anything reconsiders the hegemonic capitalist development model. In addition, it imposes a real and effective participation of the societies of those countries in this process.

Only as a means of collective autonomy, as proposed by Escobar (2017) and when inspired by its foundational postulates, can SSC be a mechanism to promote the decolonial turn (Surasky, 2013) and to reform and innovate towards new practices, new narratives, and new actors (Muñoz 2016).

A new emancipatory social imagery should be able to produce more just societies. According to Villoro (1998), power and value are equally important, as justice should be a value for seizing power and a goal. Otherwise, if power is pursued as the only goal, there is domination, violence, and injustice. Counterpower, in this sense, shall be necessary, since it is conceived as peoples' power, against domination and exploration and acts on behalf of the common good.

Thus, we propose to inquire about the ways in which SSC can benefit from Latin American and Caribbean experiences hitherto silenced, both theoretical and social practices, such as proposals on post-development (alternative to development) and the realization of communal life. We assume that Latin America and the Caribbean have always reacted to the unique model of hegemonic development in their experience as a peripheral region in the world-system (Wallerstein 2000).

In this regard, authors and peoples of the region have been proposing new concepts, political slogans, and analytical categories, which we believe offer the potential to guide the practice of SSC. This is the case of the *Quilombismo* of the Black population in Brazil, the *Buen Vivir* of the Andean Indians, the Life Projects in Colombian experiments, and the Zapatismo of the Mexican region of Chiapas. In addition to others, we believe they put these two notions in perspective and justify this debate. For subordinate groups, living with the fact of domination and enduring in the midst of it necessarily entails resistance, novelty and innovation (Escobar 2017, 35–41 – our translation). Therefore, we present this debate as follows: in the first part, we present post-development as a potential transformative framework to rethink development as an objective of public policies and, consequently, of SSC; in the second, we deal with the common as a means of redefining the practice of SSC, and in the third, we mapped out some theoretical elaborations and political struggles in the region. In the end, we present contributions to an analytical framework in order to rethink SSC as an international mechanism that can change IDC practices and challenge the current world order.

South-South Cooperation in post-development

Post-development in recent decades has become a field of study. From the critique of hegemonic development as a discourse of power, the perspective of post-development can be understood as the need to decentralize development as a characteristic of societies and countries to question the fundamental discourses for promoting development – the ideas of growth, progress, and modernity – and weaving a fabric with transformative initiatives of an alternative, plural, and autonomous nature. The idea of fabric has been widely mentioned in the field of post-development, alluding to a collective, creative construction, based on popular and community wisdom, such in Miñoso, Correal and Muñoz (2014). Svampa (2017) considers that the views of post-development are constituted by a diversity of currents with decolonizing ambitions, which propose to dismantle and disable the instruments of power, myths and imaginary that are the basis of the current model of development.

The most recent literature on the subject, present in the book *Pluriverse: A Post-Development Dictionary*, inscribes post-development in the practical and epistemic-political field that implies a wide cross-cultural compilation of concrete concepts, worldviews, and practices from around the world, challenging the modernist ontology of universalism in favor of a multiplicity of possible worlds (Kothari et al 2019). Far from being a recipe to exit hegemonic development, or what they will call inadequate development, the authors rather recognize the diversity of people's views on planetary well-being and their skills in protecting it. They seek to ground human activities in the rhythms and frames of nature, respecting the interconnected materiality of everything that lives. This indispensable knowledge needs to be held safely in the commons, not privatized, or commodified for sale (Kothari et al 2019).

In a previous work (Santos and Caixeta 2018), we already indicated the power of the post-development to inspire new alliances and practices for SSC. In order to contribute to emancipatory processes that incorporate and recognize more supportive values and more community principles, we treat cooperation between peoples (and nations) as something more advanced in relation to cooperation between countries and governments. As Escobar (2017) proposes, we are witnessing a civilizational transition that brings three different models of cooperation: development assistance, that of traditional cooperation, in which the World Bank and conventional NGOs are involved; cooperation as/for social justice, eminently based on the promotion and achievement of human rights and environmental sustainability with a strong role for different groups in society, such as OXFAM; and cooperation for autonomy or solidarity cooperation linked to post-development proposals for which the binarism of we and the others in the North and South give way to alliances and collective action networks. In the latter, public policies would be proposed from the community level, rather than planned at the state level.

In this framework, we expect that SSC, based on the ideas of the Global South, will be able to achieve and constitute a cooperation for autonomy and solidarity. In doing so, from Escobar (2017) we bring Table 2.1, which highlights the meaning of each model of cooperation and the reference for development to be promoted; the direction of the intervention initiative processes; and the forms of relationship between parties that cooperate, as well as the degree of reciprocity between them (vertical/horizontal). We conceive these three models of cooperation as a continuum with the aim of challenging the cooperation of the countries and peoples of the Global South.

SSC hosts the potential for a solidarity cooperation type, considering its principles of solidarity, respect and horizontality and its objective of contributing to the promotion of international peace, common prosperity, and well-being of all, as per the Final Communiqué of the Afro-Asian Conference – also known as the Bandung Conference (1955). Thus, as an international mechanism at the service of post-development, it would take place through collective processing between autonomous social groups or societies, based on plural and innovative realities, knowledge, and experiences, against forms of domination, dependence, subjugation, and exploitation. Surasky (2013) argues that SSC can be a decolonial instrument. From what the Global South identity represents, it can become the possibility of subverting the modern-capitalist-colonial civilization based on the phenomena of globalization and development. 'Today we see that, as part of SSC´s own discourse, visions of the South on what we call development are beginning to emerge that could well be read as attempts to respond to this call' (Surasky 2013, 8).

In this regard, recovering what was hidden or denied by colonization allows us to rethink these hegemonic conceptions, from a perspective located on the periphery of the international system and from the living experiences with marginality. Therefore, it is important to challenge SSC from the discussion on post-development. Albeit in a propaedeutic way, it is claimed for this new cooperative mechanism the rescue of alternative experiences and knowledge regarding global well-being, both introducing new technical knowledge to be exchanged and new actors participating in cooperative activities.

A starting point for seeking an approach between SSC and post-development, would be to think of them from the connection between two sides, that is, to consider the principles of SSC at the same time as the different social struggles and longings for well-being coming from the social groups that inhabit and identify themselves with the Global South.

Although nuanced by interests of national gains, the SSC's principles express a humanist guideline of the alliance of the countries of the South. They constitute a line of political action guided by solidarity, reciprocity, and horizontality, underlying the practice of countries in various areas, whether in the political, economic, or social scope (Santos 2017). As a principle, the solidarity since Bandung, from a post-developmentalist matrix, revitalizes its potential as a political category with the strength to bring together practices and theories. In this way we can count on an SSC founded on multiple rationalities and that strengthens autonomy, knowledge, and the sense of the common.

The common in South-South Cooperation

Suggesting a debate that proposes to combine SSC with the notion of the common, means to think of post-development in countries (nations) as a global common. South-South Cooperation as a proposal to reform the International Development Cooperation system (IDC) aims to innovate cooperative practices and, at the same time, to propose effective interventions in the realization of human well-being. This implies that there is both a challenge to rethink cooperation processes and to introduce new development conceptions.

However, at the present moment, SSC is linked to procedures (logical framework of projects), institutionalities (goals and objectives of the 2030 Agenda for Sustainable Development Goals – SDGs) and evaluation criteria coming from the traditional cooperation practice – the Official Development Assistance (ODA) of the Organization for Economic Cooperation and Development (OECD). Therefore, SSC seems to lack a greater link with its initial purposes and, therefore, reproduces what has been going on in the IDC. The commitment to the Global South identity, markedly plural, requires new references.

Thus, in light of the common, SSC is conceived as a cooperative mechanism for the rescue of alternative experiences and knowledge. To this end, the region of Latin America and the Caribbean not only reflects on the notion of the common, but also accumulates social experiences, usually within the so-called traditional societies of Indigenous and Afro-descendant peoples (and their diasporas) that resisted to maintain their culture and its connection with the land (territorialization) and with community principles of collective life.

As opposed to the idea of hegemony, for which the sense of the common is imposed from certain logics and lifestyles, the common is understood here as a notion to something to be constructed from the communities. In this sense, by aggregating different societies around what is common to all – common problems, interest, resources – paradoxically we can promote pluriversal politics coming from plural worlds which depend on the communities' decisions. The principle of the pluriverse brings the idea of a world in which several worlds fit, a Zapatista motto that inspired political ontology (the ontological turn) in Latin American social thought. Realities are plural and always in the making, that idea has a profound political consequence (Escobar, 2020 viii), since it relates to the how to build the common, more than to decide the common is.

Based on Latin American thought, Torres-Galarza (2018) proposes to move from common sense to the sense of the common notion. He explains that for Gramsci, common sense has historical, ideological, and political characteristics, as there are elements of human experience and its ability to observe or perceive reality without intermediation. For this reason, the common can acquire a conservative or emancipatory sense in the world order depending on the social position of those who define or use it and how they define or use it. In Latin America and the Caribbean, for instance, the sense of the common must be discussed based on its attempt to gain autonomy and authenticity in the world order.

Therefore, overcoming a global common sense that naturalizes domination and neutralizes the possibilities of being free, Torres-Galarza (2018) suggests that it is important to understand the sense of the common as a force to create a new reality that is more potent and more satisfying for humanity. Considering this, one must break with the common imposed by capitalism, and that attributed the meaning of human existence to the market and consumption as something common in globalization. So, we must generate the sense of the common in a common sense, this time attributed by the Latin American perspective,

> We speak of a common sense of the commons, of conscience and will about the new – not determined only by the past but acting in the present with a vision of the future. This is a sense of the common that determines us as communities, as cultures and as peoples, with ways of life and relationships between human beings and nature. It is a sense of the common about

the power of the commons. [...] It is about contesting the logic of the market from culture and community, contesting the meaning of having from being. (Torres-Galarza 2018, 11) (Our translation).

Such a proposal is convergent with the political project of the common by Dardot and Laval (2015). In a vast genealogy, in temporal terms (but not in spatial terms since Latin American literature on the subject was not considered by the French authors) political proposals instrumentalize the common in the view of the 21st century revolution. The common would be a new political reason to replace the neoliberal reason, which is aligned with the decolonial turn that claims the recognition of the colonial difference and the persistence of coloniality among the peoples of the South in the modern-capitalist-world-system.

Aiming at building the sense of the common according to Dardot and Laval (2015) would follow these propositions: (1) the common must be the foundation and orientation for action in favor of the common good; (2) it must guide the collective's deliberative activities in a participatory and inclusive space; (3) it brings together all groups of society around a social political obligation in co-activity and co-obligation, against the idea of belonging (national, ethical, human); (4) as part of a process to achieve a common good elected by society as a whole – it is not, therefore, an object, not even an end, but the means; (5) as a social category, it is opposed to the legal and economic category that distinguish certain goods by their characteristics or intrinsic properties, as in 'common good' or 'common heritage of humanity' that have logics adverse to the common interest; (6) as a collective practice of collectivizing, it allows communities to further decide the common character of things, knowledge and practical experiences; (7) as a practical way of governing, it institutionalizes common goods and purposes of population groups in order to make it live and exist; (8) operates both in the social sphere and in the sphere of public policy, besides it is not incompatible with private and public interests, but it must be prioritized in relation to them (in other words, the common seeks that public policies do not harm people for prioritizing private interests); (9) as a political principle, it preaches the democracy of the commons as a space to deal with public affairs and socioeconomic exchanges in a federative logic, and (10) as a social principle, it refuses social relations from the premise of the inappropriate (of what should be reserved for common use) and definition of the social destination.

Thus, one could extract from the notion of the common ideas to recreate reality with authenticity, rooted in the community(ies) to which, from which and with which collective actions are given meaning. Always from the bottom-up, the scope of the initiatives must be designed and decided as a way of making and conceiving politics in plural contexts. In this regard, what is common would come to question SSC as a mechanism for the renewal of the IDC system.

In order to put SSC to the test of this conceptual-theoretical framework, we ask: How can SSC serve to achieve the common at the global level? How can it support the construction of a sense of the common in the various contexts in which it is practiced? To enable the instrumentalization of the common by SSC, also considering the post-development framework, we propose to think of it from three constitutive elements: its objective (the well-being for all), its process (total horizontality in reciprocity) and its principle (solidarity and otherness). Figure 2.1 outlines this proposal.37

In line with what Dardot and Laval (2015) signaled, one wonders in the context of the unifying globalization of European universalism, whether there are still social forces, alternative models, or modes of social organization that would allow us to think of an alternative scenario to that of capitalism. To guide this reflection, we will present some social experiences from the Latin American and Caribbean region from which we can extract potent categories, which have both a practical-political as well as an academic-conceptual character.

Latin American social experiences

The notions of common and post-development built from the Latin American context mobilize both practical and theoretical cases. It should be noted that they should not be restricted only to the rural, Indigenous or Black groups described here, but extended to any and all initiatives that seek social well-being from their peripheral and marginal condition or situation. Supported by Escobar (2017), we defend the leadership of those who, without an ancestral mandate of living together as a community, as is the case of native-Indigenous and *Quilombola* peoples, live displaced in liberal and modern worlds that exclude and marginalize them, as migrants, internal and external, who inhabit the periphery of large cities. These social groups belong to the age of disconnection and demand recommunalization and reterritorialization. Thus, we believe that authenticity and creativity can be rescued to imagine new territories of existence and new ways of being and living in favor of an alternative world.

Quilombismo

Based on the cultural experience, historical time, and praxis of the Black community, the *Quilombismo* proposed by Abdias Nascimento questions the bases of the Brazilian development model and its racial devices that exclude Blacks from the benefits of development, elaborates a theoretical-practical proposal of a social, political, and economic transformation and articulates a logic of the communal inspired by quilombos. The word *Quilombo* originally refers to a place where runaway Blacks took shelter, even in the period of slavery. But since the 1920s, this word has taken on new political meanings of resistance. Nascimento, though, is the one responsible for the perception and initial registration of *Quilombismo* as an 'emerging concept of the historical-cultural process of the Afro-Brazilian population' (Santos and Santos 2020).

The basic purpose of *Quilombismo* is to promote human happiness, based on a free, just, egalitarian, and sovereign society, through the implantation of a community-based cooperative economy, the collective use of land and production goods, harmonious coexistence with nature and balanced with all forms of existence (Nascimento 1980). Through a manifesto, Nascimento establishes principles and purposes that guide *Quilombismo* such as, for example, a community-based cooperative economy with sharing of results of collective work, and with land and factories considered national property for collective use and management; and, in the field of the environment, a human existence designed in a relational and harmonious way with nature in all its manifestations.

With the demand for a knowledge and experience that is historically and culturally referenced in the quilombos, Nascimento also gives us the password to think about new forms of life and social organization based on an ancestral key. For him, 'the rescue of our memory means rescuing ourselves from oblivion, from nothingness, from negation, and reaffirming our presence in pan-African history and in the universal reality of human beings' (Nascimento 2019, 309). Therefore, *Quilombismo* was born from the effort to register concepts and experiences of the Black Brazilian population – going back to slavery and the colonial period, with its history of struggles, resistances, reinvention and experiences of autonomy.

Thus, from the idea of the quilombos, the community is part of a whole – which is why as a political platform recognizes the need to think about building alternatives to development based on an anti-racist, anti-capitalist, anti-sexist, anti-colonialist, anti-imperialist, and anti-land-ownership model. *Quilombismo* also prefigures a vision of society, rather than prescribing a model to be followed. Although it is inspired by the organization of what was *Quilombo dos Palmares* in Brazil, it is neither a return to a past that no longer exists – even though that past is essential for the construction of this proposal – nor an essentialist view of life in quilombos.

Contemporary *quilombos* have their contours marked by heterogeneity – the result of historical resistance processes. Thus, as a political principle, they form another contribution to help think about new forms of social organization, respect for difference, well-being and happiness, as alternatives to the hegemonic model of development. As a decolonizing perspective, in line with the ideas of post-development, they present new horizons of civilizational possibility, based on a communal and relational life with nature and ancestry.

Buen Vivir

The concept of *Buen Vivir* has always existed in the social organizations of the peoples of the Americas. It gained political and academic centrality in the 1990s by means of 'alterworldist' movements that proposed another possible world. This came in the midst of criticisms of the failure of the idea of progress embedded in the hegemonic capitalist development model and the environmental crisis due to the commodification of multiple spheres of nature.

There are at least three approaches to *Buen Vivir*. First, a generic use associated with advertising purposes. A second focuses on alternatives to development – still in the field of modernity and often based on the claims of leftist traditions. Finally, a third approach comes as a critique of development by elaborating alternatives that are both post-capitalist and post-socialist, located beyond the matrix of modernity (Gudynas 2014, 136).

The most well-known expressions of *Buen Vivir* refer to the proposals of the peoples of Ecuador and Bolivia, respectively, *sumak kawsay* in *Kichwa* and *suma qamaña* in Aymara, have become normative references. Hence, it was incorporated into state speeches and started to guide national development plans. After the first moment of euphoria, its real implementation in these countries started to be questioned as a simulation and the *Buen Vivir* paradigm itself lost social credibility. In addition, some academics consider it essentialist, without practical applicability and restricted to a philosophical idea (Sólon 2019, 22).

The idea of *Buen Vivir* intertwines multiple ontologies and diverse types of well-being that adopt different formulations in each social and environmental circumstance in which it finds itself. It is a common platform based on the practice of interculturality that aims for the future to build alternatives to development (Gudynas 2011). *Buen Vivir* launches the challenge of living with multipolarity and learning to interrelate, being more concerned with well-being (the essence of the person) than with well-living (the condition of the person) (Solon 2019).

Recent studies continue to bet on this proposal as a possible platform for building changes. The essence of *Buen Vivir* remains and can reorient imaginary alternative systemic practices around the world, as a current development model (Acosta 2014; Gudynas 2014; Santos and Caixeta 2018; Santos 2018; Sólon 2019). It is not a purely Andean political-cultural project, as it is influenced by critical currents in Western thought and aims to influence global debates on development. Discussions about what form it could take in modern urban contexts and in other parts of the world, such as Europe, are gradually advancing (Escobar 2017).

With the potential to reorient alternative systemic forms in the field of post-development, there is an ethic of overcoming statism, valuing the local and the community, protecting nature, recognizing and respecting interculturality and plurality, intent on depatriarchalization with the idea of *Pachamama* and guaranteeing real democracy (Sólon 2019).

Life Projects

The Life Projects were thought, from the ontological turn, as a theoretical landmark of the region. It is noted in it the valuation of the pluriverse and the relationality existing between living and non-living beings (the interbeing). It is a Latin American methodology for the transition design with a view to the realization of different desires and life plans. Instead of the production of knowledge (epistemology) and certain knowledge connected to a particular society (episteme), the ideas of different social groups about the types of entities that they consider to exist in the real world are valued. Thus, it defends the right to territory, and its emphasis is on the worlds and ways of building that world, both in the practices of power present in this collective creative process and in studies on interrelationships in the world, including conflicts between different worldviews.

The initiative Life Projects Network proposed by Marcos Blaser brings together a variety of experiences in the Americas that seek to promote practices in favor of the good life, coming from different places, historical trajectories and conceptions about reality. Created to oppose national development projects (with political orientations from the right or from the left), it aims to promote the exchange between different initiatives and shows that the good life is possible beyond the current developmentalist vision. The practical exercise involving Colombian intellectual Arturo Escobar and his team in the Cauca River valley in Colombia is part of this initiative. This is a response to the exhaustion of the development model in force since 1950. The agro-industrial complex based on large investments with the participation of the World Bank whose model came from the United States (Tennessee

Valley Authority) for sugarcane and livestock plantations, the Cauca Regional Autonomous Corporation (CVC) caused great ecological devastation, massive displacement of peasants and Afro-descendant communities to the periphery of Cali – the second largest in urban Latin America, after Salvador in Bahia-Brazil, whose population is more than 50% Black. Thus, the project sought to promote the autonomy of Afro-descendant communities in the region, especially activists in the Black Communities Process (PCN).

This exercise was dedicated to re-imagining the region as a bastion of agroecological production of organic fruits, vegetables, grain and exotic plants, in a multicultural format by small and medium-sized agricultural producers through a decentralized functional network of peoples and cities. It was a life project developed for the resident population, in a social and territorial reconfiguration of great proportions, which involved different social groups.

Thus, more than thinking and proposing models of development projects, Escobar (2017) concludes, based on this experience, that creating transition projects (drawing) means coordinating plural interests. There are, therefore, two crucial tasks: assembling a co-design team and creating a design space where collaborative design work advances. In a kind of laboratory, these spaces built the construction of a world view and outlined what is expected to be projected in reality. These projects take place through conversations organized for coordinated action in sub-regions – such as that in the city of the valley (Cali).

Life projects, as a possibility of real imagination, evolve from both the continuous generation of contexts, capable of feeding the idea of a transition, and from concrete projects aimed at developing certain aspects of design for social innovation. To guide such an attempt, Escobar (2017) proposes some objectives and activities in the form of a political-ontological declaration in favor of the pluriverse, a landmark that considers other development paradigms and the sustainability of life, that call us to think and act with the heart and mind (*co-razonar*), as a way of 'thinking-feeling with the Earth' (*sentirpensar con la Tierra*) inspired in Zapatism (Escobar 2014).

Zapatismo

One of the most well-known and important characteristics left by Zapatismo as a social movement is autonomy, a key concept of ontological political practice. As an ethnic-territorial movement, the Zapatista Army of National Liberation (EZLN) started a process of constituting one of the most important experiences of contemporary Indigenous autonomy. 'No other insurgent movement would elicit such continental and global solidarity, nor would it have such an impact on the emerging contentious subjectivity.' (Svampa 2016, 332) According to Escobar (2014), autonomy refers to the creation of conditions that allow changing the norms of a world from within (changing traditions traditionally) and not based on the knowledge and intermediation of external specialists.

In this regard, the Zapatistas and their experience of self-government, denial of (national) politics that comes from above and collective decision-making, asking questions, show how autonomy in political practice implies the condition of being communal. In the Sixth Declaration of the Lacandon Jungle, 2005, the EZLN establishes 'this method of autonomous government [...] comes from several centuries of Indigenous resistance and from the Zapatista's own experience. It is the self-governance of communities' (Escobar 2014, 129).

Another Zapatista contribution is the political principle of 'lead by obeying'. Instead of seeking to seize power, it seeks to build a different political practice with a view to the organization of society. Unlike the conception of politics as a specialized activity, lead by obeying determines the bidirectional relationship between authority and command. In it, the relationship between autonomy and power takes horizontal characteristics, since popular wills are debated through assemblies, and vertical ones, which presupposes a command given by the authorities that presupposes the obedience of all (Resende and Castilho 2018).

In an act of global resistance to the neoliberal model, the Zapatista struggle can be highlighted. As Aguirres-Rojas (2017) demonstrates, it has attracted a lot of interest for its antecedents, strategies and transnational dimensions in defending the location or localization of politics. According to Svampa (2016, 336), after 20 years of insurgency, *Zapatismo* opened the snails to the world through the initiative *escuelita de la libertad* to which people from the five continents make a community stay with a view to show from within the Zapatista experience regarding daily living and collective work.

In this sense, there are many convergences in *Quilombismo*, *Buen Vivir*, Life Projects and Zapatismo in terms of the categories they mobilize to propose political alternatives to the development model and the political organization for cooperation. Table 2 brings together the four proposals mentioned, their ideas and the categories of interest to later fit them into the proposed analytical framework.

It can be said that all initiatives mentioned here, of political-theoretical nature, despite having been developed under the inspiration of very specific cultural practices, acquire regional and global importance due to their potential of anti-systemic struggles. They collaborate to detach academic debates on post-development and the common to serve as a guide to political mechanisms such as SSC, contributing to make it an alternative practice. In line with what Escobar (2014; 2017) proposes, we can rethink SSC as an ontological design for the transition to a new civilizing phase.

Proposals for an analytical framework for South-South Cooperation

The peoples that inhabit the geopolitical space that we now know as Latin America and the Caribbean, from colonial invasions to the present day, design and practice forms of existence based on ancestral epistemological and ontological structures. They were anchored in the sense of relationality, community spirit, solidarity, harmony with nature and pluriversity.

Although these forms have been belittled and dismissed as backward, traditional and essentialist by theorists and practitioners of modern development, they are precursors to the criticism made today against modernity. They denounce the failure of their hegemonic development model and point out the imperative of a new civilizing parameter based on the common in the face of global problems – the threat of climate change phenomena, the burning of vast proportions of native vegetation, hurricanes and the current Covid-19 pandemic.

Especially considering an analytical framework to rethink SSC, a research agenda is suggested based on the notions of post-development and the common. As Dussel (2018) explains, universal civilization has evolved due to cooperation in technical terms but keeping the diverse cultural ethos of peoples. So, we consider SSC as this mechanism at the global level that serves as a potential to reify international cooperation principles, processes and purposes.

As for the principle of SSC, a moment when solidarity is evidenced, we would have as criteria: the SSC initiatives (1) that socialize knowledge (techniques and experiences), (2) that move from an idea of appropriation-possession to an appropriation-destiny of communities, (3) which are able to put in common the object of cooperation to all subjects and collectives, as being part of the space-time in which they intervene. To this end, ancestry, the interbeing between living and non-living beings (harmony / balance) and the pluriverse can be mobilized as key categories.

As for the process or means of implementing SSC, a moment when horizontality should be intermediating relations during cooperation activities, the analytical criteria for SSC initiatives would be: (1) it is conceived as a 'policy of the common' between the local and global levels; (2) it develops through democratic practices; (3) it connects the global to the local levels in the midst of a political and social federalism (decentralized governments), that is, it seeks to decide together on the common ones. For that, the categories that could be mobilized would be the autonomy of the subjects and communities to imagine their own reality and design the projects, interculturality and otherness / alterity in which the difference is respected and do not turn into inequality.

As for the purpose of SSC, a moment in which it seeks to achieve well-being on a global scale, the following criteria are suggested: (1) SSC as a mechanism that builds a sense of co-activity and co-obligation between subjects guided by the right to post-development; (2) the ability of SSC to connect the global plan (intercultural human rights agendas and standards) to the place where needs, imaginary and demands are; (3) SSC serves to establish the well-being of all as a global common or as a way of acting in common, a collective construct. We conclude by suggesting to considering the following categories and concepts in the South-South Cooperation as an authentic Southern discussion: alternatives to development; accomplishment of the communal; transformation of societies and world order; transition towards other paradigms (speeches in transition); territoriality (right to territory and reconfiguration of territories).

Figures and Tables

Table 2.1: South-South Cooperation in the post-development perspective. Adapted from Escobar (2017, 30–31).

Models of cooperation	References	Direction	Relationship
Assistance for development	Models from abroad (developed countries)	Top-down processing: from the State/IO/NGO to societies	Agreements between countries and international organizations (vertical)
Cooperation for social justice	Global human rights and environmental sustainability standards	Bottom-up processing: social groups with support of intermediaries	Agreement between international organizations/institutions and civil society (partially horizontal)
Solidary and autonomous cooperation	Local projects (post-development)	Collective and autonomous processing: social groups	Agreements between social groups (totally horizontal)

Table 2.2: Analytical categories proposed in the Latin American context. Source: own elaboration

	Type of initiative	Objective	Ideas and categories
Quilombismo	Theoretical-practical proposal inspired by the 'Quilombo dos Palmares' in Brazil	Happiness of the human being; free, just, egalitarian and sovereign society; harmonious coexistence with nature and other forms of existence	Community-based cooperative economy; collective use of land and production goods; ancestry
Buen Vivir	Worldview or a philosophy of life of the Andean peoples (Quechua and Aymara); from an Andean political-cultural project to a proposal for global debates	Search of balance and harmony between human beings and Pachamama, between the material and spiritual dimensions; real democracy	Interculturality; alternative to development; interrelationship between self-community-nature; difference that complements (does not exclude); cyclic space-time (non-linear)
Life Projects	A praxis based on the case of people of African descent in the Cauca River valley / Colombia	Designs for the civilizational transition; political ontology	Right to the territory; interbeing (relationality between living and non-living beings); pluriverse; collective (communal) creativity; reimagine reality
Zapatismo	Ethnic-territorial movement of certain Indigenous peoples in southern Mexico (Chiapas); transnational alternative political project	Self-government of communities and autonomy of peoples; defense of Indigenous communities' right to land	Autonomy; land rights; politics of 'asking questions' and 'ordering obeying'; action collectives (assemblies); policy location / localization

Figure 2.1: SSC and the notion of the common. Source: Our elaboration

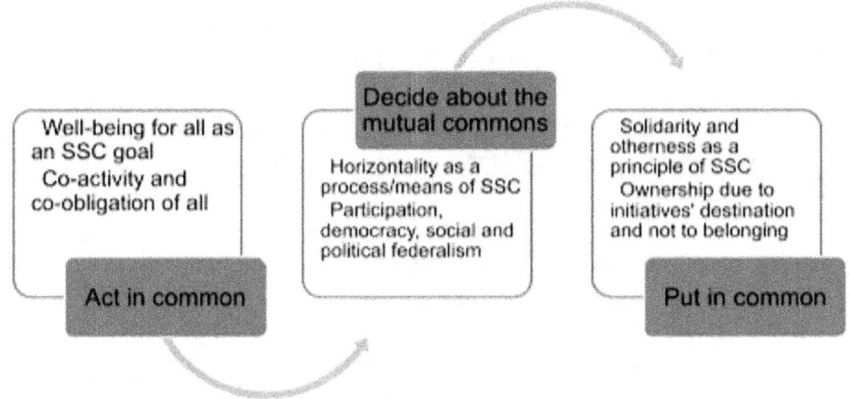

References

Acosta, Alberto. "El Buen Vivir, una alternativa al desarollo", in *Crisis Civilizatória, Desarollo y Buen Vivir* Quintero, Pablo (Comp.). Ciudad Autónoma de Buenos Aires: Del Signo, 2014

Aguirres-Rojas, Carlos Antonio, "Mapa de los movimientos antisistémicos de América Latina" Revista Theomai, n 36 (tercer trimestre 2017), 2017: 128-147.

Ayllón, Bruno Pino. "Evolução histórica da cooperação Sul-Sul (CSS)". In *Repensando a Cooperação Internacional para o Desenvolvimento,* edited by Mello e Souza, André: 57-88. Brasília, IPEA, 2014

Caixeta, Marina Bolfarine. "A Cooperação Sul-Sul: novos referenciais teóricos nas Relações Internacionais como contribuição das Epistemologias do Sul". *Conjuntura Austral* (6) 32 (2015): 4-18.

Chidaushe, Moreblessing. "¿*Cooperación Sur-Ssur o hegemonía del sur?* El papel de sur África como "superpotencia" y donante en África". In *Reality of Aid. Reporte Especial sobre Cooperación Sur-Sur 2010 Cooperación Sur-Sur: Un Desafío al Sistema de la Ayuda Medellín,* edited by ALOP (marzo de 2010).

Dardot, Pierre, and Laval, Christian. *Commun: essai sur la révolution au XXIe. Siècle*. Paris: Éditions La Découverte, 2015.

Escobar, Arturo. *Autonomía y diseño: La realización de lo comunal*. Ciudad Autónoma de Buenos Aires: Tinta Limón, 2017.

_____. *Sentipensar con la tierra: nuevas lecturas sobre desarrollo, territorio y diferencia*. Medellín: Universidad Autónoma Latinoamericana UNAULA, 2014.

Gudynas, Eduardo. "Buen Vivir: germinando alternativas al desarrollo - América Latina em Movimento☐". *ALAI*. (462). (Febrero, 2011): 1-20.

_____. "El malestar no moderno con el Buen Vivir". In *Crisis Civilizatória, Desarollo y Buen Vivir*. Quintero, Pablo (Editor). Ciudad Autónoma de Buenos Aires: Del Signo, 2014.

Kabunda, Mubya, ed., *África y la cooperación con el Sur desde el Sur*. Madri, Los libros de la Catarata/Casa África, 2011.

Kothari Ashish, Salleh Ariel, Escobar Arturo, Demaria, Federico and Acosta Alberto, eds. *Pluriverse A pos-development dictionary*. India: Tulika Books, 2019.

Menezes, Roberto Goulart, and Caixeta, Marina Bolfarine. "Desigualdades, Sul Global e Cooperação Sul-Sul: miradas desde América Latina". In *América Latina no século XXI: desigualdades, democracia e desenvolvimento*, edited by Menezes, Roberto Goulart et al., Curitiba: Ed. CRV, 2021: 111-132

Morales, Analilia Huitrón. "Del discurso a la institucionalización de la cooperación Sur-Sur". In *La constelación del Sur: lecturas histórico-críticas de la cooperación Sur-Sur*. Puebla: BUAP & Santander: Ed. UC, 2019: 165-206.

Miñoso Yurderkys Espinosa, Correal Diana Gómez, and Muñoz Karina Ochoa, eds., *Tejiendo de otro modo: Feminismo, Epistemología y Apuestas Descoloniales em Abya Yala*. Popayán: Editorial Universidad del Cauca, 2014.

Muñoz, Enara Echart. "Una visión crítica de la cooperación Sur-Sur". In *Cooperación Sur-Sur, Política Exterior y Modelos de Desarrollo en América*

Latina, edited by Lima, Maria Regina; Milani, Carlos R.S. & Muñoz, Enara E. Buenos Aires: CLACSO, 2016: 229-256

Nascimento, Abdias. *O Quilombismo: Documentos de uma militância pan-africanista.* Petropolis: Editora Vozes, 1980.

_____. *O Quilombismo: Documentos de uma militância pan-africanista.* 3. edição revisada São Paulo: Editora Perspectiva & Rio de Janeiro: Ipeafro, 2019.

Resende, Ana Catarina Zema, and Castilho, Mariana. "Educação Rebelde e Construção Coletiva de Autonomia nas Escolas Zapatistas". *Abya Yala – Revista sobre acesso à justiça e direitos nas Américas* (2) v.2, (2018): 353-371

Santos, Maria do Carmo Rebouças dos. "A cooperação Sul – Sul (CSS) para a reorientação dos imaginários e práticas do desenvolvimento: os caminhos da cooperação entre Guiné Bissau e Brasil". PdH diss., (tese). Programa de Pós-Graduação em Desenvolvimento, Sociedade e Cooperação Internacional do Centro de Estudos Avançados e Multidisciplinares da Universidade de Brasília, 2017.

Santos, Maria do Carmo Rebouças dos. "O Constitucionalismo Pluralista do Bem Viver: a reação latino-americana ao paradoxo do desenvolvimento". *Revista de Estudos e Pesquisas sobre as Américas* (1) 12, (2018): 125-153.

_____ , and Caixeta, Marina Bolfarine. "Geopolítica na América Latina e Caribe: cooperação Sul-Sul e o pós-desenvolvimento". In *Pensando as Américas desde o Caribe,* edited by Pinto, Simone. R. & Igreja, Rebecca. Lemos. Curitiba: CRV, 2018.

_____ , and Santos, Richard. "Intelectuais Negras(os) e Epistemicídio". In *Universidade Popular e Encontro dos Saberes,* editedy by Tugny, Rosângela Pereira & Gonçalves Gustavo. Salvador: EDUFBA, 2020.

"Sixth Declaration of the Lacandon Jungle" Enlace Zapatista, accessed July 20, http://enlacezapatista.ezln.org.mx/2005/06/30/sexta-declaracion-de-la-selva-lacandona/

Solón, Pablo. *Alternativas sistêmicas: Bem Viver, Decrescimento, Comuns, Ecofeminismo, Direitos da Mãe Terra e Desglobalização.* São Paulo: Elefante, 2019.

Surasky, Javier. "Una mirada a la actual cooperación Sur-Sur que ofrece Argentina". In *La cooperación Sur-Sur y triangular en América Latina: políticas afirmativas y prácticas transformadoras*, edited by Ayllón, Bruno Pino & Ojeda, Tahina Medina. Madrid: Ed. Catarata & UCM, 2013: 40-63.

Svampa, Maristela, "Pensar el desarrollo desde America Latina", accessed November 10, 2017. http://www.maristellasvampa.net/archivos/ensayo56.pdf.

_____. *Debates latinoamericanos.* Indianismo, desarrollo, dependencia y populismo. Ciudad Autónoma de Buenos Aires, Edhasa, 2016.

Torres-Galarza, Ramón. *El sentido de lo común, pensamiento latinoamericano*. 1a edición. Ciudad Autónoma de Buenos Aires: CLACSO, 2018.

Villoro, Luis. "Poder, contrapoder y violência". In *El mundo de la violência*, edited by Adolfo Sánchez Vázquez. México: Facultad de Filosofía y Letras. UNAM, Fondo de Cultura Económica, 1998: 165-175. http://ru.ffyl.unam.mx/handle/10391/1873

Wallerstein, Immanuel. *The Essencial Wallerstein.* New York Press, 2000.

3

Armed Actors in the Colombian Conflict: State vs Armed groups

DEISY MILENA SORZANO RODRIGUEZ
& ETIENNE MULUME ODERHWA

'See, we had neither bridges, nor roads, nor schools. What was asked of the State was that, please, we were Colombians, we were Tolimenses, we were humble, hard-working, honest, healthy people; but that we needed schools, we needed roads, we needed bridges. Asking for those things was a crime.'
– interview with 'Germán', a former combatant.

In 2016, the agreement for the cessation of the conflict and the establishment of a sustainable and long-lasting peace was reached between the Colombian National Government and the Revolutionary Armed Forces of Colombia – People's Army (FARC), one of the largest insurgent groups in the country, after more than fifty years of conflict. Based on the above, the chapter presents an overview of the characteristics of these two actors: it analyzes the role of the State and the FARC as the main actors in the conflict, without ignoring the fact that other protagonists emerged in this prolonged war.

First, the chapter addresses the different definitions and conceptual contributions of the state, where the state is recognized as having the legitimate monopoly of violence and force. This is emphasized in the discussions of classical authors and specialists on the subject, where the state is identified as one of the main actors in the Colombian conflict. It is evident that marginalization and exclusion have determined elements in the development and prolongation of the conflict. In addition, this chapter presents an analysis of the meaning of insurgency, discussing concepts from different lenses, which allows for a general mention of the main movements in Latin America. Colombia, in particular, witnessed the emergence of social movements with defined political traits and ideology, armed groups inspired by the socialist narrative and based on the internal and limiting narratives of the country's own political system, as detailed in the text. Lastly, the chapter provides a synthesis of the conflict in Colombia, where socio-political and economic uncertainties form important elements to further study the inefficiency of the government and institutions.

Defining State

If we are talking about armed conflict, the category of 'state' becomes prevalent given its protagonism. Multiple authors, researchers, academics and others define it while at the same time giving it its functions and laying out their criticisms. Therefore, it is necessary to clearly establish, what is really the state? Is it possible to talk about a classification of the state? Is the category of a proletarian state valid?

The meaning of state appears during the 16th century. If the contributions of Engels are taken into account, he would argue that the state presents itself to us as the first ideological power over, on the other hand, would define the state as 'a group of officials who through their representations and acts involve the community, without being a product of it' (Durkheim 1883, 58).

For Weber (1992), the state is defined as the political institution of continuous activity, which in turn contains a legal and administrative order, which makes it necessary to talk about power, domination and other categories that its analysis pertains; as well as reviewing what Marxism contributes in reference to this: The state is in no way a power imposed from outside society; neither is it the reality of the moral idea, nor the image and reality of reason.

It is a product of society when it reaches a certain degree of development; it is the confession that this society has become entangled in an irremediable contradiction with itself and is divided by irreconcilable antagonisms, that it is powerless to conjugate them. But in order for these antagonisms, these classes with competing economic interests to devour themselves and not consume society in a sterile struggle, a power seemingly above society and called to cushion the shock is necessary, to keep it within the limits of order. And that power, born from that society and which divorces from her more and more, is the state (Engels 1894).

Therefore, it is manifested as a fundamental idea of Marxism that the state is the result of class struggles and contradictions, contradictions that are not reconcilable and give rise to the category of state.

Marx argues that,

> The State is characterized, in the first place, by the grouping of its subjects according to territorial division; the second characteristic feature is the institution of a public force that is no longer the armed people. This special public force becomes necessary because the division of society into classes makes it impossible for a spontaneous armed organization of the population to spring. This public force exists in every state; and it is not only made up of armed men, but also of material accessories, prisons and coercive institutions of all kinds, which the gentile society did not know about (Engels 1894).

The elements mentioned by Engels and others such growth and ownership of the public force given the rivalry of the classes, the collection of taxes, universal suffrage, and the use of violence; provides a clear picture of the conception of the state as an instrument of exploitation of the oppressed class the basic argument about revolution and its origin for Marxist theory; as the state was born from the need to curb class antagonisms, and at the same time, in the midst of the conflict of those classes, it is a general rule that the state is that of the most powerful class, of the economically dominant class, thereby acquiring new means for the repression and exploitation of the oppressed class (Engels 1894)

Likewise, and based on the recognition of a struggle, Engels denies the idea of a state that has existed perpetually in the following manner:

> The State has not existed eternally. There have been societies that managed without it, that did not have the slightest notion of the State or its power. Upon reaching a certain stage of economic development, which was necessarily linked to the division of society into classes, this division made the state a necessity. We are now rapidly approaching a phase of development of production in which the existence of these classes not only ceases to be a necessity, but also becomes a direct obstacle to production. Classes will disappear as inevitably as they arose in their time. With the disappearance of classes, the state will inevitably disappear. Society, by reorganizing production in a new way on the basis of a free association of equal producers, will send the whole state machinery to the place where it belongs: the museum of antiquities, next to the spinning wheel and the bronze ax (Engels 1894).

The state is a special organization of force, an organization of violence to repress any class (Lenin 1917). Without this being conditioned by the exploitation of oppressed classes. A material and specific condensation of a relation of force between classes and class fractions (Engels 1894), where the unity of the bloc in power practically polarizes the interests of the other classes or fractions that are part of it, as represented in the following figure and is the basis of Marx's analysis:

The state has been classified under multiple figures such as the ancient state, the feudal state and the representative state, among others; the isolation with society can be contemplated (that is, with the social and economic relations that concern it, given the divided classes) as another defining element of the State, following this theoretical line where the divided classes would guarantee political domination to the extent that they are politically unified and the state acts as an organizer of their properly political unity, with specific interests by class or fraction (Poulantzas 1968).

Continuing with this debate and in accordance with Marx, we have the proposals of Miliband (1976), who does not share the notion of the total state of the previously mentioned Poulantzas, and denotes it not only as an instrument, but as a more complex concept; that of a systematic expression. Although they differ in some general conceptions, they coincide in the formal and therefore real separation between state and society. Other conceptions, somewhat far from the theoretical line initially proposed, contemplate that it is the state who must provide the necessary minimum of human capital without market disturbance (Becker 1964) through institutions that reduce uncertainty for development and economic growth (North and LeRoy 1976), although it has other functions to consider.

Starting from these approaches, other questions arise – such as is the classification of the capitalist state valid? Does this classification include all forms of state? Is the state a real structure of organization or domination? The role of the State as an institution within society, normative, would frame it as being 'the rector of economic development to guarantee the fulfillment of the goals of a national project, which is up to the Federal Executive (and in a mandatory way, the entire Federal Public Administration) to elaborate and execute' (López 2013, 54) so in this sense national development is its ultimate goal, development that must be comprehensive and sustainable, through all the powers that it owns and with the organs that operate. In accordance with this, the role of the state, although it has not changed, has not always been able to fulfill these stated purposes, being insufficient to respond to the needs of its population, which is added to the modes of investment of public spending.

Whether or not it is an instrument of domination, the crisis of the contemporary state, and all the decomposition and dilution of its role in socioeconomic development, cannot be ignored. Therefore, in the face of the state's failures, constant structural actions are designed to avoid perpetuating the existing pattern. To achieve this, it is necessary to eliminate the concentration of wealth, poverty and inequality and to preserve the social order.

In the words of Dabat (2010, 21):

> While in certain times and places the role of the state has been fundamental in promoting economic, social and cultural progress, in others it has been a strong obstacle to development and human progress, it has absorbed from society more resources than those that it has helped to produce, and has subsidized parasitic groups, stifling the most creative and innovative social expressions, or else it has organized huge apparatuses of death and destruction.

The State as an actor in the armed conflict in Colombia

In the case of the Colombian state, it is necessary to review two articles of its National Constitution that contain fundamental principles which indicate:

a. The Colombian territory is a social state of law, organized in a manner of a unitary republic, decentralized with autonomy from its territorial entities, democratic, participatory and pluralistic;
b. Founded on respect for human dignity, on work and on the solidarity of the people who make it up and on the prevalence of the general interest;
c. As well as aims to serve the community, promote general prosperity and guarantee the effectiveness of the principles, rights and duties enshrined in the Constitution;
d. And to ensure compliance with the social duties of the state and individuals.

Defining Guerrilla

Another conception of guerrillas can be defined as a group of revolutionaries made up of individuals with a strong ideology, in defense of social justice, having as motivation the group or collectivity, which has a greater benefit than acting individually; waiting to obtain power in order to meet basic needs and the aforementioned social justice, eliminate the oligopoly of violence against the state and open up for political participation (Harnecker 1988). But, how is it possible to arrive to this approach?

Answering this involves establishing that the origins of guerrillas have been the object of multiple studies, where it has been affirmed that its birth was due to being a self-defense group in the face of the state's opposition and for the protection of its private property. There is no single consensus on definitions and the debate is getting stronger. While for some people the term must be limited to conceptions related to ideology, for others the concept must include the meaning of sources of dissent, to which the individual interpretation that is given must be added, giving rise to confrontations and generating a degree of greater complexity.

According to this, and in order to establish the concept of war under which this chapter operates, it was necessary to review the existing definitions. The term guerrilla, according to Guillén (1969), refers to an army that is taken out of parts that make up a whole and that must act strategically with the aim of attacking the state, given favorable internal and external revolutionary conditions: economic, diplomatic, social and political aspects.

For her part, Mariguella (1969) defines the term from its origin, stating that the guerrilla is the result of the political instability of the territories, making some classifications: urban guerrilla warfare, psychological warfare or rural guerrilla warfare as forms of revolutionary war. From this, the distinction between guerrilla and delinquent is made, where the latter category differs from the purpose of the guerrilla. Although the criminal personally benefits from his actions and attacks indiscriminately, the guerrilla particularly pursues a political goal, where they attack and are an implacable enemy only to the government and therefore inflict systematic damage on the authorities and the men who dominate and wield power, with the aim of collaborating in the creation of a totally new system and a revolutionary social and political structure with the masses in power.

Consequently, Guevara (1950) agrees with the previous definitions considering that the guerrilla struggle has the main objective of liberating itself from a government that constrains it, given the forces that remain in power against established law and for this liberation people's capacity is required. In opposition to Guillen, Guevara affirms that it is not always necessary to wait for all the conditions for the revolution to be in place since the insurrectionary focus can create them. Likewise, it points out that the field and the strategy are the epicenters for the struggle in Latin America, or underdeveloped America in its terms, and it is necessary to demonstrate to the people that it is not possible to maintain the struggle for social demands within civic and peaceful spaces. Geographical and social characteristics determine the mode and forms that war and guerrillas will adopt, although the general parameters are universal.

In addition, Castro (2008) affirms that the guerrilla is an embryo of development of a force capable of taking power originated from the class struggle. Taking into consideration the Communist Party of Colombia (1973), guerrilla is defined as an organization with orientation, methods and discipline whose objective is the armed struggle for the achievement of social justice.

In the 1808–1814 War of Independence between Spain and the French Empire the term guerrilla was used for the first time, mythologizing for posterity the importance of this defensive movement. In 1809, faced with the general frustration of the Spanish civilian population in the face of the repeated defeats of its army in front of the ranks under the command of Napoleon Bonaparte, the local organization arose to attack French objectives in a surprising way. It should be clarified that the excessive mistreatment of the Napoleonic troops served as a breeding ground to generate great guerrilla leaders such as *Chaleco,* the most important guerrilla in *La Mancha*, who joined the confrontation by witnessing the *Valdepeñas* fire where his mother and brother died.

This model of fighting arose under the incapacity of traditional combat due to the asymmetry of the armies; the Spanish troops were widely outnumbered by their invaders. The uncertainty of the French about the lightning attacks carried out on key objectives for the distribution of resources, communication and roads, dismembered the Napoleonic strategy based on the war of vast armies, giving way to the establishment of a command dedicated to persecuting guerrillas, significantly neglecting the main battle fronts. The guerrillas provided key information to the army and were a fundamental piece to obtain victory, although they did not win the war properly, their appearance and combat tactics turned the French onslaught upside down (Ibid.). Examples of this model had previously been seen, however only in Spain were they strategically articulated, being indispensable to achieve victory.

The basic structure of a guerrilla model is simple; It is fundamentally composed of three elements, a group of people with access to military weapons, ideological support through the civilian population and a terrain with conditions that allow an attack on the enemy, Von Clausewitz (1832) describes that the success of a guerrilla is based on two factors: a terrain with geographical access difficulties that make it possible to protect and camouflage the guerrilla, and a civil war that encourages dissent and support for the rebel group.

The aforementioned structure, according to Mariguella (1969), is characterized by the autonomy of its movements translated into the belligerence of the area where they operate, under a functional hierarchy specialized in ambushes: surprise assaults in order to destabilize the enemy. The members that compose it are volunteers and act independently from a pre-established military command or political party; they have the popular support of a percentage of civilians and encourage the appearance of *caudillos* or visible heroes who embody the voice of the voiceless.

There are contributions of the organization in the Latin American revolutions from the Spanish yoke between 1810–1824, among the most recognized *caudillos* in command of guerrilla groups are the Uruguayan José Gervasio Artigas, the Mexicans Hidalgo, Morelos and Guerrero, the Argentine Martín Güemes, the Chilean Manuel Rodríguez, commandos that acted in order to disrupt the development of Spain on these colonies and in some cases worked hand in hand with regular armies based on independence, anti-racism, anti-colonialism and in some cases anti-property.

The mythical meaning of the word guerrilla thickens much of the history of the second half of the 20th century in Latin America, after the defeat of Nazi Germany, when the dispute for the application of a global economic model takes place: in one extreme capitalism, which is based on the free flow of the market, and on the other hand communism, based on the regularization of the market by the state. Given this situation, the southern countries of the American continent with emerging economies and due to the direct influence of the US hegemony adopt the capitalist-Keynesian system, an implementation that is achieved thanks to the influence of the newly founded International Monetary Fund and the World Bank.

This is how Latin American countries embrace an economic-social system that is alien to their culture and history, developed under multiple pro-independence coups. A series of guidelines is acquired that do not correspond to the nature of its economy. It is in this historical milestone where North American hegemony arises over the entire continent, the decision to apply this model is not made taking into account the environment itself and the existing variables in each region, it is simply limited to the replication of models from the north, without taking into account the particular conditions of this geography.

With the adoption of this model, outbreaks of deep dissatisfaction arise as well, which prompt movements extending from Cuba to Patagonia in Argentina. From there, we start from the premise that the guerrilla assumes this condition of his own free will without any pressure other than the submission of his peers, which leads to the generation of a violent clash with an evidently asymmetric force.

Highlighting the multiple organizations which were part of the guerrilla struggle in Latin America, in Paraguay, there was the emergence of the Paraguayan People's Army (EPP), known as a revolutionary and political-military organization, based on Marxist-Leninist ideology (Mariguella 1969).

For its part in Chile, the Manuel Rodríguez Patriotic Front was the main left-wing group in the country, having as its background the confrontation against the military dictatorship of Augusto Pinochet, together with the *Vanguardia Organizada del Pueblo* group, founded in 1968. In Peru the group Partido Comunista del Perú – Sendero Luminoso (PCP-SL) or Shining Path – is notable, as well as the Túpac Amaru Revolutionary Movement (MRTA), who were inspired by the leftist guerrillas forming in nearby regions. In Uruguay, for its part, the National Liberation Movement-Tupamaros (MLN-T) was present, which had its stage as an urban guerrilla and later as a political movement. Likewise, Nicaragua witnessed the Sandinista National Liberation Front (FSLN), which had its origins in left-wing political and military organizations, initially called the National Liberation Front. Argentina, with the presence of *Montoneros* as a manifestation of the armed struggle, the People's Revolutionary Army (ERP) as an Argentine guerrilla organization, and finally the Peronist Armed Forces (FAP) carried out urban guerrilla actions. In Mexico, the representation was for the Zapatista Army of National Liberation (EZLN), as a political-libertarian organization, with military origins, as well as the Mexican Popular Revolutionary Army and the Revolutionary Army of the Insurgent People. In Cuba, there was the July 26 Movement (Cuba M-26-7), as well as the Revolutionary Left Movement (MIR) founded in 1965 (Ibid.).

Finally, in Colombia, we saw the Revolutionary Armed Forces of Colombia, the people's army (FARC-EP), and the National Liberation Army (ELN). Each of these with different origins, causes, ideologies, environmental conditions and operating characteristics, under a specific motivation: to fight against the Colombian army. The FARC-EP, for their part, insisted on the existence of the class struggle, so power could only pass into the hands of the proletariat and the poor peasants through armed insurrection and the overthrow of the dictatorship of the bourgeoisie (Lenin 1960).

Armed groups in Colombia

It was in the 1960s when the first social movements emerged with a defined political trait and ideology based on internal contexts of the country – such as the narrowness of the political system. Starting as self-defense groups, and later transforming into mobile guerrillas due to the specific circumstances such as the destruction of *Marquetalia* in 1964 and the attack on *Río Chiquito*, *El Pato* and *Guayabero* at the hands of the military; as a consequence of the implementation of the LASO plan, whose purpose was to counteract the revolutionary movements, the Southern Guerrilla Bloc emerged, later called the Revolutionary Armed Forces of Colombia, FARC, which contained a revolutionary program including agrarian struggle, national liberation, a popular government, among other aspects, which identified with the politics and influence of communist thought.

Later came the National Liberation Army, ELN. It was started by young people in the region of Santander, who saw the revolutionary example of Cuba. It is one of two main guerrilla armies with leftist political ideologies that operate in Colombian territory, although militarily weakened.

M-19 was born in 1974. The movement springs up in cooperation with ANAPO, its founders being former leaders of the Communist Youth. In the same way, there are other unsuccessful attempts to form guerrillas such as Tulio Bayer, the Student and Peasant Workers' Movement, MOEC, and the Popular Liberation Army (Harnecker 1988). The EPL Popular Liberation Army emerged in 1967 in the Alto Sinú and Alto San Jorge regions, as the armed wing of the Maoist-inspired Marxist Leninist Communist Party, whose cadres come from urban middle classes, many of them of Antioquia origin. It was on 17 December, in the midst of peasant uprisings, that the first guerrilla detachment of the PLA emerged – led by Pedro Vásquez Rendón and Francisco Caraballo.

Currently, the groups with the greatest presence and participation are reduced to the FARC and the ELN, together with a strong presence of criminal gangs and organizations that do not follow a political purpose.

In 1985, the National Guerrilla Coordination (CNG) was created, made up by eight of the nine guerrilla groups existing in the country, excluding the FARC. Consequently, in 1987, the Simón Bolívar Guerrilla Coordinator was formed (CGSB) (Aguilera 2013), in order to create unity with M-19, ELN, EPL, Quintín Lame, the PRT, and the FARC-EP (Guaraca 2015).

On the other hand, it is not only the FARC, the ELN and the alliance units that have been actors at certain times in the country's conflict. Colombia has witnessed the presence of minority insurgent groups that had an armed project as stated by Aguilera (2013):

- The Popular Liberation Army, EPL – originated in the sixties, had the participation of peasants from Córdoba, banana unions, and urban sectors of Antioquia. Originally with a Maoist, militarist and abstentionist vision, it transformed its prolonged people's war scheme and considered other models (such as the Albanian one) for the construction of socialism.
- The Quintín Lame Armed Movement, MAQL – created in the 1980s, represented the Indigenous communities of Cauca, since they defended them and fought against the landowners in order to protect their territory. They also maintained the internal order of their communities without using a political-military project like the two groups with the highest representation.
- Revolutionary Workers Party, PRT – a group with similar characteristics to the MAQL in terms of the absence of a political-military project; and not being considered a militia or self-defense.
- M-19 – with high political capital, given its actions and movements. Originated in the seventies.
- Stream of Social Renewal – detached from the ELN.
- Francisco Garnica Front – made up of the EPL dissenters
- Popular People's Militias and for the people – arose in relation to the ELN.
- Independent militias from the Aburrá Valley.
- MIR – Free homeland.

Conclusion

To discuss, and to try to define, the actors of the Colombian armed conflict is a complex and ambitious task. The presence of social, political and economic uncertainty is pertinent when we talk about an inefficient state and an organized group which confronts it. From an insurrectionary viewpoint, the armed struggle is a process which vindicates the social, political and economical absences that the state has constantly provided and legitimizes the people's resistance, their right to revolt. Likewise, social unrest, originated by the presence of specific interests from the state, institutional inefficiency, socioeconomic inequality, political violence and repression, influence of foreign military forces, persecution of social mobilizations (from students, unions and other sectors of the population), Indigenous persecution, land struggle and inefficient rural policies; were detonating factors of the confrontation between the state and the armed groups. The Colombian armed conflict is part of a decolonization process whose foundation is found in the rejection of the policies of exclusion of the ruling bourgeoisie. As well as considering the genesis and emergence of armed groups in the country, it is a conflict that arises from the post-Cold War world processes because it reflects the new political order that emerged because of the conflict between the two superpowers (Pastor Beato 2013).

So, behind the political objectives of the armed actors in Colombia there was an anti-imperialist dynamic that opposed the hegemonic power and the intent to push the country towards the periphery of global capitalism. This means that for the armed actors in Colombia, there were two social groups within the state, of the privileged one and of the exploited, therefore, their political agendas had to be aligned on the side of the marginalized.

Analyzing the Colombian conflict from a decolonial perspective requires an understanding of the ways in which political power was configured in this post-Cold War Latin American country as well as how political actors operated at the time. From a decolonial perspective, one can say that the armed actors in the country of our interest correspond to the modern forms of the creation of technologies of killing because their actions have affected communities and individuals differently (Maldonado-Torres 2008).

Earlier, we identified the actors involved in one of the longest armed conflicts in the history of mankind, highlighting that the forms present in the conflict in Colombia were different depending on the particular armed group and the struggle for the defense of local lands was considered as a survival alternative against global capitalism.

This is what Maldonado-Torres (2008) calls a scream of terror made by the populations who lived under the domination of the Global north that mask its actions under a civilizational mission. The armed conflict in Colombia must be interpreted from this perspective as a turn towards socialism; therefore, some Colombian armed actors, of course, have to take into account the specificities of the capitalist policies to which they opposed.

This allows us to note that the peace agreement signed by the main actors of the armed conflict does not differentiate the political actors of the socialist side from those with capitalist tendencies, but rather it is all about recognizing that all of them were equally bad in managing the longest conflict in history Latin American.

In the Colombian conflict we see a combination of the cultural with the social and the national. In other words, this was a resistance to neoliberalism and neoimperialism (Anderson 2004) in the 1960s to highlight a process of recognition of the practices of social groups that have been historically victimized (De Sousa Santos 2018). In short, the Cold War precedes and explains the genesis of the Colombian conflict, whose actors turned to the great economic and military blocs. Although over the years, Colombia will experience the multiplication of armed groups, what they all had in common was the territorial control and therefore the control of the communities that live on those territories. Because of the exclusion from global markets that suffer those territories, they were forced to develop a kind of social economy.

Figure

Figure 3.1. Conceptualization of the state. Source: Own elaboration based on (Poulantzas 1968).

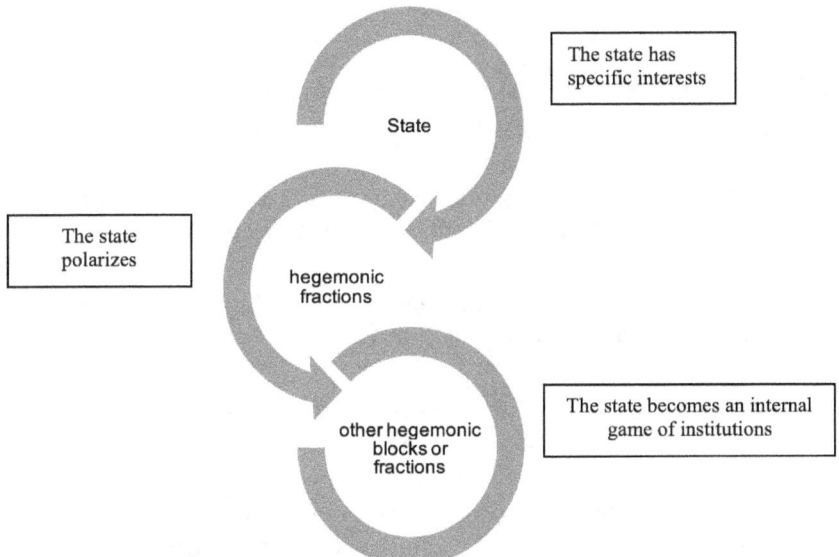

References

Aguilera, Mario. 2013. *Insurgencies, dialogues and negotiations*. Bogotá: Ocean Sur.

Anderson, P. (2004). The role of ideas in the construction of alternatives. In Chomsky, N (et al.). New world hegemony: alternatives for change and social movements. Buenos Aires: Clasco.

Becker, Gary. 1964. *Human Capital: a theoretical and empirical analysis*. USA: Columbia University Press.

Boisier, Sergio. 2003. *Development in place*. Santiago: Universidad Católica de Chile, Faculty of History, Geography and Political Science. Geo Books Series.

Castiñeira, Katiuska, and Fidel Castro. 2011. *Guerrilla of the time*. Havana: Ruth Casa Editorial.

Castro, Fidel. 2008. *La Paz in Colombia*. Havana: Political Editor.

Clausewitz, Carl von. 1984. *De la guerra*. Barcelona: Editorial Labor.

Communist Party of Colombia. 1973. *Manuel Marulanda Vélez*. Bogota: campaign notebooks.

Constitución de colombia. 1991. *Political Constitution of Colombia*. https://pdba.georgetown.edu/Constitutions/Colombia/colombia91.pdf.

Dabat, Alejandro. 2010. *State, neoliberalism and development. State and development*. Mexico: National Autonomous University of Mexico.

De Santos Sousa, B. (2018). An epistemology of the South: the reinvention of knowledge and social emancipation. Buenos Aires: Clacso and Siglo XXI.

Durkheim, Emile. 1883. *The role of great men in history. In Political Writings*. Gedisa, pp. 47–57.

Engels, Friedrich. 1894. *The origin of the family, private property and the State*. Moscow: Institute of Marxism-Leninism of CC of the CPSU.

Guaraca, Jaime. 2015. *Thus was born the FARC, memoirs of a Marquetalian commander*. Bogotá: South Ocean.

Guevara, Ernesto. 1960. *The guerrilla war*. Cuba.

Guillén, Abraham. 1969. *Challenge to the Pentagon: Latin American guerrilla*. Barcelona.

Harnecker, Marta. 1988. *Chronology of political violence. Combination of all forms of fighting. Combination of all forms of fighting*. interviewed by Marta Harnecker: Gilberto Vieira (Secretary General of the Colombian Communist Party).

Lenin, Vladimir. 1917. *The state and the revolution*. Russia: Editorial Zhizn and Znanie.

Lenin, Vladimir. 1960. *Selected works. Gospolitizdat.* Moscow: Institute of Marxism-Leninism of the CC of the CPSU.

López, N.2013. *Constitutional characteristics of the National Development Plan.* Sinaloa: Obtained from: http://www.icjsinaloa.gob.mx/medios/publicaciones/caracteristicas_constitucionales.pdf

Maldonado-Torres, N. (2008). Decolonization and the decolonial turn. In Tabula rasa. Number 9: p. 61–72. Available at http://www.scielo.org.co/pdf/tara/n9/n9a05.pdf

Mariguella, Carlos. 1969. *Minimanual of the Urban Guerrilla.* Insubordinate.

Miliband, Ralph. 1976. *The State in capitalist society.* Spain: Siglo XXI Editores

North,Douglass, and Roger LeRoy Miller. 1976. *The economic analysis of usury, crime, poverty.* Mexico: Fondo de la Cultura Económica.

Pastor Beato, N. (2013). Decolonization and Cold War in the independence of Indonesia. In Ab Initio, No. 8, p. 121–138, available at www.ab-initio.es

Poulantzas, Nicos. 1968. *Political power and social classes in the capitalist state.* Madrid: Siglo XXI de España editores.

Weber, Max. 1992. *Economy and society. Comprehensive Sociology Outline.* 2nd ed. Mexico: Economic Culture Fund.

4

Decolonizing Environmental Politics: *Sumak Kawsay* as a Possible Moral Foundation for Green Policies

VALERIA VICTORIA RODRÍGUEZ MORALES

Each nation interprets the value of each good from a different axiological scheme of preconceptions. This is the reason why the moral assumptions of each country conflict in the attempt to reach an international agreement to pursue environmental justice. It becomes difficult to coordinate an axiological hierarchy that prioritizes environmental goods over economic goods. The denial of this priority arises from the assumption that 'man' and 'nature' are two opposite concepts. The Ecuadorian economist Alberto Acosta (2010) points out that the supposed antagonism between human beings and Nature 'is the starting point to understand the conquest and colonization of America, which crystallized merciless exploitation of natural resources' (17; my translation). By contrast, in the Quechua tradition, as well as in other Indigenous traditions, we find a relational concept of Nature.

Although the Quechua concept of *sumak kawsay* is relatively recent, it is also deeply rooted in a conception of the human being in permanent relationship with Nature. The general meaning of this concept is related to living in harmony with Nature and community (Hidalgo, Arias, and Ávila 2014, 29–73). The axiological conflict between environmental goods and economic goods is demolished, because both are part of the structure of 'good living' or 'life in fullness'. Countries like Ecuador or Bolivia have included this concept in their new political constitutions (Asamblea Constituyente de Ecuador 2008; Asamblea Constituyente de Bolivia 2009). Nonetheless, their own moral assumptions often show strong colonial influence.

Which are the moral foundations that could sustain an international policy in order to pursue environmental justice? This philosophical question is hidden in the background of the present research, but it is not intended to be answered in its entirety. Since there are innumerable ways to answer that question, this chapter limits it to a particular case: could the Quechua concept *sumak kawsay* be one of these moral foundations? The answer (hypothesis) that is argued is affirmative and is based on Latin American authors such as: Eduardo Gudynas, Enrique Dussel, Alberto Acosta, Yuri Guandinango, Verónica Andino, Ana María Larrea and Salvador Schavelzon. The method used to answer this question is the critical analectic, structured by Dussel in his effort to find a decolonial methodology. Consistent with this method, the objective of this research is to dialogue about the Quechua concept *sumak kawsay* within the alterity of different moral foundations for international environmental policies, such as the concept of development.

Dussel's critical analectic method

The Mexican philosopher Enrique Dussel perceives the attempt to formulate a decolonial philosophy with Eurocentric methods as a setback. That is why he sees the necessity of a new methodology based on the critical study of the Hegelian dialectics and the Aristotelian method of analogy. To think that Dussel's method is then Aristotelian-Hegelian would be a total misinterpretation. On the contrary, the analectic method is born as a criticism of other methods and stands on its own merits.

In *Método para una filosofía de la liberación* [Method for a philosophy of liberation], Dussel (1974) introduces the analectic moment by clarifying the concept of alterity: 'the other, for us, is Latin America with respect to the European totality; it is the poor and oppressed Latin American people with respect to the dominating but dependent oligarchies' (181–182; my translation). Dussel's *other* is not an *absolute* alterity as Levinas describes the other's face. According to the Mexican philosopher, the totality is univocal; the univocity is identity. Then, the totality is opposed to alterity.

The analectic method begins with the recognition of the other as free, as beyond the system of totality; therefore starts from the revelation of the other and, trusting in his word, works, serves, creates (Dussel 1974, 182). Faith in the other's word, an anthropological faith, is the precondition of this analectic moment. According to Dussel (1974), the dialectical method is the dominating expansion of the totality from itself; the passage from potency to the act of the same (182). After this criticism, he offers a synthetic definition of the analectic method, that is: 'the passage to the fair growth of the totality from the other and to "serve" (the other) creatively' (182; my translation). The critical analectic method involves an exercise of finding similarities in the possibilities of polysemy, as he later explains in a class on this method (Dussel 2016).

The described method guides the objectives of the present chapter. As stated above, this research aims to dialogue about the Quechua concept *sumak kawsay* within the alterity of different moral foundations for international environmental policies. In order to achieve this general objective, it is necessary to go through a critical step and an analectic moment.

The first specific objective concerns the critical stage: the purpose is to question the moral assumptions of the concept development as the foundation of international policies. The reason why it is necessary to question this concept lies in its colonial influence and its harmful consequences for the environment. Furthermore, most of the mentioned Latin American authors oppose the concept of development to the decolonial alternative of *sumak kawsay*. The second specific objective concerns the analectic stage, start from the word of the other: the proposal is to understand the polysemy of the concept in Quechua *sumak kawsay* as a possible moral foundation for environmental policies. The stages of the analectic method will culminate in what Dussel calls the fair growth of the totality from the other and to serve (the other) *creatively*. Therefore, the critical study of the concept of development will bring alternatives based on different moral assumptions in order to reduce the environmental impact.

It is necessary to clarify that this chapter does not attempt to analyze Abya Yala's environmental policies in general. Its approach does not belong to the area of political science or international law. The reflection intends to be philosophical and presents some possibilities of understanding rather than concrete realities. This research is limited to the axiological and moral scope of new constitutional proposals from two specific countries: Ecuador and Bolivia. The study of the concept of *sumak kawsay* linked to the relational Andean worldview aims to question the economy-focused conception of Nature. For this reason, it is carried out from the perspective of a critical look at conventional development. That is why the term Abya Yala is used to refer Latin America, because it means 'Mature Land', according to the historic Kuna Indigenous group (Carrera and Ruiz 2016, 12). Given the maturity of this land, it does not make sense to put here the underdevelopment label.

Critical description of the concept 'development'

The Global Forest Watch's 'World forest map and tree cover change data' (2020) reveals that Bolivia ranks fourth among the countries with the highest loss of primary forests. An etiological study of deforestation in this country, between 2000 and 2010, remarks the three main direct causes: livestock in sown pastures, mechanized agriculture and small-scale agriculture (Müller et al. 2014, 20). From that decade to the present, the causes remain the same. These have only become stronger and stronger. Despite the immense food production at the cost of the destruction of primary forests, 15.5% of the population of this same country is undernourished (FAO et al. 2020, 8). This unfortunate irony stems from the hope of economic growth based on the export of raw materials.

According to Alberto Acosta (2010), from the conquest and colonization of America 'an extractivist scheme was forged to export Nature from the colonies based on the capital accumulation demands of the metropolises' (17; my translation). The contradiction between precarious food security and unbridled food production in Bolivia is the result of an economic scheme founded five centuries ago in the midst of colonial violence.

As a colonial residue, developing countries conceive development as blind economic growth without many environmental considerations. Brazil, the country with the highest loss of primary forests (Global Forest Watch 2020), carries the slogan of Order and progress on its flag. It is under discussion whether Brazil should be considered a developing country or not. This discussion considers economic growth more than its levels of inequality, extreme poverty, and environmental impact.

Amartya Sen (2000) describes as 'narrow views of development the ones that identify development with the growth of gross national product, or with the rise in personal incomes, or with industrialization, or with technological advance, or with social modernization' (3). Those narrow views had their consequences on the status quo of an unfair and anthropocentric structure. According to the Ecuadorian anthropologist Ana María Larrea (2010), the concept of development was constructed from a colonialist perspective and is now in crisis due to the poor results it has generated throughout the world (15; my translation). These poor results include environmental impact, hunger, inequality, etc. Probably, because of these consequences, this type of development cannot be sustained throughout time. This pace of indefinite progress necessarily implies a collapse due to the characteristics of the natural world, hence the need to combine the concept of development with sustainability.

Although for Wolfgang Sachs (1999) the sustainable development combination is an oxymoron, at least its intention gives us a little hope. The Uruguayan researcher Eduardo Gudynas (2003) distinguishes between traditional development and sustainable development, criticizing the first one without ceasing to discuss the second one.

The proposal is to criticize the concept of development but not to destroy it radically. It would be Manichean to think that the biased conception of development is to blame for all the ills that affect the environment and the human community. Furthermore, it would be unfair to ignore the virtues that this model has provided on the possibility of structuring large populations, granting certain food security to a relative majority. Nevertheless, it would also be naive to think that conventional development actually improves our situation in some respects without making it worse in others. In addition, it improves the situation of some beings making it worse for others.

According to Gudynas and Acosta (2011), in the 1940s, the concept of development defined as a progressive linearity or as the opposite of underdevelopment began to be formalized (73). However, the authors point out that in reality 'what is observed in the world is a generalized "bad development", existing even in countries considered as developed' (Gudynas and Acosta 2011, 73; my translation). The relationship between this bad development and the gradual destruction of the environment is decisive. The assumption of blind progressive linearity causes progressive damage as well. This type of moral assumption, where the highest good is economic value, interrupts international treaties aimed at protecting the environment. The most surprising thing about this assumption is its ability to ignore the irreducible relationship between economics and environmental justice.

One of the main notions attached to the progressive destruction of the natural wealth of the *developing* countries is extractivism. Gudynas (2015) defines this concept as 'a type of extraction of natural resources, in large volume or high intensity, which are essentially oriented to be exported as raw materials without any processing or with minimal processing' (13; my translation). This type of export condemns the Abya Yala nations to the lowest profit in economic terms and the highest loss in environmental terms. Moreover, according to the aforementioned study, third generation extractivisms have been the cause of most social conflicts in Latin America (Gudynas 2015, 24). The Uruguayan researcher not only denounces the environmental consequences of extractivism, but also its social problems and moral conflicts.

Gudynas dedicates a whole section to ethics and values in the conclusions of his book *Extractivismos: ecología, economía y política de un modo de entender el desarrollo y la Naturaleza* [Extractivisms: ecology, economics and politics from a way of understanding development and Nature] (2015). In this section, he points out that there is an axiological component that cuts across all levels: 'from the cultural bases of development strategies to extractivist implementations with all their environmental, economic, political and social implications' (433; my translation). According to Gudynas, this component is the result of an anthropocentric ethic where 'values are only assigned by human beings, and they prevail directly linked to human benefits and needs' (434). The present chapter considers that not even human benefits and needs are prioritized, since the environmental impact has enormous negative consequences on the well-being of the most vulnerable sectors of the human community. What is often prioritized is a split economic value, briefly separated from its immediate material value.

Gudynas (2015) adds that the 'recovery of other values in nature, and in particular when its own rights are recognized, is not only an antidote to extractivism, but is also an alternative to that anthropocentric ethic' (434; my translation). The moral assumptions of traditional development are determined by the conception of 'nature'.

In the 1980s, a new turn in the conceptions of nature began with a perspective originated in the economy: 'from different starting points and conceptual options, several authors began to consider nature as a form of capital' (Gudynas 2003, 23; my translation). A sample of this type of economy-focused conception is the widely used expression of natural resources. This explains the fact that countries like Bolivia or Brazil see deforestation as a form of economic progress. Developmental extractivism condemns these countries to their own wear and tear. International logic forces them to choose this kind of economy, because the moral foundation of this logic lies in the polysemic value of progress.

Due to the polysemy of the concept of development or progress, it can be used for very different purposes, even contrary to each other. A logical consequence of conceiving nature as a form of capital is the interpretation of economic progress as the exploitation of this capital. By contrast, more recent notions such as sustainability include preserving the environment as part of development. For this reason, if it is interpreted in the previous sense, the term sustainable development itself may sound contradictory.

However, even in the sustainability of a development more courteous with nature there are also moral assumptions that Gudynas would call anthropocentric. Furthermore, Sachs's critique of the concept of sustainable development reveals that this attempt to preserve the environment is ultimately an attempt to preserve the pace of economic growth.

In an article entitled 'Los derechos de la naturaleza en serio: respuestas y aportes desde la ecología política [The rights of Nature seriously: responses and contributions from political ecology]' (2011), Gudynas raises the following argument: 'if the rights of nature are taken seriously, their own values appear, but also the chains of an exclusively economic valuation are broken' (255; my translation). What the present chapter proposes is a decolonizing effort to take seriously the rights of nature.

Sumak kawsay as a possible moral foundation for environmental policies

The economy-focused conception of nature leads the paradigm of conventional development in Latin American countries. Nevertheless, cultures that bestow on nature an immense or even sacred value still inhabit many of these countries. The cases that fit the purpose of this chapter are Bolivia and Ecuador.

Although in Bolivia and Ecuador there are approved opinions that promote extractivism, there is also an attempt to explore in the Andean tradition alternatives to the dominant conception of nature. Given the oral character of this tradition, there is a possibility that the concept of *sumak kawsay* may be actually a new construction. Yuri Guandinango (2013) points out that this notion 'is not explicit in Indigenous communities; since most of the communities of the Ecuadorian highlands are traversed by historical processes that have reconfigured the experiential practices; such is the case of agroecological and sociocultural systems' (14; my translation). Nonetheless, most likely this notion is consistent with a relational conception of nature that is deeply rooted in an Indigenous worldview.

Pablo Mamani (2011, as cited in Schavelzon 2015) lists the terms that could approximate a definition or translation of the concept of *sumak kawsay*: 'richness of life'; 'knowing how to live life'; 'attitude'; 'be full of great heart'; and even 'good die'. In Bolivia, the state assumes as a principle the Aymara version of good living: *sumaj qamaña*. Javier Medina (2001) translates it to the following terms: 'good life', 'life quality', 'wellbeing', 'lifestyle', 'good living', 'happiness', 'joy', 'felicity' (26). Xavier Albó (2011) proposes other definitions for *qamaña*: 'live', 'dwell', 'rest', 'shelter' and 'take care of others'. Consequently, according to Albó, the translation of *sumaj qamaña* is: 'good living together or living well together'. Regarding the polysemy of these terms in Quechua and Aymara, Salvador Schavelzon (2015) says: 'the difficulty in defining a signifier tells us about the beginning of a journey where conceptions of life and different worlds are translated and delimited for the construction of political concepts' (181; my translation). However, thanks to this phenomenon, it is possible to apply Dussel's analectic method, where different horizons dialogue due to a possibility of analogy in polysemy.

The new constitutions of Ecuador and Bolivia introduce the concepts of *sumak kawsay* and *sumaj qamaña* as a political project. Article 275 of *Constitución de la República de Ecuador* (2008) points out: 'The development regime is the organized, sustainable and dynamic set of economic, political, socio-cultural and environmental systems, which guarantee the realization of the good living, from *sumak kawsay*' (135; my translation). Since, in its constitution, Ecuador is presented as a republic and not as a plurinational state, the principle of *sumak kawsay* is applied as a generality. In the Bolivian case, *sumaj qamaña* is an ethical-moral principle among diverse principles from other *nations* of the state. Article 8 of the Second Chapter of *Constitución Política del Estado Plurinacional de Bolivia* (2009; my translation) establishes: 'The State assumes and promotes as ethical-moral principles of plural society: *ama qhilla, ama llulla, ama sua* (do not be lazy, do not be a liar, do not be a thief), *suma qamaña* (good living), *ñandereko* (harmonious life), *teko kavi* (good life), *ivi maraei* (land without evil) and *qhapaj ñan* (noble way or life)'. The concepts extracted from the Guaraní tradition do not clash with the relational perception of nature characteristic of the *sumak kawsay*. Especially *ñandereko* and *teko kavi* have an impressive resemblance to the Andean concepts of good life. Although it would be foolish to confuse these notions as if they had the same meanings and were originated in the same traditions, they could all be presented as alternatives to conventional economic development.

Yuri Guadinango (2013) separates the academics who explain the discourse of good living from different perspectives into three groups according to their positions: 'the followers of group A promote good living as an alternative to development; those in group B place good living in line with 21st century socialism; and those in group C understand good living as part of development theories' (19; my translation). This chapter belongs especially to the position of group A, because group C suggests that the concept of *sumak kawsay* may become a reinforcement of the dominant paradigm of traditional development. However, there are reasons to present this concept as a very different alternative due to its possibility of founding environmental policies: (1) the Andean relational worldview; (2) the criticism of the logic of capital accumulation; (3) the recognition of intrinsic values in nature.

What does the notion of Andean relational worldview mean? This first reason is linked to what Gudynas and Acosta (2011) called a 'space occupied by the ideas encompassed under the label of "Good Living"' (76; my translation). Those 'ideas originated in traditional Andean knowledge, focused on the well-being of people and defenders of another type of relationship with the environment, quickly managed to influence the debate on development, and become new alternatives to it' (Gudynas and Acosta 2011, 76; my translation). The worldview that concerns the concept of Good Living does not conceive of the human being as a subject separated from the object so-called nature. The human being is only one part of the *chakana*, the 'bridge at the top', which unites nature, the spiritual world, the human community and the ancestors (Flores Rengifo 2018). Although *sumak kawsay* is not a purely ancestral concept and is mixed with very recent political projects, the coherence between this concept and the relational structure of the Andean traditional conception of nature is notorious. In the Andean relational worldview, we are not the masters and antagonists of nature, but only a part of the relation between all beings that are united by the *chakana*. Good Living is not mere human well-being, but rather a certain harmony of complementarity between all beings.

It is precisely this worldview that challenges development to decentralize its anthropocentric approach. As Verónica Andino (2010) asserts, 'the challenge posed by the Sumak Kawsay paradigm is to consciously dislodge the logic of capital accumulation, with its corollary in the concept of development, from the central place it occupied in the imaginary of the Ecuadorians of what a better society represents' (101; my translation). This is the aforementioned second reason: the criticism of the logic of capital accumulation. If the center is no longer the human being but the *chakana*, then the economy-focused logic loses its meaning. With the moral foundations displaced, the edifice of conventional development collapses and an alternative possibility of grounding environmental policies emerges.

Why environmental policies specifically? This is what the third reason is aimed at: the recognition of intrinsic values in nature. The two previous reasons converge on this one. The decentralization of value allows for moral diversification. The following statement is the philosophical complaint of Gudynas (2015): 'dissolution of ethics is what makes tolerable the repeated violation of the rights of people and of nature as a means of extractionist imposition' (434; my translation). Therefore, a reconstruction of an ethic that takes seriously the rights of nature is a *sine qua non* condition for the proposal of green policies. Gudynas adds: 'For this reason, conceptions such as Good Living or the rights of nature are undoubtedly alternatives, but they become substantial when promoting ethical changes that open the doors to other valuations, thus generating consequences on many levels' (Gudynas 2015, 434; my translation). These consequences are directly related to a mitigation of our environmental impact.

The three reasons presented support the understanding of *sumak kawsay* as an alternative possibility of moral foundation of environmental policies. The polysemy of this term is a fertile field for dialogue. This is the reason why this concept represents a decolonial point where the national horizon of Ecuador and Bolivia can meet the international horizon of the rest of Abya Yala. Environmental policies are inevitably international policies because even domestic provisions can affect the rest of the world. Therefore, it is necessary to look for different concepts such as *sumak kawsay* that can represent more nations in their polysemy than those that are represented by the univocal concept of conventional development.

Conclusions

Is the Quechua concept *sumak kawsay* one of the possible moral foundations that could sustain an international policy in order to pursue environmental justice? Throughout this chapter, an affirmative answer has been argued. As well as other notions of the diverse cultures of Abya Yala, the concept of *sumak kawsay* is a fertile moral foundation for the pursuit and consolidation of international policies that promote environmental justice.

The argumentation has gone through two methodological moments to reach that conclusion. The first step was a critical study: the concept of conventional development was questioned for its consequences on the environment. The reading of Gudynas, Acosta and Larrea revealed that this concept is based on the colonial economic system consolidated later by industrial production demands.

The second methodological moment was analectic: the polysemy of the concept in Quechua *sumak kawsay* was understood as a possibility of moral foundation for green policies. 'Life in fullness' is conditioned by harmony with nature and community. This means that the economic values that concern the satisfaction of the human needs do not contradict the environmental values. The reason lies in the relational conception of nature. This concept could constitute a decolonial moral foundation for green policies because it provides alternatives to conventional development.

Sumak kawsay is not a magical concept that will automatically solve all the environmental challenges of our time, but it could be a moral foundation alternative to the one that conceives nature only based on economic criteria. This foundation constitutes an axiological system that could morally base international agreements in order to preserve the environment in Abya Yala. At least there is already a point in common between Ecuador and Bolivia, which Dussel would call analectic.

When the national decision-making threatens environmental justice, international considerations must start from the dialogue of moral assumptions towards the search for alternatives, different from the conceptual structure that led to the harmful consequences. The premise that supports this conclusion is that even inside a country that causes and suffers an environmental impact, there may be axiological hierarchies in conflict, also conditioned by the dominant paradigm on an international scale.

References

Acosta, Alberto. *El Buen Vivir en el camino del post-desarrollo. Una lectura desde la Constitución de Montecristi.* Quito: Friedrich Ebert Stiftung, 2010.

Albó, Xavier. "Suma qamaña = convivir bien. ¿Cómo medirlo?" In *Vivir Bien: ¿paradigma no capitalista?*, edited by Ivonne Farah and Luciano Vasapollo, 133–144. La Paz: CIDES, 2011.

Andino, Verónica. "Continuidades y rupturas entre los enfoques de economía solidaria y desarrollo local." In *Diálogos sobre Economía social y Solidaria en Ecuador*, edited by Yolanda Jubeto, Luis Guridi and Maité Fernández-Villa, 59–148. Bilbao: Instituto Hegoa, 2010.

Asamblea Constituyente de Bolivia. *Constitución Política del Estado Plurinacional de Bolivia*. La Paz: Corte Nacional Electoral, 2009.

Asamblea Constituyente de Ecuador. *Constitución de la República de Ecuador*. Quito: Asamblea Constituyente de Ecuador, 2008.

Carrera, Beatriz, and Ruiz, Zara. "Prólogo." In *Abya Yala Wawageykuna. Artes, saberes y vivencias de indígenas americanos*, edited by Beatriz Carrera and Zara Ruiz, 12–17. México-España: Patrimonio Cultural Iberoamericano, 2016.

Dussel, Enrique. "Curso sobre el método analéctico crítico." Class lecture at Universidad Nacional Autónoma de México, Ciudad de México, February 3, 2016.

Dussel, Enrique. *Método para una filosofía de la liberación. Superación analéctica de la dialéctica hegeliana*. Salamanca: Ediciones Sígueme, 1974.

FAO, FIDA, OPS, WFP, and UNICEF. *Panorama de seguridad alimentaria y nutricional en América Latina y el Caribe: seguridad alimentaria y nutricional para los territorios más rezagados*. Santiago de Chile: Organización de Naciones Unidas para la Alimentación y la Agricultura, 2020.

Flores Rengifo, María Gabriela. "La Chakana y los saberes ancestrales del Pueblo Kayambi." B. A. diss., Universidad Central del Ecuador, 2018.

Global Forest Watch. "Interactive World Forest Map and Tree Cover Change Data." Global Forest Watch Map. Accesed May 20, 2021. https://www.globalforestwatch.org/map/

Guandinango, Yuri. "Sumak Kawsay – Buen Vivir. Comprensión teórica y práctica vivencial comunitaria, aportes para el Ranti Ranti de conocimientos." MSc diss., Facultad Latinoamericana de Ciencias Sociales, 2013.

Gudynas, Eduardo, and Acosta, Alberto. "La renovación de la crítica al desarrollo y el buen vivir como alternativa." *Revista internacional de filosofía iberoamericana y teoría social* 53 (April 2011): 71–83.

Gudynas, Eduardo. "Los derechos de la Naturaleza en serio: respuestas y aportes desde la ecología política." In *La Naturaleza con derechos. De la filosofía a la práctica*, edited by Alberto Acosta and Esperanza Martínez, 239–286. Quito: Abya-Yala, 2011.

Gudynas, Eduardo. *Ecología, economía y ética del desarrollo sostenible.* Quito: Ediciones Abya-Yala, 2003.

Gudynas, Eduardo. *Extractivismos. Ecología, economía y política de un modo de entender el desarrollo y la Naturaleza.* Cochabamba: CLAES-CEDIB, 2015.

Hidalgo, Antonio Luis, Arias, Alexander, and Ávila, Javier. "El pensamiento indigenista ecuatoriano sobre el Sumak Kawsay." In *Sumak Kawsay Yuyay. Antología del pensamiento indigenista ecuatoriano sobre Sumak Kawsay* edited by Antonio Luis Hidalgo, Alejandro Guillén, and Nancy Deleg, 29-73. Huelva: Universidad de Huelva and Universidad de Cuenca, 2014.

Larrea, Ana María. "La disputa de sentidos por el buen vivir como proceso contrahegemónico." In *Los nuevos retos de América Latina. Socialismo y sumak kawsay*, edited by Secretaría Nacional de Planificación y Desarrollo, 15–27. Quito: SENPLADES, 2010.

Müller, Robert, Larrea-Alcázar, Daniel, Cuéllar, Saul, and Espinoza, Sara. "Causas directas de la deforestación reciente (2000-2010) y modelado de dos escenarios futuros en las tierras bajas de Bolivia." *Ecología en Bolivia* 49, no. 1 (April 2014): 20–34.

Sachs, Wolfgang. *Planet dialectics. Explorations in environment and development.* London: Zed Books, 1999.

Schavelzon, Salvador. *Plurinacionalidad y Vivir Bien/Buen Vivir. Dos conceptos leídos desde Bolivia y Ecuador post-constituyentes.* Quito: Abya-Yala, 2015.

Sen, Amartya. *Development as freedom.* New York: Anchor Books, 2000.

5

Latin American Critical Economic Thinking and the Labor Market

ROCIO ARREDONDO & JAVIER CASTELLON

It is well known that most of the economic theory is formulated in the Western world (mostly U.S.A. and England), where it has achieved a higher status within the social sciences. However, the experience in the Latin American countries (LAC) along the 20th Century in applying the policies derived from these theories to propel economic development has been disappointing at best. One of the most notable efforts for creating a body of work that addressed the specific problems faced by the LAC has been the Latin American Structuralist School in the 1950s. Following a group of distinguished authors across the region – Raúl Prebisch in Argentina, Aníbal Pinto in Chile, Celso Furtado, Fernando Cardoso and Enzo Faletto in Brazil, and Juan Noyola in Mexico – this school of thought was able to build an analytical toolbox capable of accurately diagnosing the root causes of the ills experienced in the LAC. These efforts provided the governments with the necessary tools to implement economic policy programs that led to an accelerated industrialization, the expansion of the domestic market, outstanding economic growth and rising living standards for the next couple of decades (Bértola and Ocampo 2010).

A long time has passed since these ideas were set in motion to generate one of the most prosperous periods experienced in Latin America, and most of the economies in the region have gone through a big transformation. The secondary sector, especially manufacturing, has become a key sector in the largest economies, and some of them even have developed a large high-tech export base (Moreno-Brid and Ros 2004, 184). According to the principles of structuralism, a higher industrial base was a necessary condition for development, since it was expected to foster technological progress, raise productivity, and reallocate labor into more productive activities (Prebisch 1983) settling the basis for higher wages and a better distribution of income.

Although it is debatable if the first two propositions became true or not, one can hardly say the same for the propositions relating to the labor market. It is noticeably clear that the labor conditions had not shown much improvement compared with the period in which the Latin American Structuralist School (LASS from now on) ideas were set in motion exhibiting stagnant wages, high informality rates, and poor job quality. In the present paper, we argue that this inability for improvement comes from implementing the policy prescriptions coming from western thinking, which emphasizes the role of the market forces and pushes for deregulation, recommending measures like reducing collective bargaining and low minimum wages (Ros 2015, 51–72).

In order to have an improved policy response for these unresolved issues about the labor market, it is important to have an analytical framework that allows us to properly diagnose the root causes of the problem and take 'the right medicine' to relieve it. It is in this regard that the structuralist school provides a better approach to shed light into these root causes, since one of the main methodological features of this school of thought is the use of the historical-inductive approach, rather than the logical-deductive that is typical of the theories that had domain policy making in the last three decades.

Therefore, it is imperative to make a change in the way we approach the economic challenges of the developing world, shifting away from theories that conceived the textbook free market model as the blueprint for policy making in developing countries, and towards those that emphasizes the characteristic traits and underlying operating mechanisms in these economies, capable of elucidating the core issues that prevent LAC from developing.

The main thesis of the LASS, which was the impossibility to get out of the underdevelopment trap following the western recipe, goes hand by hand with the decolonial agenda that has been resonating a great deal in a multiple of fields of science in the last couple of decades. The decolonial authors argue that the colonial countries were able to reproduce their old dominance relations over the colonized ones through the spread (and imposition) of the euro-centric view of science, which tend to naturalize these epistemological hierarchies and create subordination structures. We can easily see that we are able to reach the same conclusion from either approach – and that the need for a development theory of our own is urgent. Therefore, in this chapter we argue that both approaches can nurture each other in order to reach this common goal.

This chapter first briefly reviews the structuralist approach in Latin America, as it is considered one of the main predecessors of the decolonial agenda, introducing its own analytical framework for analyzing development issues specific to Latin America. Secondly, an analysis of the Mexican labor market is presented as a case study, to denote the need to approach its study through new theories and approaches. Thirdly, a section on the relationship between Latin American structuralist school (LASS) and the decolonial agenda is discussed, and finally, conclusions are presented.

A brief review on Latin American structuralism

According to Bielschowsky (1998) the LASS can be described as a specific body of analysis, applicable to historical conditions proper of the Latin American periphery. Thus, the structural analysis mainly focuses on medium-long term economic and social tendencies; paying close attention to the behavior of social agents, the role of institutions, it's change over time, and the initial conditions.

Epistemologically speaking, the LASS relies heavily on the inductive method. Induction makes reference to the analytical process that goes from specific facts to affirmations of general character (Rojas 1990, 83) by the means of identification of regularities, establishing interconnections on the observed phenomena and the detection of trends. Although this method could generate theories of limited scope, the lack of universality of its conclusions is compensated with a stronger base of empirical validity (World 1969, 431).

This method seems more compatible with the normative nature of the objectives of the LASS and allows the analysis to adapt easily to evolving problems, like those typical of the developing world, without losing consistency or coherence (Bielschowsky 1998, 14). This practice departs far from the abstract-deductive method used in most of the western economic theories, which seeks universal and ahistorical laws, which seems unfitting when it comes to dealing with historical and regional specifications.

Thus, one of the main principles of the LASS is that classical economics (in the Keynesian sense of the word) has its limitations when it comes to correctly interpreting the reality of developing countries, leading to erroneous conceptions of economic policy (González 1986). Raúl Prebisch, the father of Latin American structuralism, narrates how he began to question his schooling as a neoclassical economist when he had to face the economic consequences of The Great Depression as a Subminister of Finance and the Central Banker of Argentina in the 1930´s. Then, he realized that the traditional economic policy prescriptions, derived from the traditional theories, were not enough to solve the *structural problems* (hence the term structuralism) of the region (Prebisch 1983). After he left office in the early 1940's, Prebisch was able to put together the main theoretical conclusions of his experience into the work that became the core foundations of the LASS.

The main focus of Prebisch's early work was the external vulnerability, the tendency to generate balance of payments deficits and the international distribution of the gains of technological progress. The analysis taken upon these issues arrives at the conclusion that there are uneven commercial relationships between the developed countries, the 'Center', and the developing ones, the 'Periphery'. This distinction would become one of the central pillars of structuralist analysis.

The productive disparities between these two groups of economies tend to move the terms of trade in favor of the central economies when these engage in commerce with the periphery. Therefore, if a free trade strategy is implemented in both countries, these disadvantages will perpetuate themselves in the medium-long run, preventing the peripheral economy from developing. Thus, when Prebisch joined the Economic Commission for Latin America and the Caribbean (ECLAC) in 1949, he was able to perform an accurate diagnosis for the entire region (ECLAC 1951) and suggested an inward-looking development strategy as opposed to the export-oriented alternative. This was the birth of the LASS.

After the publication of the diagnosis, several academics across the region followed Prebisch's lead and began to use the basic toolbox displayed by him – one othe ne hand, the historical-inductive method; and on the other hand the theoretical concept of the 'Center-Periphery relation' and its implications. This resulted in the flourish of a rich literature on the major issues that plagued Latin America for the next decades. The better known examples are the structuralist theory of inflation (Noyola 1953; Sunkel 1956; Pinto, 1968), which emphasized the bottleneck coming from a restricted supply of agricultural goods and the social pressure on wages; and the dependency theory (Furtado, 1971; Cardoso and Faletto 1971; Graciarena 1976) which analyzes the economic and political implications of the power structure on the light of the Center-Periphery system.

However, there is one central issue that the authors of the present chapter feel that hasn't had enough attention despite its discouraging recent performance – the distortions regarding the labor market. There have been signs of unhealthy labor markets across the region for the past couple of decades, such as strong presence of informality, insufficient growth of real wages, and, therefore, poor quality jobs.

Labor markets are strongly influenced by institutional and structural factors. The first one includes labor legislation, minimum wages, and the labor institutions that establish workers' working conditions. In addition, various actors, such as trade unions and employers, are involved in decision-making regarding the rules of the game in labor markets. The second group of factors influencing the functioning of the labor market, the structural ones, includes demographic dynamics, i.e., the age distribution of the population, the level of women's participation in society in general (and therefore in the labor market), the population's schooling, and the economic structure inherited from the past, among others.

A good example of the influence of institutional factors in the struggle for collective labor rights is Latin America. According to Cerdas Santi (2017, 215), through the development of the horizontal voice, a concept introduced by O'Donnell (1989), the power of workers through the union has contributed to reduce power asymmetries vis-à-vis the state and employers. However, in the case of Mexico, since the introduction of the neoliberal model, these types of political figures have lost collective power.

The labor market issues were not of major interest for the structuralist authors until the decade of the 80's, still there are some writings that address these problems as a consequence of other phenomena. The early structuralist thought of these labor market mishaps as a result of the transition from a mainly rural economy into an urban one with more modern productive sectors and the reallocation of the labor force throughout these sectors, a phenomenon Aníbal Pinto (1970) called structural heterogeneity. By the middle of the 1980's the labor landscape became worrisome, as the capacity of the urban centers to absorb the growing labor force was undermined. The result was a widening of the tertiary sector, which is characterized by low productivity activities and substandard jobs, exhibiting a different kind of structural heterogeneity within the big cities (Pinto 1984).

In the next decades, the policy making paradigm suffered a big shift towards a more market-oriented one, when most of the countries adopted the neoliberal agenda and started to pursue objectives like opening up the economy to international trade and capital flows – as well as the liberation of key domestic markets such as financial, telecommunications, and labor. A series of structural reforms by the International Monetary Fund (IMF), the World Bank (WB) and the World Trade Organization (WTO) were implemented to achieve these goals (Mosoeta & Williams 2012, 2). Meanwhile, the welfare state was dismantled to a minimum level leaving vulnerable sectors to the will of the invisible hand.

The expected benefits of these measures followed the mainstream narrative; a significant improvement in allocation of resources and efficiency; increases in productivity and growth; higher wages and better distribution of income; and, finally, a reduction in poverty (Toye 2003, 30–34). Needless to say, these rewards were under-delivered, as labor conditions in the Global South still differ from those prevailing in the Global North (Saad-Filho 2005). Defining Global South broadly as to the regions of Latin America, Asia, Africa, and Oceania, which can also refer to as Third World and Periphery, that denote regions outside Europe and North America, mostly (though not all) low-income and often politically or culturally marginalized (Dados and Connell 2012, 12).

Although we are aware that the individual experience across countries may be a bit diverse, we know that this situation is especially true for one of the biggest economies in the region: Mexico.

Mexico's case study

Over 40 years have passed since the publication of the 1984 Pinto's article on the situation of the labor market in Latin America, and it's alarming how similar was the labor landscape described in the 1980's and the one we are experiencing right now.

Although there has been a gradual fall in the rate of labor force participation worldwide, the trend in Mexico and Latin America had been more stable prior to the crisis caused by the COVID-19 pandemic. Thus, as of 2012, the participation rate was stable at around 68% in Latin America and 64% in Mexico. However, since the recent crisis according to ILO data (2020), more than 26 million people lost their jobs during 2020, representing a 10% drop in labor force participation in the region.

In addition, economic growth expectations for the Latin American region, and for Mexico in particular, are not favorable. Figure 5.2 shows the economic growth rate of GDP for Mexico, Latin America, and the World between 2005 and 2020. It shows a greater drop in the 2012 crisis period for Mexico (-5.2%) than for Latin America (-1.88%) and the rest of the world (-1.67%). In the post-crisis period, it can be said that Mexico's growth had been stagnant with rates ranging between two and three percent in the last decade. Even with the COVID-19 pandemic, Mexico is among the countries in the region with the steepest drop in GDP (-8.23%) in 2020, while the fall observed in the region was lower (-6.30%).

As a result of the evolution of the economic cycle, unemployment rates in the region have followed different patterns. Figure 5.3 shows that, in the Latin American region, this indicator has been above the world average throughout the period, reaching over 8% in recent years; while at the global level, the unemployment rate has followed a slightly downward trend since 2009, reaching 4.9% in 2019. On the other hand, unemployment rates in Mexico are not generally high (the highest values were recorded during periods of crisis, when they were above 5%) and since 2017 they have returned to values ranging between 3.4% and 3.3%, except for 2020, when they rose to 4.7%.

As reviewed in the previous graphics, unemployment rates are not usually remarkably high in Mexico, but having a job does not guarantee decent living conditions. Therefore, it is important to analyze other indicators that reflect the labor conditions of workers. Possibly one of the indicators that best characterizes Latin American labor markets are the high rates of labor informality, which refer to both those employed in the informal sector and those employed in informal conditions (i.e., they may be employed in perfectly constituted private or public companies, but do not enjoy certain labor rights such as social security, non-wage benefits, or have access to health institutions). Mexico is no exception and has informality rates of over 55%. As can be seen in Figure 4, the incidence of labor informality, which shows a similar pattern by gender, has shown a decrease since 2012 (after the spike recorded during the Great Recession and starting in 2007). However, despite this, the average value in 2020 is close to 56%.

Even more contemporary authors such as Ros (2015) state that the Mexican labor market in Mexico is '...very competitive and flexible, with low union density, high labor turnover rates and high labor mobility between sectors' (10). In addition, they mention that stagnation in real wages is also related to high rates of informality, a segmentation between the formal and informal labor market, within the formal sector technological conditions and different market structures lead to wage differences between industries. In other words, an increase in employment in modern sectors does not bring with it a significant increase in the real wages that these sectors have to pay (Ros 2015, 10).

For their part Levy and Székely (2016), highlight that informality rates in Latin America have remained constant, moreover in the case of Mexico there has been no improvement in the last two decades. They also argue that there is a close connection between informality and low productivity levels in Mexico, pointing out that although there have been significant advances in educational coverage, these have not been reflected in a decrease in informality rates (501).

In addition, it shows that the labor informality rate for women, between 57 and 60 percent, is slightly (a couple of percentage points) higher than that of men. Other indicators that accentuate labor precariousness are working hours and low wages. Mexico is the country with the longest working hours and the lowest wages in the OECD (OECD 2018), with an average of 2,148 hours of work per year per worker; well above the OECD average (1,734 hours). At the same time, the minimum wage is at $1.1 per hour (compared to the OECD average of $6.7 per hour). And in many cases, the labor income of Mexican workers is below the poverty line.

At the same time, there has been a stagnation of real wages and, therefore, a loss in the purchasing power of families. Figure 5 shows the evolution of the average real wage per worker, which has ranged between 330 and 350 pesos per day from 2005 to 2018, an increase of less than six percent over a 13-year period.

In conjunction, there has been a stagnation of real wages and, therefore, a loss in the purchasing power of families. According to the Mexican Institute of Social Security (IMSS) data, the average real wage per worker has ranged between 330 and 350 pesos per day from 2005 to 2018, an increase of less than six percent over a 13-year period. If we compare the evolution of Mexico's real wage with that of other Latin American countries, as shown in Figure 5, we notice that while remunerations in countries such as Peru, Chile and Brazil are on the rise; in Mexico, the purchasing power of workers is quite stagnant. This situation has been going on for more than 30 years. According to the estimates of Ibarra and Ros (2019), the average wage has not yet recovered the values prior to the 1982 crisis, which means that it has grown less than labor productivity. Hence, the wage share has been declining for decades, reaching levels as low as one quarter of the total value added.

Observing this experience, and how labor conditions seem to be worsening, the question arises as to whether precarization and bad labor conditions have become a permanent feature of Latin American development and whether it has contributed to the region's disappointing long-term performance. For this reason, it is imperative to question the current validity of certain concepts, what is happening in these societies, and the approach under which certain phenomena are studied and analyzed.

The LASS and the decolonizing agenda

One of the central ideas of the decolonizing agenda is that forms of coloniality still persist in the present, not only in modern relations of power that solidify and naturalize the racial domination of colonialism, but also in knowledge formations and modern (individualist) ways of being that colonial power imposed on the world as a hegemonic standard (Adams and Estrada 2017, 7). If we apply this principle to the problems of economic development, we have the starting point for the LASS.

As Cañón (2019, 12) puts it, the inferiority of some countries is accentuated by the inability to generate their own science, which is taken advantage of by others to exercise domination over them and classify them as underdeveloped. Thus, a handbook for development is designed and imposed on them. Although the problem may seem purely economic, it's much wider. It is for this reason that the LASS approach to economics could contribute to the decolonizing agenda, and vice versa; the structuralists could provide the methodological foundations and the study cases for elaborating an analytic body that allows underdeveloped countries to create its own tailor-made map for development; while the decolonizing authors may wider the vision beyond the economic dimension and contribute to the formation of a more overall theory.

Several decolonial authors have already mentioned the relevance of the LASS as an important predecessor for the decolonial agenda. Aníbal Quijano (2007, 95) recognizes Prebisch as the most influential author in the Latin American attempts to get away from the Eurocentric view; Restrepo & Rojas (2010, 61) mention Prebisch too as a milestone in the decolonial inflection in the social sciences; while Sérgio Costa (2019) pointed out that *dependentistas* opened a second lineage of Latin American modernity research, rejecting dualistic descriptions towards a radical relational approach to global asymmetries and inspiring current postcolonial and decolonial approaches (as quoted in Ruvituso 2020, 35).

On the other hand, there have not been many recent attempts to use the decolonial principles in economics, since it has proved to be a discipline very reluctant to change (Kayatekin 2009, 113). Nonetheless, some authors have pointed out the necessity to incorporate the decolonial toolbox into the field; Kvangraven and Kesar (2021, 5–6) emphasize that the economist's obsession for *objectivity and rigor* prevents them from uncovering its Eurocentric core hidden in the formalizations of the mainstream approach, and calls for the acknowledgement of the decolonial perspectives for a better understanding of the unequal structures that create injustice. On the other hand, Danby (2009, 1119) proposes that the adoption of postcolonial concepts in heterodox economic analysis would make it more robust, since it will apply principles like uncertainty and historical time to a broader set of institutions and transcend the Eurocentric modernity, mentioning Celso Furtado and Juan Noyola as examples of it.

Finally, in his late work, Prebisch (1983, 23) reflected furthermore on his Center-Periphery system concluding that this relationship goes far beyond just trade – the late industrialization of the periphery accentuated its tendency to imitate the center, trying to adopt its technology and its lifestyle, to follow its ideology and reproduce its institutions. Thus, this system penetrates under the social structure, creating considerable contradictions that need to be highlighted in order to be corrected. The reader can easily appreciate the close link to the decolonial principles.

Conclusion

The approaches presented in this paper show that one of the great contributions of Latin American critical thinking has been its tools to address problems intrinsic to Latin American countries. It also sets an important precedent in the creation of a body of work specific for a time and place, thus providing to the policy makers with the analytical arguments for implementing a different development strategy.

Without these approaches we could not be talking about the importance of decolonizing science and that the countries of the Global South build their own knowledge. To decolonize science is to accept that knowledge is marked by power relations, in that sense both approaches complement each other. the Center-Periphery conception of the LASS can nourish from the decolonial principles to solidify its foundations; while the historical-inductive method developed by the structuralist authors could serve as an epistemological alternative to enable the Global South to the creation of knowledge.

The purpose of conducting a study relating the need to decolonize science, through Latin American approaches, together with the study of Latin American labor markets characterized by precariousness, stagnant wages, high rates of informality and lack of labor rights, is to highlight the relevance of structural and institutionalist approaches for understanding the functioning of labor markets.

It is evident that there is a relationship between informality rates and the stagnation of real wages, caused in part by the segmentation of labor markets, which leads to greater investment in sectors with greater human capital and technology, making necessary a wage policy that redistributes income in favor of lower wage earners, to stimulate the domestic market, productivity and investment in lagging sectors.

Last, but not least, the authors would like to bring attention to the relevance of this agenda, it is of utmost importance to generate an analytical framework that delves into the roots of the economic and labor conditions of these countries, to be subsequently translated into public policies that involve all workers who have been invisible within these power relations.

Figures

Figure 5.1. Labor Force Participation Rate in Mexico, Latin America and the World (1990–2019). Source: World Bank (2021).

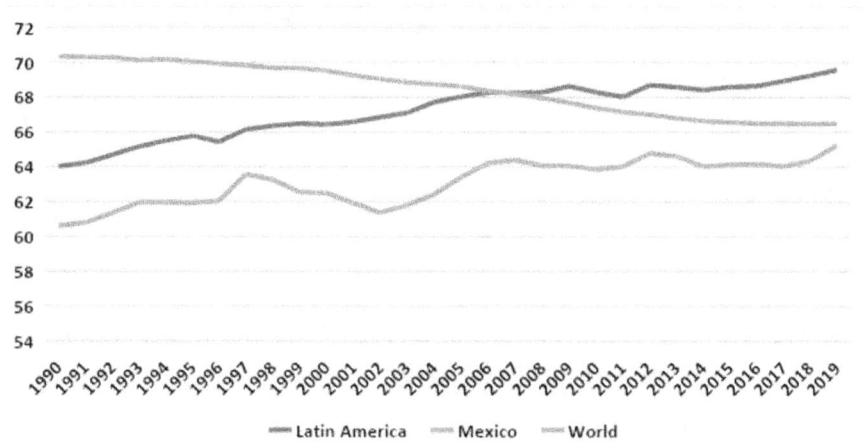

Figure 5.2. Real GDP growth rate in Mexico, Latin America and the World (2005–2020). Source: World Bank 2021. Aggregates are expressed in US dollars at constant 2010 prices.

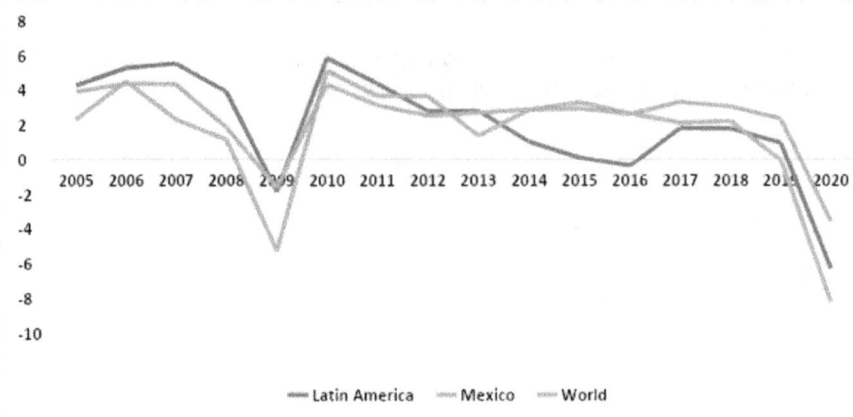

Figure 5.3. Unemployment rate in Mexico, Latin America and the World (2005–2020). Source: World Bank. 2021.

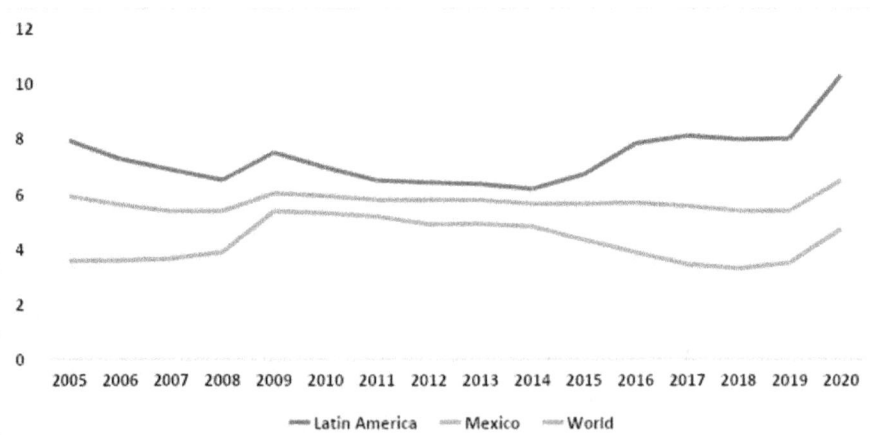

Figure 5.4. Labor informality rate by sex in Mexico (2005–2020). Source: Economic Information Bank, INEGI, 2021.

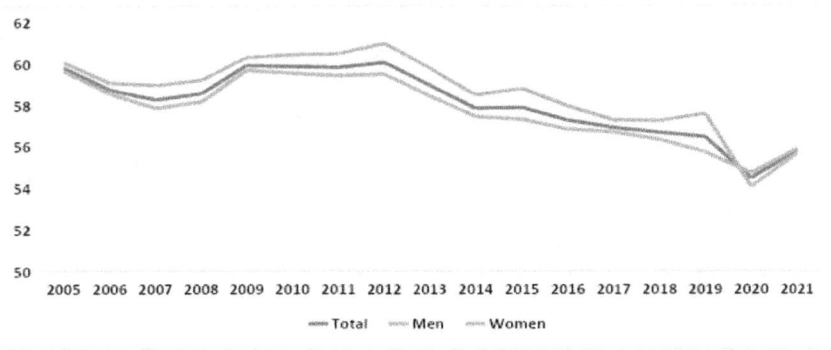

Figure 5.5. Evolution of wage remuneration in selected Latin American countries (2005-2017) (2010 = 100). Source: ECLAC 2019. Average real wage is used. Average annual index (2010=100).

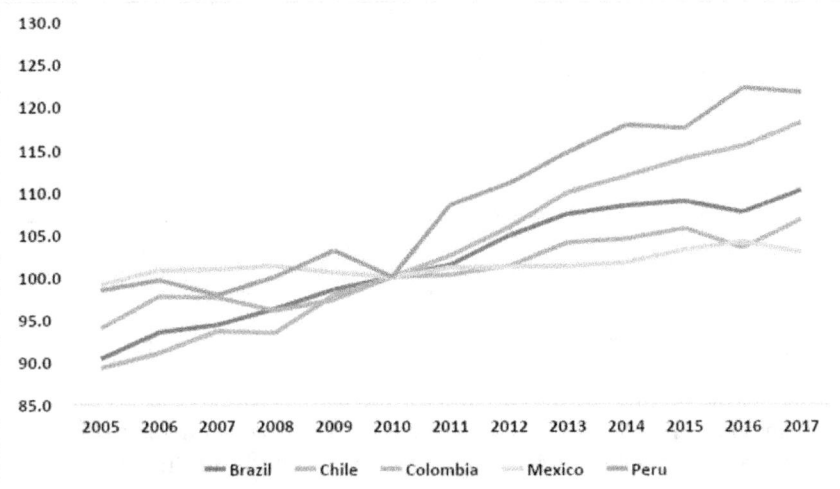

Figure 5.6. Evolution of the wage share in value added in Mexico (2003–2019). Source: Economic Information Bank, INEGI, 2021.

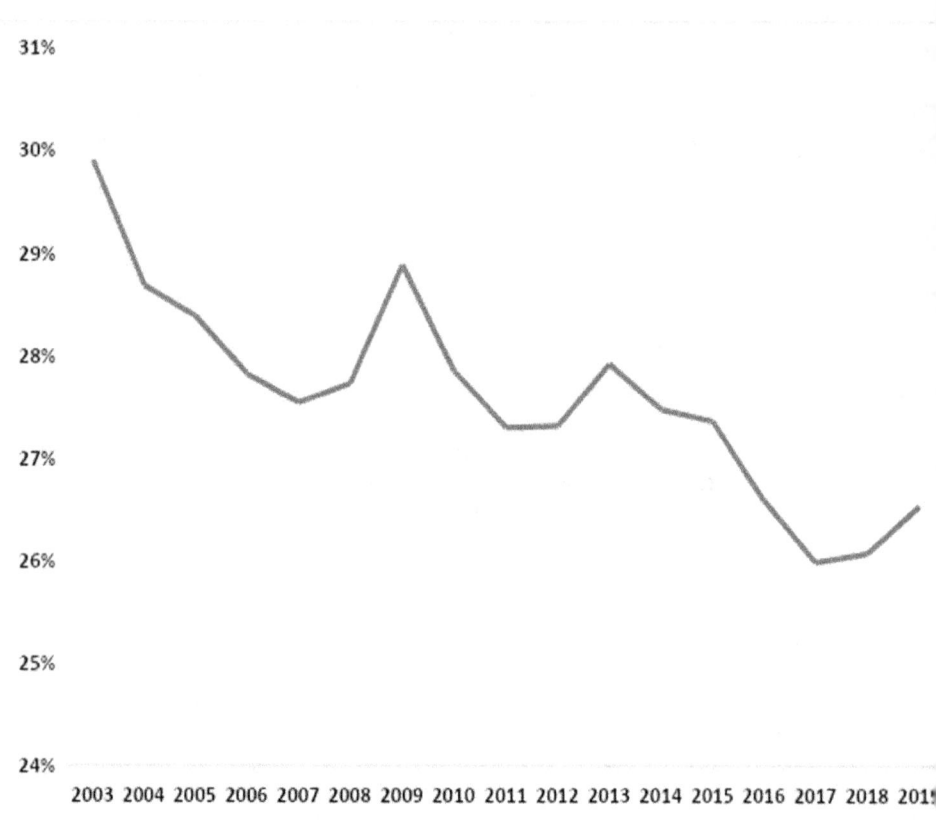

References

Bértola, Luis, and Ocampo, José Antonio. *El desarrollo económico de América Latina desde la independencia*. México: Fondo de Cultura Económica, 2013.

Bielschowsky, Ricardo. "Cincuenta años del pensamiento de la CEPAL: una reseña." *in: Cincuenta años del pensamiento de la CEPAL: textos seleccionados, 9-61 Santiago: Fondo de Cultura Económica/CEPAL*, 1998.

Cañón, J. A. "El papel de la economía en el proyecto decolonial". *Econografos. Escuela de Economía,* No.130 (January, 2019): 2–54.

Cardoso, Fernando Henrique, and Enzo Faletto. *Dependencia y desarrollo en América Latina: ensayo de interpretación sociológica*. Siglo Veintiuno Editores, 1971.

Cerdas-Sandí, D. "Derechos laborales colectivos y democracia. Una discusión a partir del concepto voz horizontal de Guillermo O'Donnell". *Revista IUS*, *12*.42, (2018): 209–230.

Costa, S. "The research on modernity in Latin America: Lineages and dilemmas." *Current*

Sociology, 67 no.6 (2019): 838–855.

Dados N. and Connell R. "The Global South." *Contexts,* 11(1) (February, 2012): 12–13.

Danby, Colin. "Post-Keynesianism without modernity." *Cambridge journal of economics* 33.6 (2009): 1119–1133.

ECLAC, *Economic survey of Latin America*. Santiago de Chile: United Nations, 2019.
https://estadisticas.cepal.org/cepalstat/portada.html?idioma=english

Furtado, Celso. *Desarrollo y Subdesarrollo.* Río de Janeiro: Fondo de Cultura Económica, 1971.

Graciarena, Jorge. "El problema del poder en los estilos de desarrollo una perspectiva heterodoxa." *El trimestre económico* 43.172 (September 1976): 1077–1101.

González, Norberto. "Homenaje a Don Raúl Prebisch" in *Raúl Prebisch: un aporte al estudio de su pensamiento*. Edited by Economic Commission for Latin America and the Caribbean, 9–12. Santiago de Chile: United Nations, 1987.

INEGI Instituto Nacional de Estadística, Geografía e Informática. Economic Information Bank. 2021. https://www.inegi.org.mx/sistemas/bie/

Kayatekin, Serap A. "Between political economy and postcolonial theory: first encounters." *Cambridge Journal of Economics* 33.6 (2009): 1113–1118.

Kvangraven, Ingrid Harvold, and Surbhi Kesar. "Standing in the way of rigor? economics' meeting with the decolonizing agenda.". *The New School for Social Research Working Paper. (October, 2021): 1–55.*

Levy, Santiago & Székely, Miguel "¿Más escolaridad, menos informalidad? Un análisis de cohortes para México y América Latina. *El trimestre económico*, 83.332, (2016): 499–548.

Moreno-Brid, Juan Carlos, and Jaime Ros. *Development and growth in the Mexican economy: A historical perspective.* Oxford University Press, 2009.

Mosoetsa, Sarah and Williams, Michelle. *Labour in the global South: Challenges and alternatives for workers.* Geneva: International Labour Office, 2012.

Noyola Vázquez, Juan. «El desarrollo económico y la inflación en México y otros países latinoamericanos." *Investigación económica* 16. No.4 (1956): 603–648.

O'donnell, G. "Transiciones, continuidades y algunas paradojas." *Cuadernos políticos, 56*.1 (1989): 9–36.

OECD. Organisation for Economic Co-operation and Development. Employment database. 2018. http://www.oecd.org/employment/emp/onlineoecdemploymentdatabase.htm

Pinto, Aníbal. "Metropolización y terciarización: malformaciones estructurales en el desarrollo latinoamericano." *Revista de la CEPAL* 24(December 1984): 17–38.

Pinto, Aníbal. "Naturaleza e implicaciones de la" heterogeneidad estructural" de la América Latina." *El trimestre económico* 37.145 (January 1970): 83–100.

Pinto, Aníbal. "Raíces estructurales de la inflación en América Latina." *El Trimestre Económico* 35.137 (January 1968): 63–74.

Prebisch, Raúl. "Cinco etapas de mi pensamiento sobre el desarrollo." *El trimestre económico* 50, no. 198 (2), (1983): 1077–1096.

Quijano, Aníbal. "Colonialidad del poder y clasificación social" in *El giro decolonial: reflexiones para una diversidad epistémica más allá del capitalismo global*, edited by Castro-Gómez, Santiago, and Grosfoguel, Ramón. (Bogotá: Siglo del Hombre Editores, 2007), 93–126.

Restrepo, E. & Rojas A. 2010. *Inflexión decolonial: fuentes, conceptos y cuestionamientos*. Popayán: Universidad del Cauca, 2010.

Rojas S., Raúl. El proceso de la investigación científica. México: Trillas, 1981.

Ros, Jaime. *¿Cómo salir de la trampa del lento crecimiento y alta desigualdad?*. Ciudad de México: El Colegio de Mexico AC, 2015.

Ros, Jaime. "¿Por qué cae la participación de los salarios en el ingreso total en México?". *Economía UNAM*, *12*.36 (2015): 3–15.

Ruvituso, C. I. 2020. "From the South to the North: The circulation of Latin American dependency theories in the Federal Republic of Germany." *Current Sociology*, *68*.1, (2020): 22–40.

Saad-Filho, A. 2005. "From Washington to post-Washington consensus: Neoliberal agendas for

economic development", in Neoliberalism: A critical reader, edited by Saad-Filho A. and D. Johnson (London: Pluto Press, 2005), 113–119.

Sunkel, Osvaldo. "La inflación chilena: un enfoque heterodoxo." *El trimestre económico* 25.100 (September 1958): 570–599.

Toye, John. "Changing perspectives in development economics." in *Rethinking development economics*, ed. Ha-Joon Chang, 21-40. London: Anthem Press, 2003.

Wold, Herman O. "Mergers of economics and philosophy of science." *Synthese* 20.4 (1969): 427–482.

The World Bank. 2021. World Development Indicators. Washington, D.C.: The World Bank (producer and distributor). http://data.worldbank.org/data-catalog/world-development-indicators

6

Latin American Antiphilosophies

CHRISTINA SOTO VAN DER PLAS

When we, in Latin America, think of theory or philosophy, the thinkers that come to mind are almost always European, and particularly German, French or English. But when we try to think of Latin American philosophers, we must dig deeper and justify why a certain thinker could be considered a philosopher within the scheme of the Western understanding of what philosophy is deemed to be, as a corpus and self-referential system. However, most of the time, thinkers operating outside of the European philosophical pedigree – whether they write and think in the European languages they have inherited or in their mother tongues – are always first seen as subjects of ethnographic inquiries or anthropological fieldwork and investigation, and never quite as thinkers in their own right. 'No Greek ever asked himself about the existence of a Greek philosophy and no Latin or medieval thinker – French, English or German – ever thought about the existence of their philosophy. They simply thought, created, ordered, established, defined. They philosophized.' 'Their heirs in Latin America', Leopoldo Zea says 'suffer from an inferiority complex. We say: This cannot be philosophy!' (Zea 2010, 11) We hear the question: 'Philosophy in Latin America?... and they question: Where are the systems? Do they have an equivalent to Kant or Hegel, etc.?' (Zea 2010, 53) Hence, philosophy is the self-conscious and confident pretension that assumes that its particular thinking is *thought*. And this kind of thought is included within the limited history of occidental reason, also known as Universal History. That is, the history of the world that, by expanding itself, has made of the objects of its expansion part of its aggressive history.

In Latin America, there is a longstanding tradition of thinkers wondering if there is such a thing as philosophy in the Americas, and several responses have been offered from different traditions, countries, and genealogies. The debate can be traced back to the earlier colonial writings by Bartolomé de las Casas (2013) where the dispute was if the Indigenous population inhabiting the Americas should be considered as possible slaves or if they should instead be treated as sons of God, due to their religious conversion. Once most Latin American countries were independent, there was a fierce inner fight over whether our governments (and hence our scientific models and our ways of thinking) should follow the French model of development after the Enlightenment, or the nascent North American capitalist model. This also happened within philosophy and economics, and most thinkers adhered to one or another model.

In late 19th and beginning of the 20th century, however, many thinkers began questioning if we were original and systematic enough to be included within the philosophical catalogue of Western reason. Augusto Salazar Bondy famously wrote a book titled ¿*Existe una filosofía de nuestra América?* (1968) following the philosophical critique first articulated by Samuel Ramos in Mexico where he affirms that in Latin America, we

> think according to theoretical frames previously conformed to the models of Western thought, particularly the European ones, importing trends of ideas, schools, fully defined systems in their content and intention. To philosophize for Hispano-Americans is to adopt a foreign *ismo*, to subscribe to certain preexisting thesis... there is no philosophical system born in Hispanic America. (Salazar Bondy 1988, 20)

Following this negative view of our capacity to articulate our philosophy, many thinkers began reflecting upon the 'problem of America' and our identity as thinking subjects from a particular region of the world.

The question that I will address in this chapter then becomes: What is particular of the kind of questions we develop from our spaces of being in Latin America? What kind of philosophy can we formulate? Can we have a philosophy more akin to our chaotic Third World experience and not to that, say, of Kant's routine that every day at the same time after drinking tea walked around the bell tower of his hometown which he never left? I argue that it is about supplementing the possibility of *ser* with that of *estar*, and tracing the poetics of their relation, not of including our being in the philosophical (capitalized) Being. For tracing this discussion, I propose going back to questioning the idea of Latin American philosophy, but from the lens of a term capable of displacing the whole discussion: 'antiphilosophy'. This debate can be productive, as Hamid Dabashi would argue, albeit coming from a different geography, even if for European thinkers Philosophy is mental gymnastics performed with the received particulars of European philosophy in its postmodern or poststructuralist registers. But unless and until those defining moments are structurally linked, thematically moved and conceptually compromised, and thus epistemically violated, they will have very little or nothing to say about the world that is unfolding in front of us' (Dabashi 2015, 6). If 'we are no longer (if we ever were) knowable to that European knowing subject... We, therefore, come together at a new gathering of knowledge and power not to mourn but to dislodge the link' (Dabashi 2015, 23). Seeking to dislodge the link, I will trace the origins of what antiphilosophy means and how conceiving of it from Latin America can help us unsettle the mental gymnastics of philosophy, not necessarily by ignoring our European heritage, but rather by understanding how conceptually we can consider our form of thought as Western philosophy's necessary sophist, counterpart and interlocutor.

Antiphilosophical Principles

The term antiphilosophy first came into being as a monstrosity of the Age of Reason. It was originally a name under which a group of self-appointed antiphilosophers assembled in a reactionary response to the *Encyclopédie* and its rationalist and materialist project. The *Encyclopédie* edited by Denis Diderot and Jean le Rond d'Alembert between 1751–72 in France had as its main goal to gather in a clear and accessible manner the accumulated knowledge of its time. But the project born out of the French Revolution was very controversial and had many adversaries, among them the self-appointed antiphilosophers. The Antiphilosophers were a group of conservative Catholics that defended faith and religious dogmas against the idea of universal reason. As we know, the ideas of the *philosophes*, the writers of the *Encyclopédie* won the debate and we remember their time as *the Age of Reason*, the beginning of modernity. And the intervention of the conservative antiphilosophers would have been lost in history if it were not for Jacques Lacan's unearthing of the term antiphilosophy.

The psychoanalyst rescued the obscure term of antiphilosophy but changed its meaning, for his own purposes. In *Perhaps at Vincennes* (1975), Lacan briefly suggests to the analysts of his School that antiphilosophy should be part of their curriculum for training, along with linguistics, logic, and topology. The role of antiphilosophy would be evidencing what he calls the indestructible root and eternal dream of the anthology of the stupidity that characterizes philosophy and the university discourse (Lacan 2001, 314). Against the commodification and fetishization of knowledge, a training in antiphilosophy would imply an *awakening* from the mere educational reproduction and transmission of ideas. After Lacan and his brief remarks,

Alain Badiou, a self-proclaimed Platonist and philosopher, took up the task of defining what philosophy is *vis-à-vis* all of its enemies, rivals and against the contemporary version of the sophists (Bosteels 2008, 155). For Badiou, philosophy can only be defined if it reaffirms itself, survives and works through all the objections and violent strokes of the antiphilosopher, his rival and shadow, who is constantly seeking to dethrone philosophy's systematic ambitions. That is why Badiou spent many years of his seminar in Paris (between 1992 and 1996) inquiring about the formal criteria and the practices of antiphilosophy over and against the claims of philosophy itself. Bruno Bosteels even argues that 'today the dominant philosophical attitude is in fact thoroughly antiphilosophical in nature, even if the label is not always used or accepted' (Bosteels 2008, 161).

Alain Badiou explains three antiphilosophical operations which are at the core of how I will conceive of antiphilosophy in Latin America. As he says, first, the movement of all antiphilosophy is the destitution of the category of truth, the 'unraveling of the pretensions of philosophy to constitute itself as theory' (Badiou 2011, 75). For antiphilosophers, the question of being and the world are coextensive with the question of language. The limits of the world are the limits of language (words are not things, and truth is nothing more than linguistic effect, the outcome of culturally specific language games or tropes), 'nominalism is the untranscendable horizon of our time' (Bosteels 2008, 163). The second operation is that antiphilosophers often seek what lies beyond the realm of the sayable, beyond sense, and this *beyond* must be understood with its mystical consequences: 'Philosophy is an act, of which the fabulations about "truth" are the clothing, the propaganda, the lies' (Badiou 1011, 75). What matters for the antiphilosopher is an idea that transforms us in an existential or revolutionary way, not merely a passive theory as they deem philosophy to be. The third operation is that there is a radically new act – implying a subject – discrediting any systematic theoretical or conceptual elaboration: 'this act without precedent destroys the philosophical act, all the while clarifying its noxious character. It overcomes it affirmatively' (Badiou 2011, 76). As for their style, antiphilosophers usually do not write in a systematic fashion and their texts are often experimental and autobiographical. It is crucial to note that these three described operations debunk the core philosophical notions of being, truth, and the subject. Antiphilosophy situates itself as the extimacy (the internal exteriority), it moves between distance and proximity, admiration and blame, seduction and scorn (Bosteels 2008, 158) – challenging and questioning such presuppositions: truth is linguistic, beyond meaning, and a radical act is necessary to dynamite theory.

In Latin America and other peripheries there are antiphilosophical tendencies, but this is not surprising: the common attitude and rule nowadays is antiphilosophical. The exception would be finding someone claiming to be a true philosopher with a systematic project and declaring to uphold the notions of truth, subject and being (like Alain Badiou himself). But what I want to consider is how from these other geographies, the antiphilosophical offensive movement is linked to what I call an *estar* – an inhabiting of experience – and not merely to debates about theory and its place in our society. The sword and the pen are one in our countries, and political theory comes after the revolution not before. As José Revueltas explains, 'Instead of the "weapons of criticism" (that is, a systematic, coherent, organized and more or less total conscience of development) preceding its material deployment, objective development begins with the "criticism of weapons", with the armed revolutionary conflict itself' (Revueltas 2020, 320). The same goes for antiphilosophy: its active and revolutionary nature always begins with the criticism of the weapons of philosophy itself. This is precisely what Leopoldo Zea also affirms: 'In Western culture… philosophy comes before action, it is its foundation, it justifies it. In Latin America first there is the action, and then comes what justifies such an action' (Zea 2010, 34). Instead of having a metaphysics as the essential base of political praxis, in Latin America political praxis seeks to find a metaphysical doctrine – or at least a philosophy – to justify its actions. In this sense, we could say that our style of philosophizing is one committed with our realities, is a kind of thought seeking to solve the immediate problems of reality and not a preemptive model for developing action.

In what follows, I will take on Leopoldo Zea's plea for a Latin American philosophy *sin más* – universal and yet located and derived from a space and time – and I will propose that the kind of thought arising from the region's political and epistemological circumstances can be characterized as antiphilosophical in nature. As Zea proposes, we need to think about 'our strange way of philosophizing' (Zea 2010, 14). I will focus on key notions from two authors to demonstrate how these operations come into play in different circumstances and historical moments: the poetics of relation of Édouard Glissant, tracing a different geography for being, and Rodolfo Kusch's Indigenous thought that articulates a form of living.

Rodolfo Kusch's Dialectics of Ser and Estar

The Argentinian anthropologist Rodolfo Kusch (1922–1979) often traveled to the Indigenous villages of the Bolivian highlands. He wanted to rescue a popular and Indigenous form of thought – he researched particularly the Quichua and Aymara cultures – at the foundations of America (he calls it *América profunda* – and of course there are echoes here of populism and its quest for *authenticity* in the Indigenous roots). In his fascinating work one can find travel chronicles alongside profoundly critical reflections of, for example, the infinitesimal meta-mathematics disputed by the logic of negation of Aymara witchcraft. As Santiago Castro-Gómez characterizes the work of Kusch and others like Carlos Cullen, Enrique Dussel and Juan Carlos Scannone, they wanted to propose a 'hermeneutics of Latin American popular culture... to understand the structures of thought different from those of dominant culture, intellectual, and "wise" of Latin American *criollismo*' (Castro-Gómez 2011, 49). One of the pillars of Kusch's work is tracing the dialectics between *ser y estar* as experiences. For Kusch, in the depths of America there are two opposite cultures: one superficial and visible, product of the European civilization and another one unconscious, and deep, of popular and Amerindian character.

For Kusch, the experience of *ser* is linked to the Europe of the sixteenth century and that of *estar* to pre-hispanic cultures. And he explains: 'the verb *estar* is very rich. We know that it comes from *stare,* in Latin, *estar en pie* (standing up), which implies discomfort... *Ser*, instead, comes from *sedere, estar sentado* (sitting down) and connotes a point of sustenance that leads us to the possibility to define' (Kusch 1975, 364). A definable world is a world without fear (comfortable) and a world subject to the swaying circumstances is a frightening world. Note that for Kusch *ser* is a matter of language, a verb. For him, *ser* requires a technique that dominates action and codifies it in the frame of the history of consciousness. In the Western ethos, we live in a constant race to *be someone* in life (*ser-alguien en la vida*), which is what happens in Latin American cities. While in the Andean setting, closer to nature *se está* or *está no más* (or even, one adopts the attitude of *dejarse-estar* in the world – to just let oneself be). It implies a territory, standing up in life, inhabiting the circumstance. The zero-point of Kusch's epistemology is *estar*. Based on these two distinctions, Kusch affirms that Latin America is constitutively divided between a modern rationality, imported from Europe, which is always theorizing in its sitting down (*ser*), and the inherent rationality of its earthly nature, which just *is,* standing up and facing life and experience directly (*estar*).

Kusch suggests that *el pensamiento americano* has two ways of dealing with philosophy, the one we learn at the university, which is based on European problems translated philosophically, and the implicit everyday thinking. In popular thinking the semantic is more important and you say *something*, while in the learned one the technique and the *how* matter more (Kusch 1975, 9). They are embedded in a dialectic, and we should not deny the technique of Western philosophy, but rather seek a language closer to our way of life. I would add that this is a kind of ontic situation crystalized in an ethical affirmation. European thought, like any other, is embedded in a way of life – just as the Latin American with *estar*. But, oftentimes, we are passive and not critical enough of the misplaced ideas that we acquire and come from elsewhere. As Roberto Schwarz argued elsewhere, there are a series of ideas out of joint or misplaced ideas, which is the mechanism of how Latin America imports European and North American ideas, but we must use and acquire those ideas with a critical distance, because they often do not fit our realities or material conditions, and they end up swiveling around falsely (Schwarz 1992, 23) in their foreign context.

Kusch claims that,

> the real distance between an Indigenous way of thinking and a way of thinking consistent with traditional philosophy is the same as that between the Aymara term *utcatha* and the German term *Da-sein*. Heidegger takes up this word from ordinary German speech, first because *Sein* signifies *being* (ser)—which allowed him to take up again the themes of traditional ontology—and second because *Da*—which means *there* —signaled the *circumstance* into which being had fallen. Heidegger's problematic is centered on an awareness of a diminished being, a *thrown* being. His merit lies in having taken up in the twentieth century the theme of being (time and authenticity) with an exactitude that befitted the lives of German middle class that had always felt the fall of being as its own, with all the anguish that implies. (Kusch 1962, 268)

Kusch proposes an equivalent of *Da-sein* in Aymara, the term *utcatha* that means *estar*. The term house is in *uta*, linked to *domo*, which means, essentially, being home. *Utcatha* also means *sitting down*, which leads us to *sedere*, *ser* in Spanish. It is a seat or chair, and it is also related to mother or womb. Its meaning reflects the concept of a mere being or *estar no más*, linked to shelter (Kusch 1962, 269). If *Da-sein* is a foreign category to Latin America, how can we accept the universality of Being? For Kusch, the answer can only come from our more essential *utcatha*, or *estar siendo*. The question is then: Do we join a branch of Western philosophy? Science, psychoanalysis? Do we open a franchise? Or do we create our own thought, our *pensamiento propio*?

In my view, Kusch's deduction establishes a fairly monstrous antiphilosophical category. A sort of teratology of reason. The gesture affirms the departing point of Latin American antiphilosophy which is the mere being or *puro estar*, a being here and now, in a circumstance and *in* language. In a truly antiphilosophical gesture Kusch says: 'I exist, then I think, and not the other way around. That is why mathematical truth is only an episode of the ontological truth. The false Western pretension, in this sense, is finding a universal science. Instead of science one can only speak of a methodic attitude. And, since existing is the most basic thing, the only possible universal is the existing itself' (Kusch 1962, 553). As Badiou recognizes, there is clearly a sophistic operation in reducing ontology to phenomenology, and in conceiving of truth as an effect of language, along with the 'biographical impulse, the taste for confession, and even in the end a highly recognizable infatuation that commands the "writerly" style of all antiphilosophers' (Badiou 2011, 88). Rodolfo Kusch's deduction of our *way of being* in the world is antiphilosophical in nature because he derives our experience from a linguistic specificity of the Spanish and Aymara languages and how they express the ways in which we inhabit our realities against the unmovable category of 'being' as *ser* that comes from a theoretical definition of Western philosophy – and from the rest of languages that can only articulate the notion of *ser*, and not that of *estar* or *utcatha*, which are specific to our realities.

Beyond Rodolfo Kusch's attempt to find in the depth of America our *pensamiento propio,* what I want to hold onto from his antiphilosophical gesture is the potential of *estar* as a way of unsettling the philosophical core of Being. This is clearly a first step in the direction of dislodging philosophy and questioning its ferrous grip in our territories when we have our own language and categories that are extremely rich and fertile in how they can articulate a different debate, one that is more in tune with our political praxis and our contradictory reality.

Glissant's Poetics of Relation

After this brief exposition of how Rodolfo Kusch conceives of *estar* as the core of being-existing (within the dialectic of *ser* and *estar*), derived from language, and how I read in it a fundamentally antiphilosophical gesture, I insert here the poetics of relation, a geography devoted to reimagining itself in this *existing*. The second antiphilosopher I want to briefly address is Édouard Glissant (1928–2011). Glissant is from the Caribbean, and he was born in Martinique, partaking in the tradition of the French Caribbean thinkers of postcolonialism including Frantz Fanon and Aimé Césaire. His work is halfway between poetry, antiphilosophical reflections, and contributions to a politics that upholds *metissage* and creolization against French essentialism. However, unlike the thinkers that defend *negritudé* and a Pan-African sense of belonging, Glissant puts forward his idea of *antilleanité*, which decenters the ideas of origins and proposes instead nomadism and the relation as a model. He conceives of the Caribbean inserted in a world of chaos – which he calls the *chaos-monde*.

Against the totalitarian, unique, and monolingual root that feeds itself of its surroundings, Glissant proposes the rhizome (beyond Gilles Deleuze, although his work is very much Deleuzian in nature), an enmeshed root system, a spreading network with no predatory ambition. The form to which Glissant clearly adheres to, like a true antiphilosopher, is the poetic form: The highest point of knowledge, he says, is always a poetics (Glissant 1997, 140). We should understand poetics as *poiesis*, creation, dynamic, energy. A poetics of relation does not imply cultural relativism where everything is the same as or is relative, which is another form of essentialism. Instead, it maintains the specificity of every space and at the same time articulates a chaotic, fluid, and relational network. In his seminal work, *Poetics of Relation* (1990) – the third volume of his *Poetique* project – Glissant thus articulates a form of thought departing not from identity or a structure, but from the relation itself, the knowledge of how the Other is within us and affects how we evolve historically and as beings, as well as how we are *projected toward* in an arrowlike nomadism.

The basis of Western thought, for Glissant, is transparency, which is not unlike what Kusch proposed in the vein of *ser*: a being we can identify from the comfort of our seats. The West says: 'In order to understand and thus accept you, I have to measure your solidity with the ideal scale providing me with grounds to make comparisons and perhaps judgements. I have to reduce to make you intelligible' (Glissant 1997, 190). Indeed, the West can only understand the 'different' by relating it to its norm. And, in order for them to admit that others exist, they should be measurable or classifiable within their system. To which Glissant, the antiphilosopher, replies in a radical maneuver: 'we need to bring an end to the notion of scale and displace all reduction' (Glissant 1997, 190). The right to difference is the right to opacity (against the transparency and clarity of Western scientific thought) where 'opacities can coexist and converge, weaving fabrics. To understand these truly one must focus on the texture of the weave and not on the nature of its components. For the time being, perhaps, give up this old obsession with discovering what lies at the bottom of natures' (Glissant 1997, 190). This means that instead of looking for the ultimate cause of things, the origin or root cause of movements and ideas, Glissant privileges the weaving, that is, the relation between opaque beings in no particular order.

At some points in his *Poetics of Relation,* Glissant also appears to embrace the philosophical language and structure, albeit in a series of aphorisms – which is a common antiphilosophical maneuver against systematic treatises. There are, for example, a series of statements where he condenses what he means with his idea of 'relation'. He advances his thinking, deceivingly, from the logic of negation, even though they can be perceived as affirmative propositions – not unlike the ones we can find in Wittgenstein's *Tractatus*. Glissant affirms: '"Being is Relation": but relation is safe from the idea of Being' (Glissant 185). Let me add two more of his propositions to confirm the antiphilosophical core of his thought. The first one: 'That which would preexist (Relation) is the vacuity of Being-as-Being' and 'Being-as-Being is not opaque but self-important' (Glissant 1997, 185). In asserting a kind of being, the antiphilosopher cannot but add that we are in fact dealing with being-as-being, which is a movement close to the *estar* and *utchatha* defended by Kusch and his *pensamiento propio*.

For Glissant, the relation – which is never to say the relationship, which is dialogical – is what preexists the emptiness of the Being-as-Being, and it contaminates, sweetens, as a principle, or as flower dust. The second proposition I want to consider is the following: 'Beings remain, as long as Being dissipates' (Glissant 1997, 186). This means that the multiplicity of beings, the beings of the poetics of relation can only exist if Being, as a notion and unifying principle, dissipates, and as long as it asserts the subject. If we wanted to translate this into Kusch's vocabulary, then the following would be true: *estar* remains when *ser* dissipates. That is, Relation is knowledge in the movement of *estar*, which risks the being of the world, 'or being-earth' (Glissant 1997, 187), *ser del mundo*. Once again, we find the idea of a kind of thought and existence that is universal and yet located and derived from a space and time, which is precisely the link and material base that Western philosophy often erases in favor of its pretended neutrality and universal ambition. Instead, antiphilosophers in Latin America recognize that they are theorizing *in* a space, *in* a language and within a certain space that determines the material conditions of their way of thinking. Recognizing this should not in any way diminish or obfuscate their relevance and theoretical power nor should it relegate them to being second class philosophers for their origin denomination, as if Glissant had to be first Martinican and then a philosopher, and not the other way around, to be understood.

Glissant is a thinker with an incredible potential to think the matter of relation, the operation of *poiesis* as a creative force and as the foundation of *chaos-monde* (there we find his mystic undertone, what for him goes beyond the limits of language). I believe this is a step forward from the dialectics of *ser* and *estar* and towards tracing the constellation between *ser, estar, da-sein, utcatha, étre, étant*. It is not about the 'West and the rest' of civilization, where we are incapable of producing our own thought (*pensamiento propio*) but of a reading that privileges the affirmation of a fluid cartography of energy that brings together heterogeneous elements of reality without striping them from their specificity. The zero-point of Glissant's epistemology, in my view, is the following: relation is knowledge in motion of the being of the universe, and it risks being in being-there (*se arriesga el ser en el estar*). Like in Kusch, there is the need of a radical act of facing the unknown of our geography and of searching our space not in that universality we pretend to yield to no end.

Conclusion

With the antiphilosophical core of these authors, I seek to begin redefining the *unthought* of Western philosophical systems via the engaged and active nature of the Latin American style of thought. The antiphilosophical operations of Kusch and Glissant give the *ser* and *estar* a genealogy (a filiation and not an affiliation) and remind us that truths, even if they are not relative or circumstantial, do exist in a site. Truths exist in a space and time and not in the vacuum that Europe pretends it to be – in order to philosophize, to preserve the character of universal history, philosophical truths, and the scientific method beyond any bias or uncertainty that history or society might infringe upon their epistemology. Such is the site of the event or a besieged state, a regime of exception. The seat of being gives consistency to the specificity and the reality of a theoretical form and how it is configured in a region. But standing up, uncomfortable, in an *estar*, we relate to a creative poetic. Our antiphilosophy needs to traverse these other knowledges in order to be-something. It also needs to doubt its zero-point, the *chaos-monde* from where it is writing, *el asiento del ser que es el estar*. Beyond dialectics of *ser* and *estar*, or of privileging one over the other, what we seek is a poetic that can be the platform for the dance of thought, its swaying critique. When we philosophize from Latin America, I hope it will be not only legible in terms of curiosity or ethnophilosophy. The historical conditions are the basis of ideas and changes are ideas that are not yet articulated: *ser y estar, ahí*.

References

Badiou, Alain. 2011. Wittgenstein's Antiphilosophy. Translated by Bruno Bosteels. London: Verso.

Bosteels, Bruno. 2008. "Radical Antiphilosophy". *Filozofski vestnik*. Volume XXIX. Number 2. 155–187.

de las Casas, Bartolomé. 2013. *Brevísima relación de la destrucción de las Indias*. 18th Edition. Madrid, Cátedra

Castro-Gómez, Santiago. 2011. *Crítica de la razón latinoamericana*. 2nd Edition. Bogotá: Editorial Pontificia Universidad Javeriana

Dabashi, Hamid. 2015. *Can Non-Europeans Think?* London: Zed Books.

Dussel, Enrique. 1973. *Para una ética de la liberación latinoamericana. Tomo I, II*. Buenos Aires: Siglo XXI Editores.

Glissant, Édouard. 1997. *Poetics of Relation*. Translated by Betsy Wing. Michigan: University of Michigan Press.

Kusch, Rodolfo. 1962. *Obras completas. América Profunda.* Tomo II. Santa Fe: Editorial Fundación Ross,.

Kusch, Rodolfo. 1975. *Obras completas. Geocultura del hombre americano.* Tomo III. Santa Fe: Editorial Fundación Ross.

Lacan, Jacques. 2001. "Peut–être à Vincennes," *Autres écrits*, Paris: Éditions du Seuil.

Salazar Bondy, Augusto. 1988. *¿Existe una filosofía de nuestra América?* Mexico: Siglo XXI Editores.

Zea, Leopoldo. 2010. *La filosofía americana como filosofía sin más.* Mexico: Siglo XXI Editores.

PART TWO

Praxis Analysis

7

The Crime of Defending a River: Domination, Racism, and Structural Violence in Guatemala

MIGUEL ALEJANDRO SAQUIMUX CONTRERAS

To my dad, who the Guatemala state is criminalising.

Structural Violence and Racism against Q'anjob'al People

Historically, Maya People have been excluded from participating in decision-making processes in Guatemala. Over the last two centuries, the state has constrained the exercise of Maya peoples' rights and denied their history (Martínez 2011), political organisation and practices (Guzmán 2016, Casolo 2020). This has been possible because the elite has built discourses that have made Maya People's lives, practices, and resistances invisible. Moreover, the elite has created a racist ideology to cement its domination and increased the gap between *Criollos*, Mestizos (Guzmán 2016) and Maya people. As a result, the Maya People have been dispossessed of their land (Castellanos 1985, Acemoglu and Robinson 2012, Casolo 2020); besides, their knowledge and practices have been undervalued and made invisible (Guzmán 2016, Casolo 2020).

Racism has played a central role in reproducing inequalities and oppression over marginalised groups from subjective means and the construction of meaning. Currently, racism as a practice is evident in the unequal life chances that the Maya population has compared with the Mestizo population. As Galtung (1969) argues, structural violence seems to be like tranquil waters, by extension, less violent than direct violence. However, it is not; maybe it does not kill or hurt people, but it makes disenfranchised social groups suffer. For instance, Maya represents 42% of all Guatemalan people (Institute of National Statistics 2018), but 39.8% is poor compared with 12.8% of Mestizo (Institute of National Statistics 2014).

Therefore, before I go further on this, it is imperative to know what Galtung understands by violence. He conceptualised it 'as the cause of the difference between the potential and the actual [conditions of life], between what could have been and what is [...] and that which impedes the decrease of this [difference]' (Galtung 1969, 170).

The previous paragraph could be understood from the original conceptualisation done by Galtung (1969), in which he explains violence has six distinctions, them being:

1. The distinction between physical and psychological violence.
2. The distinction between the negative and positive approaches to influence.
3. The distinction between whether or not there is an object that wounds.
4. The distinction between whether or not there is a subject who acts.
5. The distinction between intended violence and unintended violence.
6. The distinction between two levels of violence: the manifest and the latent.

For this analysis, only distinctions numbers two, four, five, and six are used. As the reader will see later, these distinctions will help understand the link between structural violence and racism in Guatemala. In distinction number two, Galtung (1969) says people can be influenced by punishing them when they do what the influencer considers wrong and rewarding them when they do what the influencer finds right. In distinction number four, he says, 'violence is built into the structure and shows up as unequal power and consequently as unequal life chances [...] if people are [suffering] when this is objectively avoidable, then violence is committed' (Galtung 1969, 171). In distinction number five, Galtung (1969) establishes that analyses only focused on intended violence fail to capture structural violence, which used to be unintended. However, both are necessary to analyse whether we want to understand violent dynamics and how the latter is exerted in different contexts. In distinction number six, he makes a difference in how violence can be exerted. For him, '[m]anifest violence, whether personal or structural, is observable, although not directly, since the theoretical entity of potential realization also enters the picture. But, on the other hand, latent violence is something which is not there, yet might easily come about' (Galtung 1969, 172).

The previous distinctions make it possible to cross concepts moving beyond the analyses of why societies seem to be unable to distinguish when violence is exerted or why specific groups are suffering due to social order imposed in a given territory.

Nevertheless, Galtung (1969) does not define structural violence but develops the concept through characterisations. He says that structural violence is silent, and it has two specific features, 1) stability over time, and 2) it is not possible to track people as actors responsible for exerting violence. Furthermore, Galtung (1969) says that this kind of violence in a static society 'personal violence will be registered, whereas structural violence may be seen as about as natural as the air around us' (173). On the other hand, within a highly dynamic society, 'personal violence may be seen as wrong and harmful but still somehow congruent with the order of things, whereas structural violence becomes apparent' (173).

In that order, he continues saying whether there is no subject-verb-object in a violent action; thus, it is structural and built into the structure. This kind of violence is experienced by people who have constrained their capabilities and agency due to 'lack of access to the basic necessities of life, and lack of access to resources that maintain well-being, [such as] healthcare, education, jobs, and security' (Rylko-Bauer and Farmer 2016, 51). These people are living in poverty as a result of inequalities that have been normalised by society.

However, even Galtung's concept embeds two central elements: inequalities [in Galtung's frame, this means unequal life chances] and unequal power relations. It is unclear how these two concepts – which form structural violence – can expound beyond the unequal exercise of power. Thus, by analysing the structural violence category itself, it is impossible to link disfranchisement from dominant speeches and practices founded on ideas of one group's superiority over others and how these are connected to violence. Neither is it possible to look at social movements and people as active subjects. Although Galtung (1969) says, 'behind structural violence is inequality' (175), and there are efforts to change the matrix of power, as long as the distribution of power is not equally distributed, 'inequality seems to have a high survival capacity' (175). He does not talk about domination; even people suffer due to the inegalitarian distribution of power and unequal access to resources. Therefore, it is unclear why and how this inequality is [re]produced and can survive in time and space.

Before I continue going further in the absence of the domination concept into Galtung's frame, it is imperative to echo Rylko-Bauer and Farmer's (2016) explanation of how structural violence works. For them, structural violence can survive over time because it has been *normalised* through *symbolic means*, and this standardisation has made it invisible. As a result, it is unrecognisable at the social level. Drawing on this, Farmer (2004) proposes to understand structural violence as 'the concept [intended] to inform the study of the social machinery of oppression. Oppression is a result of many conditions, not the least of which reside in consciousness' (307). Farmer's conceptualisation of structural violence, based on oppression as a central concept, is essential to bring more elements to display a violent structural frame in a given territory and society. As Vela, Sequén-Mónchez et al. (2001) explain, it is necessary to analyse structural violence since society conceives its world, social values it has, and everyday practices lived in a given context.

However, to understand that kind of inequality in Guatemala, we must depart from the fact that the Guatemalan oligarchy, which presumes its Spaniard heritage (Casaús 2010), has ruled for more than 400 years (Casaús 2000, Martínez 2011, Acemoglu and Robinson 2012). Besides, across this time, it has built an apparatus that has allowed it to grab any resource, and it has subdued Maya peoples. This has been possible in part because the oligarchy has employed its own narrative from a racist stance. As a result, Cojtí (2006) states, Guatemalan society and its state are racist; they are 'structured to act and be mono-ethnic, mono-legal, monolingual and monocultural' (103). Besides complicity with the mestizo people, the oligarchy through the state has promoted manifest and latent violence dispossession and submission of Maya peoples (Organización del Pueblo en Armas 1976, 1978).

While it is true that the dynamic of repression is no longer the same as that which disappeared, displaced, and killed thousands of Maya people over 40 years ago, the racist rationality continues making them invisible. It excludes their knowledges, desires, and everyday practices. According to Galtung (1969), this has widened the gap between the ruling elite and marginalised groups, the primary condition to talk about structural violence.

Furthermore, as Cojtí (2006) says, the Guatemala state is a racist state 'designed and structured to act against [Maya] peoples' (103). Thus, on behalf of the economic development, Maya Q'anjob'al cosmogony, knowledge and practices have been dismissed by the Guatemalan state.

Additionally, it is necessary to remember the most recent direct violent expression of state racism in Guatemala, the genocide against different Maya people in the second part of the 20th century. The Report of the Commission for Historical Clarification – CEH, acronym in Spanish (1997) – reported that Guatemala is one of the countries worldwide with the highest number of disappeared and murdered people. The CEH (1997), in its points 2894–2895, argued a high over-representation of Maya among the identified victims in this period: 83.5% are Maya, and 16.5% are Mestizos. According to the official census, this happened when Maya represented only 43% of the total population. These crimes caused a deep wound in the Guatemalan population's collective imagination (Figueroa 2019).

As a result, in Guatemala, structural violence at the social level is still discussed, because people continue talking about it, only considering direct violence as violence (Menjívar 2014). Thus, following Echeverría (1995), this position provokes that society only understands violence in part, and the state only punishes it in part without reflecting on how this is (re)produced and what motivates it. Consequently, it is challenging to address violence comprehensively.

Besides, the oligarchy has created a founding narrative (Echeverría 1995, Straus 2015, Guzmán 2016) across the time that currently hides structural violence. After all, 'whose general terms [and techniques] are familiar to and resonant with ordinary citizens' (Straus 2015, 67). This condition does not allow society to identify when the rights of the Maya people are violated. Furthermore, it also justifies the dispossession and imposition processes against Maya Peoples because, in the dominant narrative, they are considered a threat to the nation-state and that the territories they live in do not belong to them.

Therefore, racism has a real effect on how Guatemalan society, through its state, exerts structural violence over social groups considered inferior, criminal, or unworthy of being right holders. For instance, driving racist narratives and structural violence over specific groups, looking at the dominant ideas produced, and by maintaining unequal power relations which result in unequal life conditions. This is possible, echoing Quijano (2014a) because all those violent everyday social interactions are part of the racial axis that gives sense to the modern-colonial Eurocentric world. He stated, '[t]he racial axis has a colonial origin and character, but it has proven to be more durable and stable than the colonialism in whose matrix it was established' (Quijano 2014a, 777). As a result, the matrix of power imposed by the European invaders has normalised race notions (Quijano 1992).

After the previous paragraph's exposure, I argue that structural violence in Guatemala is linked with other categories, such as race as a technology of power (Casaús 2000, Valencia 2019, 2020), as an essential part of the dominant founding narrative. Therefore, the proposal is not to make the concept of structural violence broader but to make it more concrete for the

Guatemalan context. Trying to understand how structural violence actually works, and how it is made perdurable in time and space.

The previous statement leads me to refer to domination as the concept that addresses this paper's central idea, while structural violence and its link with racism function as an analysis framework. It is necessary to do this because it is a fact that Guatemalan society is only seeing violence at an individual level. It is not linking it with structural violence and the disenfranchised of these group's needs and rights because the dominant ideas have led it to believe that groups must rule over others by, for instance, social class, gender and ethnic differences.

The aforementioned is possible because domination is embedded into the colonial rationality (Quijano 2014b), which has 'not ceased to be the central character of social power today' (758). Moreover, the fact that racism was produced in Abya Yala 'as a foundation of the specificity of power relations between Europe and the populations of the rest of the world' (Quijano 2014b, 757). It led to the elaboration of 'a colonisation of the imaginary; the dominated could not always successfully defend themselves from being led to look at themselves with the eye of the dominator' (Quijano 2014b, 760).

From the preceding discussion, in this essay, domination is understood as a 'process that not only transforms the social structure of the person but transforms the subject him/herself at the same time' (Schoungunt 2012, 52). Following Bourdieu (2000), domination is exerted by reproducing ideological ideas without any reflection about the implications that have in everyday life. Thus 'domination has an indissoluble link with violence because when it comes to controlling the subject, there are only two possible ways to exert it: [direct or indirect] violence' (Saquimux 2014, 32). As Farmer argues (2004), following Bourdieu (2000), violence is a structure and structuring frame into social reality. It constricts social relations and beliefs, also makes believe that these violent forms of interaction are typical.

The previous statement is linked with Farmer's analysis of structural violence that focuses 'attention on the social machinery of exploitation and oppression – the ways in which epic poverty and inequality, with their deep histories, become embodied and experienced as violence' (cited by Rylko-Bauer et al. 2016, 47). It draws on structural violence conceptualisations made by Rylko-Bauer et al. (2016) and Gupta (2012); this phenomenon is understood as a continuum of violence over marginalised groups that consequently result in the subjugation of people and cause of suffering. Here is when Galtung's (1969) frame, which understood this one as a central part of the 'unequal life chances' (171), makes sense.

Product of the crystallised ideas of superiority of one group against marginalised groups; structural violence is rooted in hegemonic ideas (or at least dominant) that shape lives through racist, sexist and colonial speeches. Consequently, this could be (or not) in public policies or national laws, but irretrievably exists in everyday life practices. It does not matter in space and time. It could happen in state office everyday duties or in a policy-making process.

However, it is imperative to be aware that marginalised people resist and organise themselves even though material living conditions are adverse and their rights are constrained. Otherwise, it would be impossible to identify how societies and their states exert violence in different ways against excluded and disenfranchised groups. Resistance makes evident structural violence and founding narratives.

Therefore, the challenge of talking about structural violence lies in how people comprehend how the regimes 'usually [try] to maintain a status quo whether it means forceful maintenance of traditional social injustice that may have lasted for generations, or the forceful maintenance of some new type of injustice brought in by an attempt to overthrow the old system' (Galtung 1969, 184). From this theoretical stance, I argue that racism is an explanatory category to address how structural violence is comprehended and exerted in Guatemala.

Firstly, I use the category of racism following the proposal made by Casaús (2000). She understands it as an ideology crystallised in practices that (re)produce inequalities through techniques that exclude social groups by biological and cultural differences. 'The purpose of all racism is to legitimise a system of domination' (Casaús 2000, 34). Furthermore, the notion of the race here is understood as a technology of power; as Casaús (2000) says,

> racism [...] has the prerogative and the right to decide who should live or die. It exercises the right to kill or eliminate the Other in the name of sovereignty. Furthermore, it has a racial biological component (33).

In a static society like Guatemala, racism is a relationship of domination that has built a founding narrative on behalf of the state, the nation, and development. It establishes 'the main goals and principles of the state, [...] the core mission of the political project, and who [...] rule' (Straus 2015, 64). Thus, several social groups are marginalised, disenfranchised, and excluded because they are considered unworthy or an issue for policy implementation. As a result, racism creates a gap, and whenever it can, it enlarges it based on fictitious biological differences that lead to social and economic inequalities.

Criminalisation in Guatemala, a Case Study

How is it possible to identify structural violence in Guatemala without leaving peoples' resistance and advocacy avoiding colonial narratives? All the above can be identified in the case of the opposition of the Q'anjob'al people to the imposition of a hydroelectric plant on a river they consider sacred, the Q'an B'alam River, located in Santa Cruz Barillas, Huehuetenango, Guatemala – the actual names of these places are: Jolom Konob', Xibanajul, Iximulew; respectively.

To proceed, it is essential to divide the analysis into two frameworks. Firstly, it is necessary to point out that in 1997, the state of Guatemala ratified the Indigenous and Tribal Peoples Convention – ILO 169 without any reservation. Thus, the state assumed all the obligations outlined in this international treaty on human rights, '[which] is subsumed within the provisions of Article 46 of the Constitution of the Republic. This article [in the Guatemalan Constitution] categorises human rights within a higher hierarchy than the rest of the country's ordinary law' (Javalois cited by Saquimux and Castillo 2018, 8). Hence, since the planning stage, the state assumed the obligation to consult the population affected by implementing extractive projects in its territories. This obligation has the purpose of ensuring that at the time of the community consultation, this is carried out by ensuring the free, prior, and informed consent of the population. Nevertheless, it is something that all the state entities involved in the process of authorising licenses for the construction and operation of projects such as hydroelectric plants, mines, and other extractive projects never did before 2021.

However, at the same time, the coffee monoculture plantations were collapsing; thus, the oligarchy took desperate measures to expand the economic matrix to maintain the macroeconomic balance. As a result, the elite started to boost the idea that extractive projects promote economic development into its founding narrative. In order to do so, it began to encourage law reforms in the late 90s' and the beginning of the 21st century. Consequently, the Guatemalan Parliament carried out reforms and promulgated laws (Saquimux, Castillo et al. 2011) to assure foreign investment in this kind of project. Therefore, several changes were made to the economic matrix of production in response to the new international trade needs (Enfoque 2010, Saquimux and Castillo 2018).

These modifications into the founding narrative were made to inculcate a vision of a developmental nation-state based on extractive projects, mainly gold and silver mining, hydroelectric plants, and other monoculture plantations (Gutiérrez 2012, Chán 2016, Escalón 2016a, Escalón 2016b).

However, when this narrative began to create conflicts or worsen existing ones, the state's answer was to blame those who opposed installing or constructing extractive projects. As Galtung (2017) says, 'belief in modernisation, development or progress are seen as indisputable; not believing in them then speaks against unbelievers, not belief' (161).

Secondly, in 2007, when the Guatemalan state authorised one hydroelectric plant over the Q'an B'alam River never carried out any consultation with the communities living there. In response to this, the Q'anjob'al people, such as other Maya people, called for a community consultation based on the ILO 169. Communities carried it out using their local practices and basing their actions on the national legal framework, such as Municipality Act and Electoral and Political Party Act. These acts have several articles about who can call for consultations and how the results can be considered valid, legal, and legitimate. Community consultation can be done if a determined number of persons through their Municipality organise it. (Saquimux, Castillo et al. 2011, Saquimux and Castillo 2018).

In the aftermath, in 2007, Santa Cruz Barillas's communities carried out a community consultation called by the municipality. In this consultation, 46,479 people voted, which had a participation of 209% compared to the 2007 general elections, which had abstentionism of 41.63%. The result was 100% of the people who voted said *No* to any extractive project in Santa Cruz Barillas (Saquimux, Castillo et al. 2011).

Nevertheless, the state refused to recognise the results and rejected to link it with the construction permit approval process for the hydroelectric plant, alleging the lack of legality of the results due to the absence of regulations. Even the Q'anjob'al people carried out, performed, and executed the community consultations fulfilling all the legal requirements; the Guatemalan state did not recognise it because Maya Q'anjob'al people are not right holders for it.

Therefore, it is possible to identify how Q'anjob'al people were made invisible in the making-decision process in this first frame. It is also notorious that it is not considered a right-holder and does not belong to the state-nation because its worldview is deemed contra-hegemonic. Thus, echoing in Gupta's (2012) proposal, structural violence was exerted through no recognition of the Q'anjob'al population living in the territory.

For that reason, here I point out distinction five; it is obvious how the state systematically excluded Q'anjob'al people. Of course, I am not saying that the state's process of making them invisible only responds to a racist notion.

However, it was a powerful technique to weaken the capacity of incidence in the process of enabling extractive projects, which resulted, as Galtung (1969) states it, in the 'emergence of [overt] structural violence [because the] pattern of violence [was] challenged to the point of abolition' (180).

As a matter of fact, it is imperative to emphasize how the continuum of exclusion led to increasing tensions between communities and state/corporate entities (Bastos, De León et al. 2015) when the hydroelectric plant owner started the construction. Consequently, Q'anjob'al communities, after five years, using the formal legal framework and following state and government administrative processes to defend their territories, opted for civil resistance.

Consequently, the oligarchy through the state apparatus resorted to direct violence by repressing Q'anjob'al political-community actions arguing these discouraging capital investments in the area. Therefore, the Guatemalan state began to suppress Q'anjob'al communities through direct violence, such as states of alert and emergency (Saquimux and Castillo 2018). As a result, there were several murders in this period, and some people were forced to move (Bastos, De León et al. 2015). I am not going in-depth because it is not part of the analysis; nonetheless, I point out that the direct violence was the *intermezzo* between making invisible Q'anjob'al people and targeting it as criminal. It is an example of how structural violence evolved from latent to manifest because, in this period, all the Galtung's (1969) distinctions were presented.

Nevertheless, I emphasise how the manifest violence emerged from the Governmental Agreement 1-2012 (Presidency of the Republic 2012) when the former Guatemalan President Otto Pérez Molina decreed a state of emergency for thirty days targeting Q'anjob'al resistance actions as 'serious actions that endanger the constitutional order, governability and security of the state, affecting individuals and families, endangering life, liberty, justice, security, peace, private property and the integral development of the person.' Besides, the Guatemalan Parliament approved this presidential disposition by Decree Number 11-2012 (Congress of the Republic 2012).

From these state decisions, it is possible to identify the intended violence promoted by subjects who act through state institutions against Q'anjob'al people based on racist ideas targeting Maya political actions as criminal acts. Yet, this form of violence did not dismantle the Maya Q'anjob'al people's resistance and organization. Thus, as the state's repression was not enough, the state and enterprise began to criminalise them through manifest structural violence. In this chapter, being understood as criminalisation in its two branches: symbolic and judicial violence.

The former is rooted in racist ideas and in the developmental speech that promotes extractive projects as a way to reach sustained economic growth and the promise of eradicating poverty. These discourses created a narrative that targeted Maya leaders as ignorant people, responsible for the poor country's financial performance. Their actions discouraged capital expenditures, destabilised the rule of law, and provided no guarantee of due process.

All these topics were widespread at the local and national levels through radio and TV programmes. Opinion columns were another space to spread these speeches and create a notion of the enemy against development. For instance, some columnists wrote about how community consultations affected land tenure and created a wrong impression at the international level about Guatemala climate business. Others talked about how Maya practices are archaic and do not allow Maya people to live above the poverty line. Nonetheless, all these discourses are not new. The current founding narrative is based on the racist idea of the XIX century that says Maya people are 'the hindrance to the country's advancement' (Batres cited by Casaús 2000, 43). It is also rooted in the racist idea that Maya people oppose extractive projects because they are dumb, manipulated, and ignorant (Casaús 2020).

The legal criminalisation began with criminal persecution against seven community leaders in the aftermath of the state of emergency mentioned above. Seven community leaders were imprisoned for allegedly committing several crimes, such as illegal arrests, incitement to commit crimes, coercion, threats, and obstruction of justice. This kind of criminalisation was made through legal complaints that carried arrest warrants (Saquimux and Castillo 2018). All these legal complaints were related to the resistance against the hydroelectric plants' constructions in Santa Cruz Barillas and Yich K'isis (Enfoque 2018). As a result, they were in jail for more than one year, and finally, the case was processed by the First Court of Criminal Judgment, Drug Trafficking and Environmental Crimes, also known as the Highest Risk Court A.

According to the Court's sentence issued on 22 July 2016, only two of them were found guilty of the crimes they were charged of. One for obstruction of justice and another for coercion. The other defendants were found not guilty due to lack of evidence. However, the time they spent in prison was more than the time they were convicted. This happened due to the company's series of dilatory procedures, which ceased criminal prosecution at the beginning of the oral and public debate.

Moreover, echoing Saquimux (2021), it is imperative to point out that this type of Court attends criminal acts that represent a greater risk to the personal safety of judges, magistrates, prosecutors and judicial assistants and the people on trial, witnesses, and other parties involved in the proceedings who require extraordinary security measures. The crimes considered to be of most significant risk are: genocide, forced disappearance, torture, murder, femicide, kidnapping or abduction, organised crime, drug trafficking, money laundering, terrorism, among others, all of which fall under the jurisdiction of these courts. However, none of the community leaders was charged with any of these crimes.

Therefore, the intention to negatively influence public opinion regarding the Maya and community resistance by damaging the image of community organisation by considering the autonomous process of community consultation, the defence of the land and a river as criminal behaviour become evident. In this case, the state, through its institutions and the company, were the ones that intentionally generated racist violence against the Maya Q'anjob'al people. Besides, the symbolic sphere appealed to racist stereotypes that categorise the Maya people as ignorant and criminal Indians and incapable subjects who can be manipulated. Therefore, it simplified the exercise of rights to a potential threat to the state's economic development.

In both cases, Q'anjob'al demands are rendered invisible and denaturalised. For example, during the process of legal criminalisation, community authorities were removed from their territory. The legal process was in Guatemala City, more than 350 km away from Santa Cruz Barillas, Huehuetenango. In this way, the state sought to dismantle community resistance. This was also done to reduce the discussion of who exercised violence in a given context and to deform the resistance rationality and the forms of political-community participation of the Maya Q'anjob'al people and reinforce the Maya stereotype in resistance as criminal Indians. Furthermore, once again, the community consultation on the defence of the land and the river was made invisible.

Likewise, it is imperative to point out that the legal criminalisation against Q'anjob'al people was embedded into the megaprojects imposition state policy. Something that the Guatemalan State did systematically. It imposed several extractive projects, such as the hydroelectric plant projects La Cascata, Pojom I and Pojom II, and the Marlin and San Rafael mines, around the country without the population's free, prior, and informed consent. Consequently, several communities, NGOs, and law firms appealed to the Constitutional Court, forcing the state to listen to and respect community decisions.

Nevertheless, the Court only recognised the violation of the right of consultation that people must exercise their right to decide their historical future and self-determination. However, it also agreed that the Parliament must decree a law to regulate communitarian consultations after the Ministry of Work and Social Prevention proposes a law initiative. As Cetina (2020) says, this resolution 'ignores the diverse epistemologies that peoples have possessed since before the arrival of the Spaniards' (28). Besides, it 'legalised the violation of the right of consultation' (Xiloj cited by Saquimux and Castillo 2018). Thus, the Guatemalan State excluded Maya people from public decision making and made their political practices invisible once again. The Guatemalan State's highest institution decision reinforced the racist narrative and modern-colonial idea that ancestral knowledges and practices can be standardised, denying diversity and worldviews (Cetina 2020). As Xiloj (El Colectivo 2017) argued, the Maya political-community organization forms were reduced to an administrative procedure.

These reflections adhere to Valencia's (2020) necropolitics theory which is understood 'as a form of continuum of colonial control that seeks to exterminate racialised people who appear redundant to the neoliberal project' (7). In this context, this form of governance is based on 'racism [...] as a technology of governance that allows the extraction of material and social capital through the inflexion of violence towards marginalised populations from non-marginalised populations' (Valencia 2020, 7).

Conclusion

In this chapter, I have shown how the imposition of a megaproject in Guatemala exacerbated historical conflicts in a given territory and reinforced the structural violence against people or social collective. However, structural violence is an analytical category that falls short of identifying the causes of the unequal opportunities of life and power.

In the specific case developed in this paper, I start from the premise that structural violence cannot be understood from a modern academic and political point of view because it leaves aside domination as the primordial form of violence. While it is true that over time some authors have included oppression as a concept to identify and understand the dynamics of structural violence, it cannot explain how this type of violent dynamics can be sustained in time and space. On the other hand, domination as a concept does allow for this by connecting narratives with practices that, by endowing them with meaning, make the connection between rationality and practice evident. In the Guatemalan case, the Guatemalan State's racist and developmental rationalities, and the systematic exclusion of the Maya Q'anjob'al people in decision-making processes and its unequal chances of life. Therefore, structural and racist violence make invisible Maya political-community dynamics.

The fact that all the state institutions involved – starting with the authorisation of the licence for the construction of the hydroelectric plant and the Constitutional Court ruling recognising the violation of the right to consultation – have never considered Maya cosmogonies and rationalities in decision-making and political participation was due to the lack of questioning against the Guatemalan oligarchy's narrative, especially considering that it is the dominant foundational narrative in the country. Therefore, it was the one that sustained the symbolic and judicial criminalisation of the Maya Q'anjob'al people by demanding the right to be part of the decision-making process and to decide on their historical future.

However, I recognise the historical structural violence against the Maya Q'anjob'al people, since the Spanish invasion and the continuous dispossession of their territory by the oligarchy, has resulted in the Q'anjob'al limitation of life opportunities and constriction of their needs and rights. As mentioned above, this has been possible because the Guatemalan oligarchy for 200 years has maintained control of the state institutions that are a legacy of the colony (Acemoglu and Robinson 2012). This has been achieved through a racist foundational narrative that has allowed it to monopolise resources and subjugate Maya peoples by arguing a biological difference between *Criollos* and Maya through the crystallisation of racist ideas in the social imaginary. This has resulted in structural violence being normalised and the processes of dispossession being considered part of state policy.

The aforementioned brings me to the last point of this paper, domination as the nodal point of state action and the promotion of violent acts through direct or structural means against the Maya Q'anjob'al people. This last point is evidenced in the criminalisation process in its two branches: the racist narrative that reduced community resistance to criminal action, which made the Q'anjob'al Maya rationality invisible throughout the process of symbolic and judicial criminalisation. Besides, the normalisation within the judicial process of the criminalisation processes for opposing the imposition of the hydroelectric plant. As a result, there was never any discussion of the motivations for opposition or the systematic denial of the rights to self-determination and consultation. Nor was there any discussion of the effects on the communities of the states of alert and emergency decreed in Santa Cruz Barillas, which triggered structural violence against the Maya Q'anjob'al people.

For these reasons, I affirm that, although structural violence as an analytical category allows for the identification of systematic violence against a people or a social group, if lacking domination and racism as guiding concepts, cannot explain how specific patterns of violence can be continuous in time and space. At the same time, it provides meaning to the subjective and objective actions that crystallise racism in state actions. Therefore, in order to have a comprehensive understanding of structural violence, it is imperative to understand the processes from the rationalities that motivate the imposition of ways of life that lacerate historical processes and reduce non-Western lifeworlds to criminal actions. Despite all the historical structural violence against the Q'anjob'al people, a historic triumph stopped the hydroelectric plant's construction on their sacred Q'an B'alam River.

References

Acemoglu, Daron, and James Robinson. 2012. *Why Nations Fail. The Origins of Power, Prosperity and Poverty*. London: Profile Books, LTD.

Bastos, Santiago, Quimy De León, Dania Rodríguez, Nelton Rivera, and Francisco Lucas. 2015. "Despojo, movilización y represión en Santa Cruz Barillas." In *Dinosaurio reloaded*, edited by Manuela Camus, Santiago Bastos, and Julián López, 271-302. Guatemala: FLACSO: Fundación Constelación.

Bourdieu, Pierre. 2000. *La dominación masculina*. Barcelona, España: Editorial Anagrama, S.A.

Casaús, Marta. 2000. "La metamorfosis del racismo en la élite del poder en Guatemala." *Nueva Antropología* 27(58): 27–78.

———. 2010. *Guatemala: linaje y racismo*. Guatemala: F&G Editores.

———. 2020. "Guatemala: Así se expresa el odio contra indígenas y mujeres en las redes sociales." *Nómada*, February 25, 2020. https://nomada.gt/identidades/guatemala-urbana/guatemala-asi-se-expresa-el-odio-contra-indigenas-y-mujeres-en-las-redes-sociales/

Casolo, Jennifer. 2020. "Derechos ancestrales, dinámicas territoriales, despojo y defensa del pueblo maya Q'eqchi' Comunidad Plan Grande, El Estor, Izabal." In *Abelino y las comunidades q'eqchi'. Peritajes para su defensa*, edited by Laura Paz y Paz, 55–144. Guatemala: F&G Editores.

Castellanos, Julio. 1985. *Café y campesinos en Guatemala, 1853–1897*. Guatemala: Universitaria.

Chán, Alejandro. 2016. "Reconfiguración del territorio: empresas hidroeléctricas, Estado y Pueblos Indígenas. -El norte de los Cuchumatanes, Huehuetenango." *Enfoque* 39: 1–33.

Commission for Historical Clarification – CEH (1997). "Guatemala: Memory of Silence." from https://www.derechoshumanos.net/lesahumanidad/informes/guatemala/informeCEH.htm

Cetina, Carla. 2020. "La reglamentación de los procesos de Consulta Previa, Libre e Informada: una violación a la autodeterminación de los pueblos indígenas." *Estudios Interétnicos* 31(26): 17–42.

Cojtí, Demetrio. 2006. "Insumos y criterios para el diseño y factibilidad de políticas públicas contra el racismo y la discriminación." In *Diagnóstico del racismo en Guatemala. Investigación interdisciplinaria y participativa para una política integral por la convivencia y la eliminación del racismo: perspectivas y visiones ciudadanas*, edited by Marta Casaús and Amílcar Dávila, IV: 99–117. Guatemala: Serviprensa, S.A.

Echeverría, Bolivar. 1995. *Las ilusiones de la modernidad.* México, D.F.: Universidad Nacional Autónoma de México.

El Colectivo. 2017. "Consultas comunitarias: ¿Pertinencia cultural o Estado de derecho?".

Congress of the Republic. 2012. Decreto Número 11–2012. Congress of the Republic. Guatemala.

Enfoque. 2010. "Entrevista con Sergio Tischler. La violencia viene con los mismos megaproyectos porque es un despojo." *Enfoque* 12: 2–22.

———. 2018. "Criminalización y presos políticos en Guatemala: una historia de continuidad -segunda parte-." *Enfoque* 55: 14–16.

Escalón, Sebastián. 2016a. "La nueva era del saqueo." *Plaza Pública*, November 6, 2016. https://www.plazapublica.com.gt/content/la-nueva-era-del-saqueo-0

———. 2016b. "Los muchos favores del Estado a la minería." *Plaza Pública*, October 21, 2016. https://www.plazapublica.com.gt/content/los-muchos-favores-del-estado-la-mineria

Farmer, Paul. 2004. "An Anthropology of Structural Violence." *Current Anthropology* 45: 305–325.

Figueroa, Carlos. 2019. "Guatemala: El recurso del miedo." In *Antología del pensamiento crítico guatemalteco contemporáneo,* edited by Ana Monzón, 271-283. Buenos Aires: CLACSO.

Galtung, Johan. 1969. "Violence, Peace, and Peace Research." *Journal of Peace Research* 6(3): 167–191.

———. 2017. "La violencia: cultural, estructural y directa." In *Cuaderno de Estrategia 183. Política y violencia: comprensión teórica y desarrollo en la acción colectiva,* edited by Instituto de Estudios Estratégicos, 147–168. España: Ministerio de Defensa.

Gupta, Akhil. 2012. *Red Tape. Bureaucracy, Structural Violence and Poverty in India*. Durham and London: Duke University Press.

Gutiérrez, Alejandra. 2012. "De monocultivos, la lucha por el espacio y los desarraigados." *Plaza Pública*, June 13, 2012. https://www.plazapublica.com.gt/content/de-monocultivos-la-lucha-por-el-espacio-y-los-desarraigados

Guzmán, Carlos. 2016. *Donde enmudecen las conciencias: crepúsculo y aurora en Guatemala*. Guatemala: Catafixia.

Institute of National Statistics. 2014. *Encuesta Nacional de Condiciones de Vida - ENCOVI*.

———. 2018. *Census Report*.

Martínez, Severo. 2011. *La patria del criollo: ensayo de interpretación de la realidad colonial guatemalteca*. Guatemala: Fondo de Cultura Económica.

Menjívar, Cecilia. 2014. *Eterna violencia: vidas de las mujeres ladinas en Guatemala*. Guatemala: FLACSO.

Organización del Pueblo en Armas. 1976. *La verdadera magnitud del racismo (Racismo I)*. Guatemala.

———. 1978. *La verdadera magnitud del racismo (Racismo II)*. Guatemala.

Presidency of the Republic (2012). Decreto Gubernativo Número 1–2012. Presidency of the Republic. Guatemala.

Quijano, Aníbal. 1992. "Colonialidad y modernidad/racionalidad." *Perú Indígena* 13 (29): 11–20. https://edisciplinas.usp.br/pluginfile.php/5698653/mod_resource/content/2/quijano.pdf

———. 2014a. "Colonialidad del poder, eurocentrismo y América Latina." In *Cuestiones y horizontes: de la dependencia histórico-estructural a la colonialidad/descolonialidad del poder*, edited by Danilo Assis Clímaco, 777-832. Buenos Aires: CLACSO.

———. 2014b. ""Raza", "etnia" y "nación" en Mariátegui: cuestiones abiertas." In *Cuestiones y horizontes: de la dependencia histórico-estructural a la colonialidad/descolonialidad del poder*, edited by Danilo Assis Clímaco, 757–776. Buenos Aires: CLACSO.

Rylko-Bauer, Barbara, and Paul Farmer (2016). "Structural Violence, Poverty, and Social Suffering." In *The Oxford Handbook of the Social Science of Poverty*, edited by David Brady and Linda Burton, 47-73. United States of America: Oxford University Press

Saquimux, María. 2021. Contra y más allá del derecho. La guerra legal contra las luchas comunitarias en Guatemala. México.

Saquimux, Miguel, and Max Castillo. 2018. "De la invisibilización a la criminalización." Presented at the *Central American Conference of the Latin American Council of Social Sciences -CLACSO- 2017*. Guatemala.

Saquimux, Miguel, Max Castillo, and Mónica Aguilar. 2011. "Consultas populares, el dilema del movimiento de reivindicación del territorio en Guatemala." Presented at the *XXVIII Congress of the Latin American Sociology Association – ALAS*. Recife, Brazil.

Schoungunt, Nicolas. 2012. "La construcción social de la masculinidad: poder, hegemonía y violencia." *Psicología, Conocimiento y Sociedad* 2(2): 27–65.

Straus, Scott. (2015). *Making and unmaking Nations. War, Leadership and Genocide in Modern Africa*. Ithaca and London: Cornell University Press.

Valencia, Sayak. 2020. "Borderization and Live Regime." Lectured December 2020 at The Sawyer Seminar, The University of Arizona. https://sawyerseminar.arizona.edu/december-borders

Vela, Manolo, Alexander Saquén-Mónchez, and Hugo Solares. 2001. *El lado oscuro de la eterna primavera. Violencia, criminalidad y delincuencia en la Guatemala de post-guerra*. Guatemala: FLACSO.

8

Decolonising Social Movements in Latin America: An Approach over the Internationalization of the Landless Workers Movement (MST)

ELLEN MONIELLE DO VALE SILVA & GUILHERME DE LIMA SOUZA

Along with the historical brutality and devastation catalyzed by the diffusion of the modern/colonial, the social movements, however, consolidate new dimensions of their own senses reinvented in the circumstances and, as established by Porto-Gonçalves (2006, 25), 'they resist because they exist; therefore *re-exist*'. The Latin America driving forces of social movements for territorial struggles are interconnected along collective trajectories in the confrontation of capitalist globalization's predatory effects. Regarding the peasant movement that will be discussed in this paper, more specifically the Brazilian Landless Workers Movement (MST), it is important to note that MST has been at the forefront of *re-existence* to the modern/colonial ties, capitalism and deterritorialization (Porto-Gonçalves 2006).

Although in Brazil, the development of capitalism was able to stimulate the concentration of land, in 1984, the rural workers converged at the 1st National Meeting for land democracy, in Cascavel, Paraná. There, they decided to establish a national peasant movement, the MST, with three main objectives: fight for land, fight for agrarian reform and fight for social change in the country (MST, 2021). Thus, in order to analyze the articulation of the MST in its internationalization process, this paper aims to comprise the perspectives that consolidate the transnational actions and dialogues between Latin American peasant movements. The methodology used in the construction of this paper relates to a conceptual and bibliographical review, based on a qualitative and decolonial theoretical approach. Initially, it examined the notions of Anibal Quijano's concepts of coloniality of power and capitalist development, such as Arturo Escobar's conceptions on territory, land and place, connecting to the rise of the MST.

Thereupon, the internationalist articulations of the MST will be historically analyzed, emphasizing the engagements with networks, organizations and epistemologies for the land struggles in Latin America; for instance, La *Vía Campesina* movement and the Liberation Theology, standing out their common demands. In this section, this paper introduces the main struggles that are implied in the peasant movements, such as the complaints about neoliberal globalization and the productive systems of transnational capitalism – which are interconnected and integrated along with demands for land use and land reform. Comprehending the decolonial ideas, as aforementioned, related with territorial and land disputes between social movements and large landowners as a collective point of departure alongside the region, the MST's internationalization process, consolidated since its origins, will be explained as a mechanism of transnational class solidarity and regional resistance strategy to structural dilemmas.

Hence, the MST's actions are discussed as a unifying element of struggles to face transnational challenges of extractivism and decomposition of the peasant economies of Latin America. As said by Escobar (2015) over the Zapatista dictum 'u*n mundo donde quepan muchos mundos*', the struggles that are embodied by the MST international engagements in Latin America establish a light on the pluriversal historical narratives of the region that are encountered and reunited as an act of *re-existence* in the capitalist system.

Coloniality, territory and the rise of MST

Within the discussions regarding decolonial thinking, the concept of coloniality of power, initially developed by Quijano, in 1989, is widely used to refer to associations that did not end with the destruction of political-historical colonialism and, therefore, are understood by the maintenance of colonial forms of domination (Ballestrin 2013; Grosfoguel 2008). Based on this aspect, according to Quijano (2002, 4), coloniality of power accounts one of the founding elements of the current pattern of power, settling a social classification around the idea of race.

Quijano (2002) states that the notion and social categorization based on race was originated 500 years ago along with America, Europe and capitalism, as well as Enrique Dussel (1993) highlights the myth that we are experiencing the idea of modernity, conception based on the *beginning* of Latin America in 1492. Consequently, modernity, inseparable and intrinsic to coloniality, is based on the construction, rise and consolidation of the capitalist system of production. With the establishment of its dynamics of relations, the forms of labor exploitation and production-appropriation-distribution, consolidated in the historical constitution of America, were supported by the foundation of this new forgoing form of production and its new global standard control of work, resources and products (Quijano 2002).

That being said, the expression of colonial domination that was imposed in the course of the expansion of European colonialism is still profound and lasting (Quijano 2002; Mignolo 2003; Escobar 2015). The new historical identities produced around the idea of race, in the modernity/colonial context, were related to the nature of roles and territory/place in the new global structure of labor control (Quijano 1997). Nevertheless, Quijano (1997, 118) expresses that 'both elements, race and division of labor, were structurally associated and mutually reinforcing, although neither was necessarily dependent on the other to exist or to transform itself'.

As the manifestation of power characterizes a type of social relations constituted by the co-presence regarding elements of domination, exploitation and conflict, what is now called *globalization* is the moment placed in the development of such pattern of power. Recognizing this global ordainment and its distribution of resources taking into account the process of formation of the world power, the vast majority of the exploited and discriminated, are exactly the members of the 'races', 'ethnic groups' and 'nations' in which the colonized populations were categorized from the conquest of America onwards (Quijano 1992, 12). On this matter, the enslavement of Black and Indigenous people consolidated by the idea of race was not only a central component of colonialism, but of global capitalism as well.

Furthermore, given this power structure, it is also valid to point out that the moment of globalization, capital expansion and its colonial and dependent links, in practice, manifests itself in an inversion of reality, as emphasized by Florestan Fernandes (1972). According to the author,

> (...) as if the central economy were to reproduce itself in the peripheral economy in reverse, to feed not its development, but the development of the dominant economy. As a result, the freedom of the economic agent can be postulated and

represented by the same categories of action and thought, prevailing in the central economy – since the ideology of a colonial, neo-colonial or dependent society, maintaining the conditions of *normal* heteronomy, comes to be the ideology of metropolitan society. (Fernandes 1972, 174)

Considering this dominant asymmetry of the global 'frenzy' panorama and its capacity of transformation, Milton Santos (1994, 255–256) states that even in places where the vectors of globalization are more operative and effective, the territory creates new synergies, resulting in an expression of its affective and symbolic value. As this globalization frenzy takes control, the territory and its significance as a place has disappeared, creating 'profound consequences on our understanding of culture, knowledge, nature, and the economy' (Escobar 2000, 68). By place, it is understood the commitment and experience of a particular location with some measure of rootedness, limits and connections to everyday life. Even when its identity is constructed, place continues to be important in the lives of most people (Escobar 2010, 30).

Although transnationalized, the struggles concerning the conceptions based on territories demonstrate a defense of particular constructions of place, including its reorganizations (Escobar 2010, 78–79). The Latin America territory is frequently read in dialogue with social movements, their identities and their use as an instrument of struggle and social transformation, settling the landless workers experience on the agenda (Haesbaert 2020, 268). The Latin American accelerated process of agricultural modernization, conceived by the high technology of seeds, chemical inputs and agricultural equipment, known as the Green Revolution, gave room for the capitalist accumulation regime to benefit large rural companies.

Thus, the neoliberal conditions created a particularly dire context for the rural population. In this scenario of agricultural modernization reinforced by national development, MST was formally born at the First National Meeting of Landless Workers, in 1984 (Figueroa 2005; Rubbo 2013). Hence, the ties to territory and culture allows social movements, such as MST, the proper setting to develop place-based strategies. This plan of action uses the ties aforementioned to enact a politic *desde abajo*, that allows to interconnect the experience of the Global South due to the typology of policies to which it belongs (Escobar 2010, 32).

In this outline, the domination of space, capital and modernity, which are central to the discourse of globalization, created grounds for movements such MST to re-conceive, re-construct and re-affirm perspectives of non-capitalism, culture and territory/place (Escobar 2000, 69). Escobar (2016, 24) exposes that territorial struggles are producing new types and/or rescuing knowledge for cultural and ecological transition to face this modernity scenario. Expressly, here, the need to highlight that several forces influenced the formation of MST, moreover, Liberation Theology (TdL) played a central role in its form of organization, unconditional support for land occupations and, mainly, in the effect of stimulating an internationalist perspective of the movement through international solidarity.

Also, some broader perspectives, movements and cosmovisions that encounter strong adherence in Latin America and the Global South has its level of importance in shaping the MST, such as the Altermondialist Movement, *Fórum Social Mundial* networks that have raised, in a heterogeneous and unified manner, the agendas of environmental protection and in-depth reform of the economic system; and *La Vía Campesina*, one of the main peasant movements of contemporaneity that has been standing out on the international conjuncture confronting the political decision-making related to agriculture (Milani 2008, 290; Silva and Alves, 2021). Therefore, the Landless Workers Movement gradually built several relations with popular movements in Latin America (Rubbo 2013).

Bearing this in mind, the struggle for territory and the politics of place, an expression mentioned by Escobar (2010, 67), are resulting in the emergence of a new form of politics. Thereby, it is necessary to create a new political imaginary based on the possibility of constructing a multiplicity of actions in the plane of daily life, whereas the experiences of subalternized people are necessary to understand struggles and decolonise political constructions of territory/place. Also, territorial strives are, nonetheless, pronounced by a cultural struggle for autonomy and self-determination within a capitalist system and its ties to the context of modernity/coloniality (Quijano 1992; Escobar 2010, 79).

Transnationalization, Social Struggles and the Landless Workers Movement in a Globalized World

The driving forces of neoliberal globalization, in consonance with centuries of colonial land expropriation over Latin American territories, imply multiple challenges for the confrontation of systematic oppressions and dominations alongside the predatory capitalist mechanisms. Besides years of historical suppression of the colonial economic regimes, from far-right political leaders to the most progressives, the neo-extractivist paradigms of intense land concentration in the power of the agribusiness sectors still determines obstacles for democratic access to the means of production and living for the peasant and traditional communities of the region (Acosta and Brand 2018, 31–54).

This case-scenario suggests the analysis, which is the central point of this paper, that the problems faced and confronted by local social movements encounter similar bases on common struggles and experiences in Latin American. In the same way that the categorization of global peripheries represents a direct reflection of dynamics of the transnationalized capital accumulation system over a collectivity of territories, its resistance should also constitute a space of organized transnational confrontation (Milani 2008, 291–294). Furthermore, as it is pointed out by Escobar (2005, 80), the cooperation among social movements can be a producer of revolutionary identities by the *glocalization* of common struggles, both standing for the local dilemmas and articulating global spheres of action.

That being stated, since its origins, the MST had constituted significant transnational coalitions with other movements in Latin America, most importantly, assuming the premise that structural problems reinforced by international scales of accumulation entails international responses. The sense of transnationality comprehends the contents and extension of the land conflicts, as part of ways of production that goes beyond national borders, alongside problems that aren't limited to the local scale, which directly implies the necessity of multilateral arrangements between different governments and social actors (Sachs 1998 *apud* Milani 2008, 299).

The transnational action of the MST, despite their local differences in their forms of action and claims with other social movements, becomes a possible space to construct cohesive collective identities with networks of action, increasing the bargaining power of its objectives in the international arena (Bezerra 2004, 121). Moreover, these kind of processes can be described, as is highlighted by Escobar (2015, 22), by the idea of the construction of territorial identities based on the pluriversal existence and resistance of social struggles, converging movements to the defense of an ontological perspective of the world in alternative to the capitalist globalization patterns. The common points of departure regarding the resistance to the predatory effects of transnational neoliberalism, the decolonial approach to the globalization process, and the religious aspects over the access of lands for the poor communities become elements of influence to the international solidarity of class (Rubbo 2013, 75).

The Liberation Theology, as mentioned before, claims through the Universalist perspectives of solidarity with the poor and of humanity in its wholeness, which is reinforced with Christian movements aligned with land struggles and strong critics against the dependency relations of peripheral capitalism materialistic interests that suppress the spirits of communitarianism (Rubbo 2013, 75–82). Afterall, as it is pointed out by Enrique Dussel (1973,

49) the praxis of liberation originated with service to the Others that are suppressed by the system and, in that case, the historical role of the church in Latin America should be committing to the liberation of the peripheral world. Mostly disseminated in Brazil in the 70s by the Christian social movement *Comissão Pastoral da Terra (CPT)*, founded during the repressive apparatus of military dictatorship in the country, those internationalist aspects of solidarity and the global south refuse to dependency were fundamental to the foundational scope of the Landless Workers Movement in the next decade.

The first internationalist attempts in the MST where highly conceived through articulations with *La Vía Campesina,* an autonomous transnational social movement that integrates plural groups that struggle with the access to productive land, mostly from Latin America, into the presence in the international arenas of discussion, coalitions and protests (Milani 2008, 298). Thereupon, the participation of the Landless Workers Movement in those spheres was initially perceived on the 'Continental Campaign: 500 Years of Indigenous, Black and Popular Resistance' (1989–1992), international event convened by peasant organizations that alongside with *La Vía Campesina* establishes the creation of the *Coordinadora Latinoamericana de Organizaciones del Campo* (CLOC-VC).

The CLOC-VC articulations aligned with *La Vía Campesina* international sector proposes perspectives for the collective anti-imperialist and anti-capitalist coalition in the Americas. Above all, the international coordinator brings to light spaces of popular masses mobilization in solidarity with Cuba's revolutionary regime, socialist movements and for the defense of peasant and sustainable agricultural systems affected by neoliberal policies (Batista 2019, 137).

The Continental Campaign represents a point of inflexion in the internationalist trajectory of the MST, despite some previous years of punctual foreign solidarity with social movements and transnational peasant causes, the Brazilian landless movement begins to institutionalize an international relations sector in its structure from the beginning of the '90s onwards (Rubbo 2013). Furthermore, Batista (2019, 154) emphasizes that the Landless Workers Movement also gets to work as an international advocate, gathered with CLOC-VC, for the political themes of integral and popular agrarian reform and peasant rights over transnational frameworks of decision such as the Food and Agriculture Organization, the World Bank, the International Monetary Fund and the World Trade Organization.

This historical process highlights strong evidence that even though Latin America precedes a pluriversal world of social struggles in the local territories, the articulation in scales where MST starts to be composed represents the redefinition of transnational identities, reunited in the defense of the subalternized world (Milani 2008, 298–299). From the end of the '90s to the first years of the 21st century, this transnational scope of collective territorial identities is well translated in the so-called Altermondialist Movement, represented with the creation of the *Fórum Social Mundial,* celebrated for the first time in 2001. In this context, the Landless Workers Movement and *La Vía Campesina* started to significantly contribute with the debate of social and political problems, integrating relevant arenas of coalition among anti-neoliberal organizations, parties and movements and reuniting local problems with global revolutionary solutions (Rubbo 2010, 6–7). About the participation of social movements in the mentioned event in the years of 2001, 2003 and 2008, Milani (2008) highlights:

> (…) environmental networks and movements in Latin America represent more than 55% of the total of organizations participating in the processes of the Fórum Social Mundial, which claims to integrate the banner of sustainable development and environmental defense in their struggles. On the total of 102 organizations and movements from Latin America and the Caribbean, 80 are from Brazil, 4 from Uruguay, 3 from Ecuador, 2 from. Argentina, Chile, Panama, Peru, and Paraguay. (Milani 2008, 294)

It is clear that the main principle that instigates the transnational action of these social movements in Latin America is to integrate multiple voices and struggles that encounter demands over the impacts of neoliberal politics in the region and its repercussions on the territorial occupation. However, how is it possible to unify such different nationalities and specificities of political claims into one greater purpose? According to Bezerra (2004, 126), the transnational convergence that composes the Altermondialist Movement is built in a process of continuous interactions over time, in which the common identities are reinforced not in a way of equalization of the movements' struggles and requests, but based instead on the perceptions of a similar obstacle to be defeated, in this case, the global neoliberal apparatuses of land expropriation.

Political Strategies for the MST's International Actions

From its initial articulations in the '80s to the present moment, the Landless Workers Movement has built capacities and interactions to maintain strong transnational relations and to be a sphere of dialogue with the peasant and socialist movements of the subalternized world. The transnational action is mostly encouraged by the values of 'solidarity, humanism and internationalism' for the historical legacy of the working class and the idea that there are no borders for the political resistance to human exploitation (MST 2021). Besides, the MST's national leader Gilmar Mauro points out, in an interview for Rubbo (2012, 26), that the movement historically made efforts for the exchange of political strategies with transnational activists, actions of international political-ideological training workshops and the participation of solidarity actions in countries going through revolutionary moments.

Beyond the participation in wide-ranged organizations like *La Vía Campesina*, the internationalization of the MST is operationalized in multiple forms of action, embracing opportunities for transnational solidarity in its own national territory, but also scattered throughout other countries as well. Apart from self-organized actions observed in the international experience of the movement, the Collective for International Relations (CRI) of the MST has been working to embrace the resistance, construction, improvement and awakening of the peasant and socialist social bases and values among transnational partners (MST, 2021). Those values are well represented also in the testimony of the MST's national leader and responsible for the CRI, Cassia Bechara, in the 2020's National Encounter of Landless Women:

> The MST has internationalism in its fundamental principles. We are clear that the construction of socialism can only happen from an international construction of forces (…) This strengthens both our movement and these sister organizations. It strengthens the internationalist feeling of unity of the working class.(Poznanski 2020).

Additionally, the transnational principle represented in the MST's struggles for the land is a major factor to understand why the solidarity of class among the Latin America movements is not only a reality, but an autonomous process for the suppression of the colonial past that still maintains its effects in action over the region. In that sense, the articulations and demands that permeate the movement actions, from a national to an international scale, in search for land sovereignty also felt as global demands for peasant revolutionary acts in the Global South. Furthermore, the historical recognition of the MST's political impact had managed to conquer international sympathy for the agrarian cause in Brazil, mobilizing the transnationalization of debate and inspiring the constant multiplication of support and solidarity committees and international brigades for the movement in several foreign countries (Rubbo 2013, 147)

At least, until 2015, the Landless Workers Movement had brigades in 'Venezuela, Haiti, Cuba, El Salvador, Paraguay, Mozambique, Peru and Bolivia', besides many of them being articulated with support of *La Vía*

Campesina, which also collaborated with MST for the construction of the *Instituto Agroecológico Latinoamericano* in Venezuela (Tygel 2015). It's also valid to punctuate the existence of the *International Brigade Apolônio de Carvalho* that operates in the Venezuelan territory since 2006, working on projects of 'agro-ecological production, food sovereignty, seed production, cooperative work, political education and student exchanges' (MST 2021). Therefore, the MST had considerable international experience over the years and consolidated important networks of actions that also worked as inspiration, cooperation and resistance in the globalized world.

Final Considerations

The ascendancy of capitalism has presented challenges to popular movements in Latin America. Based on the length of what has been discussed so far, it is observed that the MST seeks to disintegrate with the forms of colonial domination and, thus, to interrupt the perspective of identities based on the idea of race and established with the coloniality of power and its context of modernity. Furthermore, the globalized world guided by this scenario involves a new global form of division of labor, while misrepresenting the meaning of territory/place and creating profound consequences in the understanding of the factors that guides it.

The reflections developed with the present analysis highlight the idea that despite being created on a basis of local issues and the particularities for the land access in Brazil, the MST seeks to collaborate with international movements that struggle with common structural problems. Therefore, it is important to point out that the internationalist interests articulated over the MST unveil the rural and land dilemmas that take part of the Latin American context as a peripheral region affected by agricultural-centered and dependent economies, constantly reaffirmed with the capitalist neoliberal globalization forms of production. In this way, participation through international coalitions, movements and networks, beyond the establishment of relations with the Global South, is an act of resistance by raising voices and occupying spheres of decision and advocacy against the predatory effects of transnational capitalism.

Hence, through decolonial lenses, it is clear that the MST re-allocates and re-affirms itself as producers of knowledge and practices, far from the Eurocentric narratives, in the context of territorial struggles. Notwithstanding, recognizing that this entire dispute crosses borders in the capitalist/modern/colonial world, as well as other agrarian movements involved in the struggle for land – the MST expands and solidifies itself internationally through solidarity.

Summarizing the main efforts and methodologies of action executed along the MST internationalist trajectory, it is recognized that the strategies articulated in partnership and cooperation with *La Vía Campesina* and the CLOC-VC movements were fundamental to expand possibilities of transnational presence. The very high presence of Latin America movements in Altermondialist events, such as the *Fórum Social Mundial*, is a direct result of the same process in which MST is inserted.

Therefore, it represents an important piece of a bigger process on which the movements articulate the defense of a pluriversal territorial identity as a radical counterbalance for the deterritorialization of colonial modernity. Those elements of collective demand, despite the differences among the social movements of Latin America integrated in the MST agenda are encountered in the idea that a revolutionary process against the neoliberal globalization must construct its bases on an internationalist perspective, otherwise, it won't have the strength to confront a system so transnationalized like the capitalism itself.

References

Alan Tygel. "MST participa de conferência sobre internacionalismo no século 21", 2015   Accessed July 3, 2021. https://mst.org.br/2015/11/09/mst-participa-de-conferencia-sobre-internacionalismo-no-seculo-21/

Alberto Acosta and Ulrich Brand, "Pós-extrativismo e decrescimento", São Paulo: Elefante, 2018.

Ândrea Francine Batista, "Movimento camponês e consciência de classe: a práxis Organizativa da Via Campesina Internacional na América Latina", (PhD diss. Universidade Federal do Rio de Janeiro, 2019).

Aníbal Quijano. "Colonialidad del poder, cultura y conocimiento en América Latina" Anuario Mariateguiano, Lima: Amauta, 1997.

Aníbal Quijano. "Colonialidad y Colonialidad/Racionalidad" Perú Indígena.,13 (29): 11–20, 1992.

Aníbal Quijano. "Colonialidad, poder, globalização e democracia" Novos Rumos 17, no. 37, 2002.

Arturo Escobar, "El lugar de la naturaleza y la naturaleza del lugar: ¿globalización o postdesarrollo?", in La colonialidad del saber: eurocentrismo y ciencias sociales org. by Edgardo Lander, 113–143. Perspectivas latinoamericanas Buenos Aires: Flacso, 2000.

Arturo Escobar, "Thinking-feeling with the Earth: Territorial Struggles and the Ontological Dimension of the Epistemologies of the South", Revista de Antropología Iberoamericana 11, 11–32, 2016.

Arturo Escobar, "O lugar da natureza e a natureza do lugar: globalização ou pós-desenvolvimento?", in A colonialidade do saber: eurocentrismo e ciências sociais organizated by Edgardo Lander, 133–168. Colección Sur Sur: CLACSO, Ciudad Autónoma de Buenos Aires, Argentina, 2005.

Arturo Escobar, "Territorios de diferencia: Lugares, movimientos, vida, redes", Bogotá: Envión Editores, 2010.

Carlos R. S. Milani, "Ecologia política, movimentos ambientalistas e contestação transnacional na América Latina", Caderno CRH 21, no. 53 (May/Aug), 289–303, 2008.

Carlos Walter Porto-Gonçalves. "De Saberes E De Territórios: Diversidade e emancipação a partir da experiência latino-americano" GEOgraphia 8 (16), 2020. https://doi.org/10.22409/GEOgraphia2006.v8i16.a13521

Deni Irineu Alfaro Rubbo. "Campesinos cosmopolitas: um estudo sobre a atuação política internacionalista do MST na América Latina" Master diss., Universidade de São Paulo, 2013.

Deni Irineu Alfaro Rubbo. "Do campo para o mundo: em busca de um internacionalismo continental para o MST – Entrevista com Gilmar Mauro", Lutas Sociais, no. 29, 21–30, 2012.

Deni Irineu Alfaro Rubbo."Aspectos preliminares sobre a internacionalização do MST - Movimento dos Trabalhadores Rurais Sem-Terra", Simpósio Lutas Sociais na América Latina IV, 1–9, 2010.

Ellen Monielle do Vale Silva and Fernanda Caroline Alves Bezerra de Melo. "Da teoria verde ao ecofeminismo: mulheres na África Meridional frente às mudanças climáticas", e-cadernos CES, 2021. https://doi.org/10.4000/eces.5704

Enrique Dussel, "1942: O Encobrimento do Outro (a origem do "Mito Modernidade")", Conferência de Frankfurt. Petrópolis, Rio de Janeiro, 1993.

Enrique Dussel. "Caminos de liberación latinoamericana II: teología de la liberación y ética". Buenos Aires: Latinoamérica libros, 1973

Florence Poznanski. "Representantes de vários países participam do Encontro Nacional das Mulheres Sem Terra", 2020 Accessed July 3, 2021. https://mst.org.br/2020/03/13/representantes-de-varios-paises-participam-do-encontro-nacional-das-mulheres-sem-terra/

Florestan Fernandes, "Sociedade de Classes e Subdesenvolvimento", 2.ed., Rio de Janeiro: Zahar. Revista Direito Em Debate, 12 (20), 1972.

Luciana Ballestrin, "América Latina e o Giro Decolonial", Revista Brasileira de Ciência Política, no.11 (May/Aug.), 89–111, 2013.

Manuel Víctor Figueroa, "América Latina: Descomposición y persistencia de lo campesino", 2005, Accessed June 03, 2021 http://www.scielo.org.mx/scielo.php?script=sci_arttext&pid=S0301-70362005000300003

Milton Santos. "Técnica, espaço, tempo: globalização e meio técnico-científico informacional" São Paulo: HUCITEC, 1994.

MST. "Brigada Apolônio de Carvalho – Venezuela", 2021. Accessed July 3, 2021. https://mst.org.br/brigadainternacional/brigada-apolonio-de-carvalho-venezuela/

MST. "Quem somos". 2020. Accessed July 3, 2021a. https://mst.org.br/quem-somos/

Ramón Grosfoguel, "Para descolonizar os estudos de economia política e os estudos pós-coloniais: transmodernidade, pensamento de fronteira e colonialidade global", Revista Crítica de Ciências Sociais, no. 80, 115–147, 2008.

Rogério Haesbaert, "Do Corpo-Território ao Território-Corpo (Da Terra): Contribuições decoloniais", GEOgraphia 22 (48), 2020. https://doi.org/10.22409/GEOgraphia2020.v22i48.a43100

Vicente Amaral Bezerra, . "A cooperação transnacional de movimentos sociais: o caso do MST", Fronteira, 109–133, 2004.

Walter Mignolo, "Histórias locais/ Projetos globais: colonialidade, saberes subalternos e pensamento limiar", Belo Horizonte: Editora UFMG, 2003.

9

Messages from the Meek: Dynamic Resistances at the Edge of Amazonian Colonization and Capitalism

CHRISTIAN FERREIRA CREVELS

Braves and Meeks in the Amazon

Three days remaining until the end of the year 1907, the newspaper *O Malho*, of the city of Rio de Janeiro, displayed under the title 'in the far north of Brazil', what seems to be the first photograph ever published of individuals of the Madihadeni Indigenous people. Those photographed (three men, six women and an infant), unsurprisingly, show some common native Amazonian dressing, such as headdresses, necklaces, small cotton skirts and bands tightly tied below the knees. They are all barefoot, have their hair trimmed the traditional old ways and are not covered with western clothes. Almost everything points towards a time where the relations between them and the surrounding society were few and sparse. They also carry long bows and arrows on full display, a fact that is commented right in the description of the picture:

> A group of Indians of the Jamamady tribe, of the Xeruan river, photographed at the Juruá river, at the *seringal* Manichy, by the amateur photographer Mr. Josué Nunes. They have their weapons of choice, including the *cabocla*... with the child to the side. Unfortunately, the civilization action of the *seringal* still permits the exhibition of pictures of such order. (O MALHO 1907.)

The term *cabocla* is the feminine version of a *caboclo*, thus referring to an Indigenous woman. It is a way that Indigenous Peoples were historically called in Brazil, now outdated due to its pejorative weight and prejudice. Sometimes translated as a *rubber plantation*, a *seringal* is, nevertheless, not a plantation, but rather an extractive site located deep within the forest. Hardly structured, it consisted mostly of a series of trails connecting the trees of latex-producing *hevea brasiliensis* and a storage shed, the *barracão,* that doubled as a market store. The *seringal* was the center of rubber production in the Amazon in the early 20th century, during what is called 'the Amazonian rubber boom' (Weinstein 1983). At the time, the River Juruá was experiencing the intensification of traffic and rapid occupation of its margins following the pursuit of the so-called 'white gold' of the Amazon.

The geographical references and some additional historical documentation leave no doubt that those photographed are the ancestors of a group of the Madihadeni that today still populate the same river. A few years later, in 1920, the anthropologist Paul Rivet and the priest Constant Tastevin would also find the *Jamamady* in the same region and write about the fast development of the rubber endeavor (Rivet and Tastevin 1921, 463). At the time, it was not yet known that those people denominated themselves as Madihadeni, and it would take yet another half a century for the first ethnography about them to be written. The ethnonym *Jamamady* is still today directed to some groups of the region and was probably used in a broader fashion by the settlers that made contact with them (Crevels 2021).

Both the local lore and academic narrative frequently state that the settlers and merchants, entering and occupying the region almost exclusively through the main rivers, created a double migration movement among the different Indigenous groups that resided there. Some established (somewhat) peaceful commercial relations and were attracted to the margins of the bigger waterways. Others, less keen to relate and/or belligerent, fled upstream crossing the small riverbeds onto dry land and deep forests. The first ones, then, in contact, gave the generic denomination they used for the latter ones, themselves isolated. Some authors, both now and back then at the first decades of the century, noticed that the ethnonym *Jamamadi* and its variances (*Jamamady, Iamamady,* and alike) seem to possibly derive from the terms of the Indigenous languages of the Arawa linguistic family for 'forest' (*zama* or *jama*) - and 'people' (*madi*). Therefore, it would mean something like 'forest people', or 'wild people'. This way, many groups were called indistinctly under the same name. The term signified less a distinct group than a specific disposition to (or not to) engage in relations with the extractive endeavors and/or the merchants that roamed the basins of the Purus River and Juruá River. On this distinction, during a huge, but disorganized, economical and colonial endeavor, the lack of intention to trade and to produce rubber by the part of some reluctant Indigenous groups took moral outlines: they were deemed as savages, aggressive, cannibals and so on. A whole sort of mystery, histories and descriptions was disseminated to convey the separation of the Indigenous peoples between the *meeks*: amicable dwellers of the rivers, willing to trade and to work; and the 'braves': violent residents of the dense forest and far creeks, obstacles to the full disclosure of the country and the development of the region (Taussig 1993).

The lexical use is, of course, not out of context. *'Brabo'*, a regional version of the word *'bravo',* can have its origins well translated as 'brave'. However, in the Amazon region and the context of the *aviamento*, the term came to be used also to refer to the rubber tappers in the very specific time when they had just arrived at the *seringal*. Most of the time migrants from the arid northeastern Brazil, strangers to the ways of the forest and the crafts of the duty, were considered in need to be 'tamed', *amansados*. Also, newcomers were often seen with cautious suspicion, as they were regarded as more prone to rebel than seasoned tappers. After some time getting acquainted with the ways of the rubber, and with a bigger debt accumulated, both moral and financial, the *seringueiros* would then be considered and referred to as now being 'meek', *mansos*: loyal to the system and the *patrão*, non-violent and hardworking rubber tappers.

In many ways, the colonization process of the Amazon that derived from the rubber boom and its main economic system, the *aviamento*, are regarded as truly violent, brutal or even sadistic. More so, it seems that there is a consensus that violence was an inherent and a structural part of it (Taussig 1993; Weinstein 1983; Soares 2017). As such, a whole poetic and semantic lexicon of violence and terror was devised within the system, closely related to the creation of debt and the enslaving of the native and migrant people. To Taussig, this configures a magical realism of terror that is, nonetheless, no less 'real' and essential to the organization of labor in the *seringal* (Taussig 1993, 88).

The practice of distinguishing Indigenous groups according to their stance in relation to society, as 'brave' or 'meek' is not a phenomenon exclusive to the Amazon region. On the contrary, it seems to be distributed throughout Brazilian history and territory. Furthermore, it is deeply rooted in the colonial process as it was not only the setting of a kind of cultural interpretation about the natives, but almost single-handedly ruled how Brazilian colonial society would deal with them in each kind of situation. The definition of some groups as 'isolated', 'pacific', 'brave', or 'meek' concretely guided official action, policies, as well as financed tutelage, persecutions, diasporas and even massacres, and still does (Oliveira 2016). There were two possible futures devised to Indigenous Peoples, each regarding how there were set in the two opposing definitions: to the meek, integralization (and so, disappearance amongst the general society); to the brave, war and decimation (Carneiro da Cunha 1992).

These processes, of course, were always guided in terms for the expansion of colonial power and, in the Amazon, the grasp of newly discovered resources and Indigenous workforce and their immersion into the functionality of capitalism. As Aníbal Quijano states, the main ways of control of labor in the expansion of capitalism, outside Europe and particularly in Latin America, were not free paid work, yet still in favor of the global capital. Thus, exploitation and domination were as much a colonial process as a capitalist one. For that, 'race' was one of the main frames of social dividing of work (Quijano 2000).

Back to the description under the old photograph, it is clear that the Madihadeni weapons (which are designed for hunting, by the way) are shown as a sign of the supposedly uncivilized state of savageness of those people, a flag of their bravery. There is no more information to be found concerning the photograph in that number of the newspaper, or the Indigenous, or even the Amazon in general, for that matter. The picture does not follow a report or an article, as it is displayed with no more explanation than the description reproduced above. It is presented somewhat like a novelty or curiosity fact, in contrast to the urban, *avant-garde* and modern concerns of Rio de Janeiro, the capital of Brazil at the time.

However, keen eyes and some familiarity with the descendants of the same people can unveil other clues that remain unspoken by, or unnoticed to, the editors. The small skirts used by the women are apparently made out of industrially woven cloth, instead of the dangling locks of wild cotton strings that would be traditional. The infant also seems shrouded in industrial cloth, as does one woman, only partially visible, who wears a long skirt. As described, they do wield their weapons, but not in an aggressive or menacing stance: they seem to display them. Uncommonly, two girls hold the arrows; one carrying a whole set, and the other just a single one. Those are masculine artifacts and belong certainly to the men with the bows. The Madihadeni hold deep concerns regarding the handling of weaponry by women, and fear that it might render the owner *zukherade,* non-lethal, when hunting. It is a belief shared by many other Indigenous peoples in the Amazon. This suggests that the photograph was, at some level, staged. At least, the display of weapons was possibly a demand of the very photographer, who claims attention to the stage of 'savageness' of his subjects. Further, it is mentioned that the encounter happened on the Juruá

River's margins, thus necessarily involving some travel by the Indigenous that resided at a distance. It is impossible to know whether they got there by their own means or were taken there by the owner of the *seringal*. Likely, it was a trade visit, even if there is not a single merchandise visible. Also, there are no cargo baskets in the frame, even though they are always present on travels. The goods can be elsewhere, even at the canoe, ready for departure.

Either way, even if the newspaper uses its rhetoric to showcase those Indigenous in an untamed light, and so condemns the 'civilization action' as innocuous, the photograph and its characteristic details point towards the opposite: the existence of some commercial relationship between the settlers and the Madihadeni that was, if not pacific, cordial at the very least. As to this day, trading is regarded as one of the main forms of relation with alterity by the Madihadeni (Crevels 2021). In spite of the hunter's bows and arrows, the Madihadeni do have weapons for battle, the *uruvitha* (something in between a spear and a war club) but they do not wield them at the scene, attesting one more time they were not there for war.

Dealing with Braves: Shamans and Settlers

Conversely, in the worldview of the Madihadeni, the non-Indigenous settlers and merchants are the ones that seemed almost hopelessly 'wild': the *karivadeni*, as they call them, came as brute men traveling mostly without women or children in their loud barges, most constantly inebriated. They were capable of ruthless acts of violence and at that were very lethal with the power of their firearms. On the other hand, they also represented a whole new world of possibilities, with their fantastic merchandise, useful tools and all sorts of interesting new things.

Since their very first interactions, sometime during the last decades of the 19th century, until the 1960s, the Madihadeni only knew those involved with the extractive endeavor as the representatives of the surrounding society, be it the passing merchants, the settlers, or the infamous *patrões*. Because of such history, for everything that matters, the societal attributes of this segment became an interpretation model of *all* the non-Indigenous society, and for the Madihadeni it meant that to deal with modern western society was to deal with those settlers and their views of the world, thus heavily guided on the images of the 'meek' and the 'brave' that settlers carried. In other words, the definitions of 'meek' and 'brave' were made inescapable to deal with, from the perspective of the Indigenous peoples that they were projected upon.

The Madihadeni are actually composed of a set of groups that experienced contact with the surrounding society, each in their own situation, but whose histories are all fairly similar. Today, when they tell how they first met rubber tappers, they frequently do it focusing on key elements that are: the risk of attack from those people armed with superior weaponry; the possibilities of access of goods and merchandise; the attempts to control the situation by use of communication of non-violent intent (by the part of the Madihadeni); and the success of the negotiation consolidating a relationship of commerce and work, in the terms of the extractive industry:

> When they (ancestors) were fishing, they heard the *karivadeni* at a distance and ran. They said: "there were *karivadeni* over there, that's why we came back". Others were thrilled: "Let's go! Let's see the *karivadeni*!". Kavazu, however, said that they shouldn't: "Don't do it, the *karivadeni* will kill us, they will shoot us. Don't you do it!". Then, the others got afraid.

> Two nights afterwards, however, another woman, Kavarini, pleaded: "Let's meet the *karivadeni*. Let's buy food and merchandise from them!" and the others agreed. They traveled downstream, quite afraid, until they found one *karivadeni*. He had a gun and, when he saw them, started to load it. "Wait, wait, wait!" someone screamed: "Don't shoot us! We are nice, nice people, don't shoot!". Then, he put the gun away and asked for their names and said: "I almost shot you, if you hadn't said a thing, I would have fired at you!". After he got to know them, he called them to see his house and his companions, a bit downstream, where he offered coffee and crackers. There they met some other *karivadeni*. They ate and then one of them said: "I came here looking for latex, if you want your things, your own coffee and merchandise, you can bring me latex, and you'll have it". So, they were thrilled when they traveled back home, bringing all the stuff along, they said to their relatives: "The *karivadeni* did not kill us. You can also go there and work for them, give them latex, and you will also have all those things for yourselves", he said. (Field notes, 7 June 2016).

Thus, the non-Indigenous individuals they knew carried what were for the Madihadeni several of the attributes of a true (and, thus, dangerous) alterity: they had access to fantastic and otherwise unreachable goods; followed their own and somewhat inscrutable purposes and reasoning; and sustained an intimate and prowess relation with violence and lethality. For so, the merchants were seen as much alike the shamans, and such comparisons are frequently made up until this day. Both figures (the shamans and the merchants) live in the middle of the intertwined and opposite symbols of violence and abundance, danger and access. The association between them is vast and based on the myth of the shaman Tahama, who travels downstream and turns into a *karivadeni* merchant:

> There was a very powerful *zuphinehe*, Tahama, whose guardian spirit gave him everything. Every day, the spirit gave food to all the village: manioc, coffee, meat. Everything the spirit would give, and everybody could eat without work. If the shaman wanted, he could choose a spot where a house would appear fully constructed by the morning; if he wanted to drink the juice of wild fruits, when everyone was asleep, the spirit would put a jar of juice in the middle of the village: by dawn, it was there. So, it was with everything.
>
> One day, the shaman said to the others that he would make the engines for the canoes and left with his spirits and his kin. He said he would come back with big engines for boats. They left, with the spirits, and made the engines, and made other things as well. When they came back, they were already *karivadeni*. Before that, there were no *karivadeni*, only Madihadeni. It is said that, once the *karivadeni* got to the Xeruã river, another shaman said that those people were to be called *karivadeni*, and told the story of Tahama, because we did not know how to call them. (Field notes, 13 May 2015)

The daily relations with the *zuphinehedeni*, the shamans, and with the foreigner merchants both have risks involved, for which special care is seen as due. They are powerful and suspicious, capable of mislead and mischief, and possess weird motivations that are hard or impossible to predict or understand. It's the desire of people whose interests are *different* in a radical way (Viveiros de Castro 2018), that resist the scrutiny. Memories of violent shamanic rampants are numerous, as they are felt as plagues and epidemic episodes. In part, the fragmentation of the Madihadeni in two groups residing in two different rivers is the result of a shamanic event of that sort. Also frequent are accounts on how easy the *karivadeni* resort to unmotivated aggression. It seems the shamans and the *karivadeni* could kill on frivolous disagreements – 'shooting' either their guns or spells.

The firearms of the non-Indigenous settlers and merchants are a dominant part of the Madihadeni imagination and memory concerning the first interactions. Especially, it is the central concern on how to avoid them. In spite of the primordial success in avoiding the lethal confrontation, the risk never fades completely, and there are several instances in history where it turned into reality. The assassination of an esteemed Madihadeni leader in 1983, is a bitter reminder of the lethal fury of *karivadeni*.

On the other hand, the western world, which the Madihadeni could partially access through their relations with the merchants and settlers of the Purus and Juruá basins, had things and goods that were unique to it, impossible to attain elsewhere or through other means. The power of mobility in a specific and restricted part of the cosmos defines what is foreign. The shamans have a special vessel *zarava*, which they use to travel to the sky *nemebakhu*, house of spirits and other beings with whom they realize their shamanic prowess. Also, in unimaginable ways, they can access the underworld *namibupe*, and the interior of the water world *pashubudi*, equally communicating and negotiating with the beings that reside there. The shamans draw their powers from those spaces. The *karivadeni*, very much alike, have their barges and engines, airplanes, and automobiles – which they use to circulate throughout the cities where the goods and merchandise come from. In their own respective worlds, the *karivadeni* and the shamans have the knowledge and information necessary to act and to move, and those are somewhat unreachable to the common Madihadeni, or at the least very hard to obtain. In sum, they possess the capacity to communicate with the residents of foreign places (such as the knowledge of the Portuguese language or the spiritual etiquette); the knowledge of the way of the trade, bargain, and negotiation; or the capacity to recognize the risks involved in the interaction and how to avoid them. Such abilities set this special type of people apart from the others, conceding them power.

Trading: A Desirable Relation

Mythically, the classificatory association of the non-Indigenous people and the shamans is elaborated through the myth of Tahama, as shown above. However, it is necessary to state that the Madihadeni people regard more close attention to the figure of the *patrão*, the *boss*. The *patrão* can either be the owner of the *seringal* or the seller of the merchandise for which the extractor production is delivered as trade. In other narratives, we see that after the shaman Tahama and its companions leave the company of the other Madihadeni and effectively move into a different *locus* in search of something inaccessible in any other way, who that returns is *karivadeni*, and more specifically a merchant *patrão,* with his motorboat loaded with goods for trading with the native production. The shaman even prepares those that stay, advising them to collect certain products of the forest while they wait for his return, in a manner very similar to the speech of the rubber tappers of the first contacts: 'cut latex, and I shall return with merchandise'. Without doubt,

Tahama is a mythical adaptation posterior to the arrival of the extractive industry. The way that this narrative was constructed, and which setting is presented there, shows the interpretative effort of the Madihadeni and their conclusion about what to make sense out of the presence of the settlers and merchants.

At the same time, the myth presents the underlying association of shamanism and commerce. The activities of a shaman are considered his *work iburei*, and are negotiated with interested clients. The most common job of the shaman is to deal with illness: from the simpler to the most complex, all of the affections are in their realm of action because they are also seen as products of foreign shamanism. When someone falls ill, to receive treatment, payment is due. Such payment is said to be *manakuni,* a special concept that is translatable as *payment*, *money*, *dowry*, *vengeance*, and so on. The value of the *manakuni* varies from what it is assumed as mere cost price, like a small jar of ground tobacco powder *shina* aspirated by the shaman in any work; up to the most valuable items, such as hand-woven hammocks or expensive utilities bought in the cities, like televisions and radios. They say an envious shaman can spell someone or their children just to ask the object of desire as payment *manakuni* for their cure. In spite of what some religious missionaries wrote about the Madihadeni, their shamanism is profoundly commercial, for the shaman himself establishes constant trades and negotiations also with the spirits with which he deals daily.

Faced with the powers of dangerous alterity, be it the spirits, the shamans or the non-Indigenous settlers, the common Madihadeni have few strategies to mitigate the risks regarding them. The most important of them is to engage in trading, transforming potential aggressors into commercial allies.

The anthropologist Oiara Bonilla, who did extensive fieldwork with the Paumari of the Purus River, affirms that the commercial relationship is the most important model of what it is to relate in the Paumari cosmos, which is populated by entities engaged in never-ending trade and commerce, and where the Amazonian patronage political system transverses the limits interspecies. The Paumari people also dwell on the Purus River basin and share linguistic and cultural proximity with the Madihadeni. For them, several animals are themselves *patrões* that possess employees and clientele and maintain with them the type of relationship that humans do. As an example, the manatee is the *patrão* of the lakes and waters. Even predatory interactions, so significantly prototypical in Amazonian ethnology, are considered under the commercial lexicon by the Paumari: the catch of the huge *pirarucu* fish (*Arapaima gigas*) is described as being a trade act of fishing material from the fisher for woven mats of the *pirarucu* owner entity (Bonilla 2005, 51).

For the Madihadeni as well the commercial is the preferred relationship with alterity, although I have not seen such sophisticated cosmological examples. The term that embodies those relations is, as mentioned, *manakuni*, used for a vast array of different cosmological situations, like for the Paumari. It invests the trading partners in a known and structured dialogue that is, as so, rather predictable. The establishment of a commercial relationship with foreigners is the first clue that it can be a tamable relation, and that is why the Madihadeni invest so much on it, since the very first contacts.

Pacifying Oneself and, thus, the Others: Relation as a Mean of Control

War as a symbolic framework of the relation with alterity has been, more than once, extensively studied through anthropological literature. In Brazilian ethnology, the case of the Tupinambá groups stands out, where war is deemed fundamental on the construction of sociality (Viveiros de Castro 2002). Likewise, contemporary situations have shown how warfare can take the form of new political configuration and communication in interethnic relations (Turner 1993).

The images (and self-images) of the 'Indigenous warrior' populate both the common imagination and spaces of interaction with Indigenous peoples. In contrast, the Madihadeni present themselves as being proudly *peaceful*, or even *meek bukherade*. In their pacifist presentation, the Madihadeni let it be known their aversion (and abandon) of warrior or violent dispositions that are considered by them as 'bad speech' *ima hirade*, either amongst themselves or in the relations with the *karivadeni*. They prefer otherwise the ways of commerce, of trade.

The proud pacifist stance was noticed by the ethnographies that studied with the Madihadeni. After the first Ph.D. thesis that took them into frame (Florido 2013), the general understanding of the ways the Madihadeni dealt with colonization developed from 'participation in the dynamics of the *seringal*' (Aparicio 2011, 117), to that of a 'movement of pacification perpetrated by merchants and missionaries' (Mendes and Aparicio 2016, 10). Nonetheless, it remains rather inadequate to understand the Indigenous stance as one of passive response. That would still be the reproduction of the *brabo* and the *manso,* in colonial terms. In such a way, the occurrence of a speech of self-presentation of the Madihadeni as *pacific* people turns into a conjunction of the categories, making the Madihadeni *pacifism* a *pacified* one: the discourse would be then a reproduction of an internalized prejudice. Such understanding is common when regarding the Indigenous peoples as victims of colonialism, but it is urgent to abandon it as it empties the active efforts of Indigenous peoples in controlling their own histories.

Much on the contrary, as we see in the native narratives, the Madihadeni positioning in a peaceful and trade-willing manner is a conscious act. To present themselves as *pacific*, *meek*, or *good people*, since the very beginning, is the stance chosen as the most adequate to deal with the perils of the *seringal*'s bosses, as such it is with the shamans. It is a means to convey the message they insistently deliver: 'you need not attack, we are harmless'. In such a way, they seek through communication and confirmation of themselves as *pacific* to induce in their listeners the very same 'pacifism' and willingness to trade and work together.

It is a powerful message, although a strange one. By means of it, the Madihadeni found a way of surviving menacing times and maintaining agency on their history as a group, even when dealing with dangerous colonial circumstances with a more powerful acquaintance. At the same time, the assumption of a peaceful stance derives from an etiquette of 'relations with the unknown alterity' in order to neutralize warlike, violent, or predatory potentialities of the encounter. It is an adjustment of a cosmological positioning of the part in interaction that happens beforehand. It is not only used for the surrounding society, but to other Indigenous groups as well, and even non-human entities.

Then again, that strategy has its historical referential framing. The Madihadeni do not say that they were always peaceful, but quite the opposite. They assure this disposition started after a time of widespread violence, war and shamanism, during which many people died and several groups perished altogether. Whether this time consists of a mythical or a chronological one is debatable, as so if it is related to the arrival of non-Indigenous people in their territory. Regardless, the Madihadeni concluded afterward about the antisocial consequences of violent conflict and its ultimate inefficacy. 'We are not violent, not anymore', they explain (Florido 2013, 131–132).

It is a strategy of resistance that regulates the conduct of an alterity by adjusting one's own behavior. To accomplish it, of course, it is necessary to have as much knowledge about those others as possible. For that reason as well, it pays to remain near and familiar to them.

To *pacify* the non-Indigenous people is a rather common perspective and stance among several Indigenous peoples. In the book *Pacificando o Branco*, organized by Bruce Albert and Alcida Ramos (2002), a compendium of such experiences is well detailed for the Waiwai, Waiãpi, Yanomami, Tikuna, Baniwa, Wapichana, Macuxi and others. Its reading elucidates much of the Madihadeni case, particularly the descriptions of Catherine Howard on the domestication of merchandise. As mentioned, another case published elsewhere by Oiara Bonilla, regards the Paumari people (2005, 2007). For them, the perspective of a symbolic economy of predation (Viveiros de Castro 2002) is even more clear: they concern controlling the predator-like *patrões* by assuming themselves the position that evokes the familiarizing domestication, thus avoiding the dangerous condition of prey, and so negating the *patrão* the full condition of predator in what can be effectively described as a 'counter-domestication' (Bonilla 2007).

What distinguishes the Madihadeni case and sets it apart is how much the 'resistance' is based on the intensification of the relationship with the surrounding society; and how they managed their relative positioning by strategic thinking in the terms and concepts of the other, like the 'meek' and the 'brave'.

Conclusions: Cooperating to Resist?

Throughout its development, Anthropology has been concerned and sometimes struggled to make fair descriptions of the Indigenous societies when in interaction with the modern western world. Either by describing a very deterministic system of cultural and social responses to contact that strips the Indigenous peoples of any agency in their history; or, on the other hand, by vesting them in well-intentioned but romantic and incongruent voluntarism. Or yet by describing them as a sort of *negative* that is defined as the symmetrical opposite of modern society: almost an incarnation of the *anti-west* anxieties that, contradictory, belong to the very west itself. The images of the Amazonian Indigenous Peoples and their resistance strategies are, very often, victims of a process similar to that of *Orientalization*, especially as they are becoming increasingly renowned for their political agenda questioning the modern western ways (Ramos 2012).

For some time now, several Indigenous peoples have been at the vanguard of recent environmentalism. However, it is important to notice that this is not the case for all Amazonian Indigenous peoples. Neither their strategies in regards to the relationship with modern society is necessarily one of the two options: to oppose or to submit. A lot of the time, these societies had to devise clever and inventive ways to deal with and coexist with a colonial process without directly opposing it, but still managing to maintain their own sense of agency and control over their world.

The Madihadeni case in question serves as an example of resistance and maintenance of autonomy that involves the use of strategies of controlled cooperation to avoid retaliation and conflict, thus making further negotiations possible on the terms of the relationship. For it to be successful, the

Madihadeni had to comply with some expectations of the setters, putting themselves under a foreign concept as *meek*, but in counterpart they managed to avoid being rendered to another conceptual position they have all reasons to fear: that of the victims, of the *prey*.

Even if the greater scheme of the colonial venture looks largely the same; in this situation, the detailing of the local history is crucial to an understanding of how those same colonial relations were given, and how the intersubjectivity of coloniality came to reach groups otherwise with great difference in ideology (Quijano, 2000). Concepts and ideas locally emergent like that of the *meek* and the *brave*, that implies little to nothing in the center of modern society and capitalism, control the conceptual framework by which whole histories are developed through its fringes.

References

Albert, Bruce, and Alcida Rita Ramos, eds. 2002. *Pacificando o Branco*: *cosmologias do contato no Norte-Amazônico*. São Paulo: Edit. UNESP: Official Press of the State.

Aparicio, Miguel. 2011. Panorama contemporâneo do Purus Indígena. In *Álbum Purus,* edited by Gilton Mendes. Manaus: EDUA.

Bonilla, Oiara. 2005. O bom patrão e o inimigo voraz: predação e comércio na economia paumari. Mana. Estudos em Antropologia Social, n. 11(1): 41–46. Rio de Janeiro: National Museum, UFRJ.

Bonilla, Oiara. 2007. Des proies si désirables: soumission et prédation pour les Paumari d'Amazonie brésilienne. PhD diss., École des hautes études en sciences sociales - EHESS.

Crevels, Christian. 2021. Patrões selvagens: história e poética Madihadeni da alteridade. MA diss., Universidade Federal do Amazonas.

Florido, Marcelo. 2013. Os Deni do Cuniuá: Um estudo do parentesco. PhD diss., Universidade de São Paulo.

O Malho. Newspaper. Rio de Janeiro, 28 December 1907, year VI, N.276. Public Domain: Available archive of the Digital Library of Brazil, Hemeroteca Digital Brasileira in: http://bndigital.bn.gov.br/acervo-digital/O-malho/116300

Mendes, Gilton, and Miguel Aparicio, eds. 2016. *Redes Arawa: ensaios de etnologia do médio Purus*. Manaus: Edit. EDUA, 2016.

Oliveira, João Pacheco de. 2016. *O nascimento do Brasil e outros ensaios: "pacificação", regime tutelar e formação de alteridades*. Rio de Janeiro: Edit. Contra Capa.

Quijano, Aníbal. 2000. Colonialidad del Poder, Eurocentrismo y América Latina. *La Colonialidad del Saber: Eurocentrismo y ciencias sociales* edited by E. Lander. Buenos Aires: Perspectivas latinoamericanas. CLACSO.

Ramos, Alcida Rita. 2012. Indigenismo: um orientalismo americano. Anuário Antropológico, Brasília, v. 2011, n. 1, p. 27–48.

Rivet, Paul, and Constant Tastevin. 1921. Les tribus indiennes des bassins du Purús, du Juruá et des régions limitrophes. La Géographie XXXV, Société de Géographie. Paris.

Soares, Gabriel. 2017. Não existem cordas para nós: relações de produção e pertencimento dentro do sistema de aviamento na região do Médio Purus. MA diss., Universidade de Brasília.

Taussig, Michael. 1993. *Xamanismo, Colonialismo e o Homem Selvagem*: um estudo sobre o terror e a cura. Rio de Janeiro: Edit. Paz e Terra.

Turner, Terence. 1993. Imagens desafiantes: a apropriação Kaiapó do vídeo. Revista De Antropologia, 36.

Viveiros de Castro, Eduardo. 2018. *Metafísicas canibais: Elementos para uma antropologia pós-estrutural*. São Paulo: Ubu Edit.

Viveiros de Castro, Eduardo. 2002. *A inconstância da alma selvagem*. São Paulo: Edit. Cosac Naify.

Weinstein, Barbara. 1983. *The Amazon Rubber Boom 1850–1920*. Stanford: Stanford University Press.

10

Development Or Bem Viver? The Xukuru Do Ororubá People's Vision of Sacred Agriculture as a Counter-Hegemonic Proposal for the Relationship between Human Beings and Nature

IRAN NEVES ORDONIO, CARLA LADEIRA PIMENTEL ÁGUAS & MARCOS MORAES VALENÇA

The word 'development' is polysemic. It can be understood as economic growth, as a promise of well-being through the satisfaction of needs or it can be linked to ecological prudence, through sustainable development. Whatever the interpretation is, this concept has been criticized over time by various theoretical currents (dependency theories, post-developmental, postcolonial, decolonial theories, etc.). Currently, our crisis amplifies this questioning about the linear, modern and western idea of development, pointing to a search for other civilizing paths. One of those perspectives is the concept of *Bem Viver* (Living Well) created by Indigenous peoples. It is a counter-hegemonic conception of the world, as well as another way of relating to the environment and life itself. It respects the world's diversity and it is inspired by the resistance of subordinate groups.

We use the decolonial conceptual framework and the concept of Bem Viver (Acosta 2016) to present the *Agricultura do Sagrado* (sacred agriculture)

associated with the spirituality of the Xukuru do Ororubá Indigenous people, located in the state of Pernambuco, Brazil. Our goal is to compare the hegemonic concept of development with *Bem Viver*, based on the sacred agriculture practiced by this ethnic group, which is characterized by respect for Mother Earth, as a place of food production that leads to health, as well as a place where the *Encantados* (Enchanted) spirits live. Methodologically, from a qualitative approach, we will carry out a dense description (Geertz 1989) to think about other relationships between human beings and nature.

On the subject, it is important to note that the separation between human beings and nature is a philosophical basis of Western thought. This dichotomy is extremely important to understand our current context, which is characterized by a web of crises that challenge the very survival of humans – as well as other living species – on our planet. Marques (2018, 475 [free translations]) describes the historical course of this schism between humans and their environment starting from Greek mythology, through the myth of Prometheus: he 'represents the ruse that steals the secrets of nature from the gods who hide them from mortals; the violence that seeks to overcome nature with the intention of improving men's lives'. That is, the Promethean attitude reduces nature to an object belonging to the human subject. As time went by, nature became progressively alienated, until we reached the Modern Age, which turned it into quantity.

Therefore, this historical process with ancient roots generated, in the West, a 'slow and gradual process of differentiation and distancing of the human beings from all other species and from nature in general. In this process, nature meant at the same time the non-human, what is around the human' (Ibidem, 476–477). From this perspective, Nature becomes a natural resource, to be controlled and conquered.

As we know, this paradigm jumped from Europe and spread to other parts of the world through colonization. In this sense, colonial rule was not only conquest of territories, but also of imaginaries. With the end of the colonial regimes, as we will see below, the colonization of the imaginaries maintained its existence through the emergence of the idea of development in the post-war period: The North's way of life remained an example and a goal, which continued to invisibilize other society models, other epistemologies, and logics of relationship with nature.

The consequences of this trajectory, as we see today culminates in an unprecedented environmental crisis, which is accompanied by a range of other crises – ethical, political, health crises, and so on – that challenge us to rethink the framework of modern Western civilization. More than ever, it is important to pay attention to other paradigms that have been systematically ignored or destroyed since the beginning of colonization. These 'other voices' have a lot to say about how to find new ways out of the dilemmas generated and perpetuated by the westernization of the world.

In this chapter, we bring a contribution to that discussion: after a brief analysis of different approaches about development, we counterpoise this concept to the Indigenous perspective of *Bem Viver*. Then, we finally present a living example of these other ways of relationship between human beings and nature, through the discussion about the sacred agriculture practiced by the *Xukuru* do *Ororubá* Indigenous people, which inspires to think about other civilizational paths that do not lead humanity to collapse.

Development for Whom? Views on the Concept

The polysemy of the word development allows for multiple interpretations. The concept, originally used in Biology, characterized the evolutionary processes of living beings to reach their genetic potentialities. With Darwin, the word came to express the transformation of species, from a more backward state towards a more advanced, more evolved state (Santos et al. 2012). From its varied connotations, we will characterize the concept from three approaches: development as economic growth, as satisfaction of needs, and as an element of environmental sustainability.

The first approach has its antecedents in Adam Smith's *The Wealth of Nations*, originally published in London in 1776. Defending the idea that the desire for profit is naturally beneficial to society, the author created the famous idea of the invisible hand of the market as a metaphor to characterize the self-regulation generated from the tendency to balance supply and demand. Therefore, there emerges the seed of an idea, later elaborated, of development as a driving force capable of promoting the accumulation of wealth, for its subsequent distribution (Santos et al. 2012).

But the actual division between a developed and an underdeveloped world occurred years later, in 1949, during US President Harry Truman's inaugural speech. This was the first time that the word 'underdevelopment' was used to characterize a large part of our planet that suffered from various social and economic problems:

> More than half the people of the world are living in conditions approaching misery. Their food is inadequate, they are victims of disease. Their economic life is primitive and stagnant. Their poverty is a handicap and a threat both to them and to more prosperous areas (Truman 1964 in Escobar 1995, 3).

Once the diagnosis was made, the solution was announced. For the US President, 'greater production is the key to prosperity and peace. And the key to greater production is a wider and more vigorous application of modern scientific and technical knowledge' (Truman 1964 in Escobar 1995, 3). Time has shown, however, that the promise was not real: 'Quite the contrary, the gap between rich and poor countries has widened. Growth is necessary, distribution not so much' (Santos et al. 2012, 48).

The gap between developed and underdeveloped countries was a new model, intended to replace the separation between metropoles and colonies of the colonial period. According to Escobar (1995), in the 18th century the domination of the South by the North was justified by the technical and racial superiority of the European – known as the white man's burden, whose task was to exploit natural resources and help inferior populations to evolve. In the 20th century, new concepts have arisen in the post-war period converted 'the poor' into 'the assisted'.

These continuities between the power matrix established by the colonial period and the hierarchies of the post-independence period have been called coloniality by several Latin American intellectuals. This term, proposed by Quijano and used by the Modernity/Coloniality group draws attention to the perpetuation of the subalternity of peoples, countries, contexts, and subjectivities in different dimensions - coloniality of power, of being, of being and nature.

For Quijano (2005), the coloniality of power refers to the economic and political control that structures the modern world-system - today divided between developed and underdeveloped countries. The coloniality of knowledge is based on Eurocentrism and does not admit the coexistence of knowledges and ways of life, in order to consider only the expert's knowledge as really valid (Restrepo and Rojas, 2010).

According to Maldonado-Torres (2008), the coloniality of being is the way the colonizing process affects subjectivities, generating effects such as racism, control over sexuality, and so on. On the other hand, the coloniality of nature, according to Walsh (2012), refers to the rupture between the biophysical, human, and spiritual dimensions, which means the exploitation and quest for control of nature, which threatens ways of life based on ancestral wisdom.

Thus, this change between the poor into the assisted, according to Leal Santos and his colleagues (2012), launched in the imaginaries a kind of 'race' between the advanced countries (in the global North) and the backward ones – those that needed help to reach the same level as their rich peers. So, underdevelopment is elaborated as a stage before development, which would consist in the final destiny of all countries, as denounced by the Modernity/Coloniality group.

Therefore, much more than semantics, this change of discourse – called by Escobar as 'poverty modernization' – meant an adjustment of new mechanisms of control and dependency. Many painful adjustments would be necessary for the achievement of a new stage for the supposed beneficiaries of development. A 1951 United Nations' publication (Escobar 1995, 4) warned that 'ancient philosophies should be scrapped, and old social institutions should be disintegrated'. In the same way, 'bonds of cast, creed and race should be burst' (Idem). All these in the name of economic progress, which required a high price.

In the Latin American context, a broad critique of these promises was developed by dependency theorists in the beginning of 1960s. Several authors, such as Gunder Frank (1983) and Theotônio dos Santos (1972) warned that the world's division between developed and underdeveloped countries became the path for the imperialist advance, composing a scenario that maintained the so-called 'Third World' as a commodities' exporter. According to this approach, the two sides were not located at different steps within an evolutionary scale; in fact, both were axes of the world economy that only brought advantage to the rich countries.

Furtado (1974, 79) said that 'the accumulation process tends to widen the gap between a center in increasing homogenization and a constellation of peripheral economies, whose disparities keep growing more and more. In his turn, Marini (2017) analyzes, through the concept of dialectic of dependency, the idea that the dependent economy is a necessary condition for world capitalism, and not an accidental phenomenon of its formation. Thus, the super-exploitation of labor is a central aspect and a foundation of dependency in the Latin American context.

Other perspectives have added to the dependency theorists' critique, such as Arturo Escobar. Influenced by postcolonial and post-structuralist studies, he warns that the idea of development is a discursive formation based on forms of knowledge, systems of power, and forms of subjectivity:

> I propose to speak of development as a historically singular experience, the creation of a domain of thought and action, by analyzing the characteristics and interrelations of the three axes that define it: the forms of knowledge that refer to it and through which it comes into being and is elaborated into

objects, concepts, theories, and the like; the system of power that regulates its practice; and the forms of subjectivity fostered by this discourse, those through which people come to recognize themselves as developed or underdeveloped. The ensemble of forms found along these axes constitutes development as a discursive formation, giving rise to an efficient apparatus that systematically relates forms of knowledge and techniques of power (Escobar 1995, 10).

The second approach to be discussed here links development to the idea of welfare. This perspective goes beyond the discourse of economic development to think about the importance of the achievement of citizen protection systems. In this way, the principle of growth and accumulation of wealth based on the GDP is replaced by the principle of basic needs, linked to the welfare state. Therefore, the use of social indicators emerges as an important tool for measuring life quality.

The main exponent of this line of thought is the Indian economist Amartya Sen, author of *Development as Freedom* (Sen 2000) and winner of the Nobel Prize in Economics in 1998. From his perspective, development should be understood as the expansion of freedoms: instead of taking the Gross Domestic Product as a reference, the country development should be measured by a complex set of aspects linked to citizenship, such as access to education, health, civil rights, and so on. Despite Sen's great influence in several areas, this approach is criticized, especially regarding the liberal character of his theory.

According to Brum (2013, 92), this conception of freedom presupposes a model of rational agent that can enjoy it, which makes it inadequate for a broader concept of justice: 'By insisting on a foundation of justice based on individual rationality, the author denies such justice to groups devoid of it, which renders it blind at the theoretical level and thus unable to provide effective protection to such groups at the practical level'. In her turn, Fraser (2005, 70) underlines the transformations that globalization causes in the concept of justice, arguing that 'many observe that the social processes shaping their lives routinely overflow territorial borders. They note, for example, that decisions taken in one territorial state often have an impact on the lives of those outside it, as do the actions of transnational corporations, international currency speculators, and large institutional investors'. The result is a new sense of vulnerability to transnational forces.

The third approach to the concept of development discussed here focuses on the environmental dimension, *i.e.*, it criticizes the idea of infinite accumulation of wealth, alerting to the limits imposed by nature itself in view of the exploitation of resources. Thus emerges, especially from the 1960s/70s, the Eco-development approach, advocated by natural scientists or non-governmental organizations and based on the 'zero-growth' model, to freeze the expansion of population as well as capital (Santos et al. 2012). From a Marxist perspective, Löwy (2009, 50) warns that the economic and ecological crises of our times signify a civilizational crisis, based on the 'commodification of everything'. Therefore, he defends the concept of ecosocialism as a critique of commodity fetishism and as an argument for the predominance of use value over exchange value.

Environmental concern has also led to the concept of sustainable development, a kind of middle way in which economic growth is permitted and desirable, as long as it is accompanied by ecological prudence. The concept was first published in the document 'Our Common Future' – better known as the Brundtland Report. Sustainable development was defined there as a kind of development that meets the needs of the present without compromising the needs of future generations (Comissão Mundial sobre Meio Ambiente e Desenvolvimento, 1988).

For Sachs (2007), sustainable development is an ambiguous concept, which can have a strictly ecological interpretation, as well as ethical, social, economic and so on. This term bets on preventive actions, depolluting technologies, alternative energies, among other paths, to find spaces of conciliation between economic growth and life sustainability. However, quoting Kothari, Sachs warns that, in the absence of an ethical imperative, environmentalism risks being reduced to a technological formula laced in the hands of technocratic businessmen.

About this concept, the Brazilian Indigenous intellectual Ailton Krenak asks: 'Natural resource for whom? Sustainable development for what? What needs to be sustained?' (Krenak 2019, 12). He argues that the West must rethink its civilizational foundations, in which society and nature remain apart: 'The idea of us humans detaching ourselves from the earth, living in a civilizational abstraction, is absurd. It suppresses diversity, denies the plurality of life, of existence and of habits' (Krenak 2019, 12).

Bem Viver and the World View from the Global South

Based on the recognition of the planet's cultural, epistemological, and socio-environmental diversity, we will now discuss some fundamental aspects brought by native peoples in order to understand their cosmologies, conceptions, ways of life, relationship with nature, political and social organization, among other aspects, which are opposed to the hegemonic concept of development and its exclusionary colonialist roots.

From the Andean peoples, arises the concept of the *Bem Viver* (Living Well) – which in Quechua is called *Sumak Kawsai*. These subjects from the Global South, in particular the native peoples from Bolivia and Ecuador, represent the excluded, invisible, oppressed – in Paulo Freire's (1987) conception. They are considered people without knowledge, who remain, through the coloniality of power, being and knowledge (Quijano 2005) tied to the colonial process that hierarchizes and subordinates the *other*, classifying them as inferior beings and devoid of knowledge.

From these people from Global South, emerges this conception of life in which culture and nature merge, remaining inseparable. Human beings and non-human beings are part of nature; they don't dominate nature, they don't exploit it, they don't perceive it from an idea of domination, but from a perspective of respect and care. Ancestrality and spirituality are inseparable components in this conception. According to Acosta, the *Bem Viver* represents:

> A proposal of harmony with Nature, reciprocity, relationality, complementarity and solidarity between individuals and communities. By its opposition to the concept of perpetual accumulation, by its return to use values, the *Bem Viver*, an idea under construction, free of prejudices, opens the door to the formulation of alternative visions of life (Acosta, 2016, 33).

Ailton Krenak warns that the hegemonic idea of human being – whom we call colonizer and patriarchal – does not consider himself as part of nature and so he consumes the Earth. Krenak points out that 'we are bodies that are inside this biosphere of Planet Earth. The *Bem Viver* is not the distribution of wealth. The *Bem Viver* is abundance that the Earth provides as the very expression of life' (Krenak, 2020, 17). Abundance! Nature is not seen as a resource, but as sacred. Krenak says that native people talk to rivers and mountains, also remembering that there are people who like to talk to their cars.

This materialistic relationship to the world results from the understanding that natural *resources*– raw material for a car, for example – are necessary for human domination that leads to accumulation. This conception of the world, as well as this conception of life and economy, is close to the previous discussion about (sustainable) development. From another perspective, the relationship with this sacred living organism – called *Pacha Mama* – is based on complementarity and reciprocity.

According to Acosta (2016), the *Bem Viver* is based on Human Rights and rights of nature. The principles of this conception of world and life arise from these ways of life that are far away from the mainstream, being built by people placed on inferior positions within the Eurocentric social pyramid.

We emphasize how far is communal life, based on self-sufficiency and self-management, from the accumulation of material assets. The former is the opposite of the concept that generates social, cultural, and environmental devastation through accumulation, efficiency, and maximization of wealth. Let's remember that, for the idea of development to exist, it is necessary to generate the idea of underdevelopment, just as it makes necessary the relationship between center versus periphery, civilized versus savage.

This hegemonic thinking ignores the struggle of these peoples, who bring with them the depth of their knowledge. In these Indigenous perspectives and practices – that is, with this practical knowledge – these peoples show how important education is for their ways of life, which go far beyond the scholar knowledge. The Amazonian Indigenous leader Márcia Kambeba states:

> Education in the Indigenous village does not follow classroom standards. It is an unhurried learning, calm and without clock time. Teaching how to fish, how to row, how to plant, how to produce flour, how to build the house, how to weave the straw, how to prepare *pajauaru, caiçuma, beijú*, how to sing, dance, how to make handicrafts, how to respect the people's cosmology, how to silence and listen to the advice of the elders persons, how to heal with herbs, how to feel the good energies coming from nature and people, and so on; these are lessons that are learned from the break of day (Kambeba 2018, 62–63).

According to the *Bem Viver* concept, all beings – human and non-human – exist and are considered in a relationship between subjects, what is different from a relationship between subjects and objects. Beings should live in harmony, in a collective life permeated by democratic logics of community rootedness. Therefore, *Bem Viver* is complex, as a counter-hegemonic and subversive proposal that contributes to the decolonization of the world-system hegemonic paradigm. In synthesis,

> If development tries to *westernize* life on the planet, the *Bem Viver* rescues diversities, as well as values and respect to the *other*. The *Bem Viver* emerges as part of a process that allows us to undertake and strengthen the struggle for the vindication of peoples and nationalities, in tune with resistance actions of broad segments of marginalized and peripheral populations. In

conclusion, the *Bem Viver* is eminently subversive. It proposes decolonizing exits in all areas of human life. The *Bem Viver* is not a simple concept. It is an experience (Acosta 2016, 82).

After this discussion about development as a hegemonic conception, and *Bem Viver* as an alternative conception, we will present an example from the *Xukuru* de *Ororubá* Indigenous people, located in the state of Pernambuco, Brazil, through their relationship with nature and with the agriculture's sacredness.

Sacred Agriculture

The *Xukuru* do *Ororubá* Indigenous people live in the semiarid biome, in the Northeastern region of Brazil, in the city of Pesqueira, Agreste region of the state of Pernambuco. They have an organizational model that allowed their political articulation in the 1980s and 1990s. The Indigenous population was until then dispersed and unaware of their ethnic identity. However, the mobilizations that took place in that period allowed self-determination and the claiming of rights that occurred parallel to the processes of self-demarcation.

In addition to the *Xukuru* Association and the leadership council of the 24 communities that make up the *Xukuru* territory, the socio-political organization also presents the councils of health and education, and the collective of youth, women and agriculture. The annual *Xukuru* assembly takes place between 17–20 May, with the purpose of evaluating the *Xukuru* life project and, based on collective decision-making, to direct actions and activities for the management of the sacred land of *Ororubá*, keeping in mind the principles and values of the *Xukuru* way of life – *Limolaygo Toype*.

This organizational model enables a management that is based on collective decision-making and has the participation of children, youth, women, adults and elders in its elaboration, naturally conducted by the social dynamics that occurs through the circuits of the sacred – which also ensure the voices of the forest and the Enchanted spirits. There are also dialogues with the *Xukuru* institutions, such as the Leadership, Education, and Health Council. From the *Xukuru* sacred rituals come the guidance of the spirits through the Science of the Enchanted Ones, so that the ritual space is an arena for consensus construction. It is interesting to note that ritual time is distinct from everyday time, as signaled by Catherine Bell:

> Ritualization is a matter of various culturally specific strategies for setting some activities off from others, for creating and privileging a qualitative distinction between the 'sacred' and

the 'profane,' and for ascribing such distinctions to realities thought to transcend the powers of human actors (Bell 1992, 74).

For the (re)construction of the *Xukuru* life plan, several processes have ressignified the uses and occupation of the territory, taking into consideration principles guided by the 'culture of subtlety'. This culture implies low-impact activities based on the observation of the behavior and manifestations of nature itself, as well as on the guidance of spiritual beings.

The integration with the land is founded on intimate relations of physical and spiritual existence, based on the centrality of natural elements such as stones, water, soil and forests, considered by the *Xukuru* cosmology as homes of the Enchanted spirits. Thus, the distribution of land to live on, and agricultural and livestock production activities were preceded by the definition of sacred spaces, understood as Spiritual Power Points. It is from these points that sustainability strategies are thought out, going beyond the idea of simply distributing land among the Indigenous communities.

Complex models of relationship between production and Mother Earth have guided the processes of social organization and land use, with the necessary care for nature and the sacred. To this end, the *Xukuru* organizational strategies seek to promote, through research, experiences and reflection, practices that value the knowledge and traditions of the elders, as well as considering the relationship between the people and the sacred territory in the construction of the life plan. In this way, this people work with sustainable practices and knowledge through events, training and the building of solidarity networks that promote the traditional knowledge of care and healing, food and agro-food systems.

The Agriculture Group *Xukuru* do *Ororubá* – *Jupago Kréka* has been defending the 'agriculture of enchantment/sacred agriculture', as a way of life that, in addition to planting, cultivating, harvesting and eating, promotes the culture of the Enchantment of *Ororubá*. Thus, it necessarily requires care for the processes of social and environmental regeneration. Its conception brings the Science of the Invisible as an epistemological basis that has been enabling practices through agricultural-spiritual systems that allow the management of ecological landscapes and agro-forestry with arrangements in biodiverse polycultures (Altieri 2010). The management is shared with the seed guardians, *Xukuru* men and women who are dedicated to this practice and are guided by the Enchanted Light to conduct the relationship between human beings, animals, plants, the sacred topography and the spirits.

The *Jupago Kreká* is located in the sacred complex of the Agriculture Center *Xukuru* do *Ororubá* (CAXO), in the Boa Vista community – *Xukuru* Indigenous Land, and fosters experiments in sacred agriculture as a promoter of the *Ororubá* culture of enchantment. With the resumption of this way of life, this group started to disseminate practices of production with care, having as its epistemological basis the Science of the Invisible, from which emerges an idea of sustainability that does not admit the development logic.

The goal of this organization is to produce care from a holistic vision of agriculture-health-education for the maintenance of the *Bem Viver* on Earth and *for* Earth itself. This implies to plant/harvest/eat/heal/celebrate with sacred nature. When practicing sacred agriculture, one cares for physical nature through the living forest, understood among the *Xukuru* as the *Greatness of Green Kingdom*. Thus, the Enchanted Nature, the world of the spirits, is present, because the trees, the stones, the soil, and the waters are the dwellings of the Enchanted Kingdoms of the *Ororubá*.

Sustainability understood from the Science of the Invisible can only be achieved through the logic of involvement. From this perspective, the people in movement involves strategies of articulation, mobilization, thought, and systematization of the traditional agricultural practices and way of life. These practices include, for example, the 'good eating' and traditional gastronomy, the manipulation of plants and the traditional system of healing, as well as the idea of reciprocity economy and social dynamics of sharing and solidarity. This vision is opposed to an agriculture that uses agrochemicals, promotes burning and deforestation, carried out by the agribusiness.

Through the *Jupago Kreká*, people dedicate themselves more intensively. This process takes place through the activities of the *Terreiro Sagrado da Boa Vista*, a space within the forest which is constituted as a set of social and religious equipments – such as the *Casa de Sementes Mãe Zenilda*, the *Barraca do Bem Viver*, the *Casa de Cura Xeker Jetí*, among other places – that promote social and sacred flows and dynamics, as well as allow the enchantment to live and materialize. These activities aim to create regeneration experiences, not only to maintain the loyalty to the old world, but also as a way of adding efforts for the common *Bem Viver*.

The resumption of ancestral ideas and practices around sacred agriculture resurfaced in the early 2000s in the framework of the discussions about *Xukuru* life project, after the reconquest of the traditional territory. The group took on the challenges of managing the territory based on the principles of *Lymolaygo Toype* (*Xukuru's Bem Viver*) and on the commitment to break up with the system of land exploitation left by the predatory cattle ranching model that dominated the territory – generating negative environmental impacts such as biodiversity loss. This scenario destabilized the *Xukuru* way of life, compromising the viability of agricultural systems, their practices and knowledge, such as traditional cuisine, ancestral medicine, healing practices, and the reciprocal economy.

Jupago coordinates processes that enable the identification of sustainable experiences among Indigenous families, the systematization of these practices and the socialization of the results among the Indigenous communities. Through joint and planned actions, it promotes the recovery of agrobiodiversity in degraded areas, and the valorization of practices and knowledge of a way of life connected to the ancestral world, producing as results useful goods for material and spiritual life. Soon after its creation, *Jupago* built the sacred complex CAXO da Boa Vista, as a reference area for sacred agriculture. It adopted a collective management model with the participation of *Xukuru* youth and women organizations, and with collaborative actions for the maintenance of sustainable experiences – such as biodiverse productive spaces with polyculture arrangements, planting of native seeds as a strategy for food and medicine production, as well as a strategy for the regeneration of native vegetation and control of environmental degradation factors.

The whole of this experience, which goes through a process of retaking sacred agriculture, understood as the basis of the *Xukuru* cosmology, is experienced throughout the 27,555 hectares of demarcated traditional territory, as well as beyond it. This process occurred due to the mobilizations for the retaking of traditional lands, that was started in 1990, and enabled a social reorganization, which, guided by spiritual forces, motivated the (re)construction of a life plan and a model for territorial and environmental management. In practice, it broke with the concentrating model that standardizes and simplifies agricultural systems and causes social disenchantment.

Conclusions

The *Xukuru* Indigenous people, through the agricultural movement promoted by the *Jupago*, develop their conception and their practices and bring in this collective process of thinking and acting together the understanding of regeneration as the reestablishment of the balance of body, mind, spirit and care for sacred nature. This conception is guided by Enchanted Kingdoms, which teach about 'Good Eating', the *Kringó Kronengo*, as well as about the real food that nourishes body, mind, and spirit – maintaining the respect and protection to nature and to the Enchanted spirits.

Within the *Xukuru* cosmology, ethnic identity is characterized by an intimate relationship with nature, based on sacredness. It is understood that the human is nature, because everything related to Mother Earth is nature. It is also based on the idea that the human being is filled with spirit, the essence of life, and that nature, including humans, is the sacred home of the *Ororubá* Enchanted Kingdoms, understood as the world of spirits, which constitute the essence of the *Xukuru* being. Through them comes the strength and wisdom for the collective reconstruction of the *Xukuru* life plan.

This philosophy promotes practices of caring for people and other beings, as well as caring for the natural elements (soil, water, and stones), and especially for spiritual beings. It acts to reestablish the relationships, the flows, and the social and sacred dynamics that guarantee the identity of the people who, as humans, are guardians of the culture of caring for life on Earth, without compromising the care that guarantees the biological and spiritual life of Earth itself.

This enchanted and spiritual view of the world contrasts with modern Western thinking, which is rooted in the fundamental separation between human beings and nature. As we saw earlier, this perspective has an ancient history and is foundational to the currently dominant civilization, which is based on the superiority of humans and on the perception of nature as inert – it exists to serve humanity, and therefore must be controlled and conquered. This division in the philosophical field has laid the groundwork for many other dichotomies, such as the separation between body and mind, as well as the separation between sacred and profane.

This Western vision spread around the world through European colonial expansion, becoming hegemonic. With the end of the colonial system, the hegemony of the global North remained through coloniality, that is, through new mechanisms capable of maintaining power structures. In this process, the proposal of development played a central role, through the supposed existence of *advanced* and *backward* peoples, as well as through the need for infinite economic growth to achieve general well-being.

But hegemonic thinking is not the only thinking. People from different parts of the world have been alerting to the need for a careful listening to the cultures defeated by the colonial process, so that it is possible to build new answers to the questions that challenge us today. In the Brazilian context, for example, Krenak (2020) calls attention to the enormous difference between welfare, a concept created by the global North – in which it is up to the economy to generate wealth to meet the infrastructure, health, and education needs of a population – and the concept of *Bem Viver* or *Sumak Kawsay*, which is not only distribution of material resources. *Bem Viver* is abundance provided by the Earth, this living organism of which each one of us is a part. This abundance, as the author states, is the very expression of life.

Sacred agriculture, as a promoter of the enchantment culture, allows to be in nature, for (re)production and guaranteeing life. The knowledge and practices of care seek to heal, through agricultural-spiritual systems, the negative environmental impacts generated by territorial invasion. It seeks to free invaded minds, avoiding practices incompatible with the *Xukuru* life plan. It also seeks to identify and promote the processes of restoration of environmental conditions, the practices and knowledge of care for the maintenance of balance between body-mind-spirit and its dimensions, for the materialization and living of the Enchantment.

References

Acosta, Alberto. *O Bem Viver: uma oportunidade para imaginar outros mundos.* São Paulo: Autonomia Literária / Elefante, 2016.

Altieri, Miguel. "Agroecologia, agricultura camponesa e soberanía alimentar", *Revista NERA*, A. 13, n. 16, 2010: 22–32.

Brum, Henrique. "Capabilities para quem? Uma crítica a Amartya Sen." *Diversitates*, v.5 n.1 2013: 92–108.

Comissão Mundial sobre Meio Ambiente e Desenvolvimento. *Nosso futuro Comum.* Rio de Janeiro: Editora FGV, 1988.

Escobar, Arturo. *Encountering Development: the making and unmaking of the Third World.* New Jersey: Princeton University Press, 1995.

Escobar, Arturo. "O lugar da natureza e a natureza do luga: flobalização ou pós-desenvolvimento?" In *A colonialidade do saber: eurocentrismo e ciências sociais. Perspectivas latino-americanas*, by Edgardo Lander, 63–79. Buenos Aires: CLACSO, 2005.

Frank, Gunder. *Reflexões sobre a crise econômica mundial.* Rio de Janeiro: Zahar, 1983.

Fraser, Nancy. "Reframing justice in a globalized world", *New Left Review*, n. 36, 2005: 69–88.

Freire, Paulo. *Pedagogia do Oprimido*. Rio de Janeiro: Paz e Terra, 1987.

Furtado, Celso. *O mito do desenvolvimento econômico*. Rio de Janeiro: Paz e Terra, 1996.

Kambeba, Márcia. *O lugar do saber*. São Leopoldo: Casa Leiria, 2018.

Krenak, Ailton. *Caminhos para a cultura do Bem Viver*. Rio de Janeiro: Escola Parque, 2020.

—. *Ideias para adiar o fim do mundo*. São Paulo: Companhia das Letras, 2019.

Lövy, Michael. "Ecossocialismo e planejamento democrático". *Crítica Marxista*, São Paulo, n. 28, 2009: 35–50.

Maldonado-Torres, Nelson. "A topologia do Ser e a geopolítica do conhecimento. Modernidade, império e colonialidade", *Revista Crítica das Ciências Sociais*, n. 80, 2008: 71–114.

Marini, Ruy. "Dialética da Dependência". *Germinal: Marxismo e Educação em Debate*, v. 9, n. 3, 2017: 325–356.

Marques, Luiz. *Capitalismo e colapso ambiental*. Campinas: Editora da Unicamp, 2018.

Quijano, Aníbal. "Colonialidade do poder, eurocentrismo e América Latina." Em *A colonialidade do saber: eurocentrismo e ciências sociais. Perspectivas latino-americanas*, de Edgardo Lander, 117–142. Buenos Aires: CLACSO, 2005.

Restrepo, Eduardo; Rojas, Axel. *Inflexión decolonial: fuentes, conceptos y cuestionamientos*. Popayán: Editorial Universidad del Cauca, 2010.

Sachs, Ignacy. *Rumo à Ecossocioeconomia. Teoria e prática do desenvolvimento*. São Paulo: Cortez, 2007.

Santos, Elinaldo, Vitor Braga, Reginaldo Santos, e Alexandra Braga. "Desenvolvimento: um conceito multidimensional." *Desenvolvimento Regional em Debate*, 2012: 44–61.

Santos, Theotonio. *Dependencia y cambio social.* Santiago: CESO, 1972.

Sen, Amartya. *Desenvolvimento como liberdade.* São Paulo: Companhia das Letras, 2000.

Walsh, Catherine. "Interculturalidad y (de)colonialidad: perspectivas críticas y políticas". *Revista Visão Global*, v. 15, n. 1/2, 2012: 61–74.

11

'El pueblo manda y el gobierno obedece': Decolonising Politics and Constructing Worlds in the Everyday through Zapatista Autonomy

SEBASTIÁN GRANDA HENAO

The most known story of the *Zapatista* uprising tells that on 1 January 1994, a group of Indigenous peoples and peasants rose against the Mexican state to oppose the reforms on land and trade. Those legal modifications were mandatory for the inauguration of the North American Free Trade Area (NAFTA). Since then, they have declared to be in rebellion and have resisted the spread of capitalist narratives of progress and development. As such, they have argued that capitalist, neo-liberal globalisation threatens their modes of living, as well as of 'poor and simple people' all around the world at the margins of that system (EZLN 2005). Locally, they struggle for the preservation of their communities and the defence of their rights and dignity as Indigenous peoples and peasants. Despite changes in the discourses and their political ventures along these years, they have consistently tried to build spaces of autonomy, resistance and dignity.

Also, it is well known that since the late 1970s and the early 1980s, a group of urban insurgents from the National Liberation Front (FLN, *Frente de Liberación Nacional,* in Spanish) entered in the Lacandon Jungle, becoming familiar with this inhospitable environment to clandestinely regroup in order to have access both to the Guatemalan border – in case of defensive retreat – and the Yucatan peninsula – to dislocate from there to the northern and western regions of Mexico. As such, the *Ejército Zapatista de Liberación Nacional* (hereinafter EZLN, *Zapatista* National Liberation Army) came out as a proposition by the FLN insurgents to establish guerrilla blocs throughout the country in a revolutionary strategy of taking over the state; however, it seems to have blossomed in Chiapas as it became ever more Indigenous than urban (Gunderson 2013 414; 452).

However, in the Lacandon Jungle there existed a multiplicity of social and political forms of organisation around the everyday issues of the communities. They preceded the formation of the EZLN, the support bases in the communities and the networks of activism and solidarity that compose the *Zapatista* movement we know today. Most of those organisations began with the migration of peoples that looked after a land to call their own – due to the land redistribution and agrarian reforms of the Mexican government since the 1940s – and escape from the bad life and working conditions in the old-time colonial *fincas* [Specific type of estate that used Indigenous Peoples as slaves for agricultural production]. Along with them, Theologists of Liberation, Maoism, ancestral Mayan knowledge and others also expanded the frontiers of the Jungle coming together in a communitarian sentiment that sustained those organisations (Leyva Solano & Ascencio 1996). Hence, *Zapatista* autonomy, emerges not only from the politico-military organisation that became the EZLN, and the *Zapatista* movement that develops around and along it, but also from the communitarian horizon that the communities construct in a longer framework of struggles for land and territory, political and religious militancies, collective works and everyday political practices of resistance and conviviality.

This chapter aims to bring forth different interpretations on the *Zapatista* autonomy experience as one based on a conception of life, development and politics *otras* – in their own terms, agendas and tools. This work takes in part some of the discussions on my PhD thesis (Henao 2019) in which I write about the experience of engaged, multisited ethnographical approach to the issue of security along with the *Zapatista* communities in resistance in 2018.

Nevertheless, here I thread rather with the written word. As such, different texts are brought forward to give testimony of the reflections, interpretations and voices about *Zapatista* autonomy as a project of good life shared elsewhere. It tries to portray how, in scholarly terms, 'autonomy' enacts a lively project of decolonising politics (see: Mora 2008), not only in its discourse but also in its everyday practices. These are some insights on how *Zapatista* autonomy offers a communitarian horizon and organisation to collectively face the challenges of Capitalism/Coloniality/Patriarchy (see: Gutiérrez & Navarro 2019; Gutiérrez *et al.* 2017), seen as the true enemy that threatens both communities in Chiapas and humanity as a whole (EZLN 2016).

It is also relevant to highlight that although sources here are predominantly from writings, the reflection as a whole is based on a multisited ethnography, revealing the multiplicity of voices that seek to interpret the meanings and directions of *Zapatista* autonomy while linking locations and sites of enunciation. As a disclaimer, it is not intended to practice academic extractivism or overlap the Zapatista voices on their own references to the self-will or that of other scholars and activists, rather I try to collect, from different sources and my feel-thinking, the sense of this lively concept and thus be able to argue in favor of it as a practice towards decolonization.

The lived project of *Zapatista* autonomy is as a proposal through which the communities intend to construct alternatives to war, based on the San Andrés agreements signed between diverse Indigenous groups, collectives, activists and the *Zapatistas* themselves and the Mexican government (see Chiapas 2003; CNI 2016). Here, I show three of the many possible interpretations that *Zapatista* autonomy may embody: first, the system of governance of the autonomy is portrayed, intending to show how autonomy also means resistance, and how resistance needs organisation to move forward. Second, *Lekil Kuxlejal*, the good life for Tsotsil and Tzeltal communities, is shown as the onto-epistemological basis for the incarnation and socialisation of a theory and practice of collective life in the communities. Third, I intend to look at a larger framework, situating the struggle of Indigenous rights and defence of land and territory, in *Zapatista*'s terms, as one of global scope, in the face of the 'Capitalist Hydra'. Finally, I reconvene my own interpretation of this discussion wondering if it is possible to look at *Zapatista* autonomy as an everyday theory and practice of decolonising knowledge, politics and security.

Autonomy Means Resistance: on *Zapatistas' Gobierno Autónomo* and Doing Politics in their Own Terms

In 2003 the *Zapatista* communities decided that it was time for them to exercise self-determination and self-government as was proposed in the San Andrés Agreements – a law proposal that the Congress altered after being set with government, *Zapatista* and civil society representatives – and that they were going to do it with or without the authorisation of the Mexican state. They founded the *Caracoles* and walked along the principles of *Mandar Obedeciendo* (Ruling by Obeying, in free translation) to guide the political practice of Zapatismo and its networks.

Each *Caracol* is seat of a JBG, whose members are elected by naming of the members of each community and MAREZ to solve issues, coordinate collective works, mediate grievances and serve justice among *Zapatista* populations and also with non-*Zapatistas* (Alonso 2003, 51–53).

Still, the emergence of the *Caracoles* is not the same as the beginning of *Zapatista* autonomy as a political and organisational project. Autonomy is the very heart of the *Zapatista* experience. Autonomy is only the name they call what is in construction in the rebel territories; of the project present since the first years and inscribed in the San Andrés Agreements (Baschet 2018, 53). What is different, nonetheless, is the inauguration of a new stage and form of organisation, to deepen and concentrate in the different actions, forms of resistance and struggle, enacted as autonomy.

Zapatista autonomy, beyond the practice of an 'other' political organisation based on collective and shared works, has brought improvements in the day-to-day life of the *Zapatistas*. This is something that *Zapatistas* express in every conversation I was able to have with the people in the communities and that is emphatically stated by the *Juntas de Buen Gobierno* (Good Government Councils, JBG) I was able to interview in *La Garrucha* and *La Realidad*.

These improvements are perceived in terms of the initiatives in areas such as education, health, justice, women's rights and economic alternatives led by the JBG. For instance, in the documentary ¿*Quién vive mejor?* Spajel Kuxlejalil (*comparando vidas*) (Tercios Compas, 2017) they make evident the improvements that organisation and the practice of *Zapatista* autonomy have brought, in comparison to their neighbours and other non-Zapatista communities. The first of them is the recovery of lands, which has allowed having spaces for other improvements such as collective crops, to set a place for JBG and the activities for their peoples; it has allowed the construction of *Zapatista* schools and healthcare centres. Nevertheless, autonomy may also be seen as a form of open government whose benefits are enjoyed by non-Zapatistas in the disperse and expanded territory that *Zapatistas* occupy (Ornelas 2005).

Autonomy should not be confused with co-existence with Mexican government structures and its rules. On the contrary, the constitution of autonomous municipalities (MAREZ, *Municipio Autónomo Rebelde Zapatista* in Spanish) is a direct challenge to Mexican sovereignty and legitimacy of the official government. Autonomy has faced many challenges as well, as it is placed as a form of resistance to state's power and a response to its low-intensity warfare and counter-insurgent strategies (Henao 2019; Baschet 2018; Martínez Espinoza 2007).

In the testimonial of Doroteo, a member of the Caracol No. 1 in the MAREZ La Realidad he explains about the constitution of autonomy as a system of governance:

> Our resistance in the autonomy began in the year 1994 with the publication of our autonomous municipalities. We began by forming the autonomous municipalities even though we did not know how to begin, but we did it anyway. We did it in spite of not knowing how to govern, in spite of all our villages and zones being militarised. We did it without the need of creating political parties, because we think they are not useful, we did it without knowing whatever could happen afterwards; [...] Also, years later, [the Mexican government] betrayed us in the dialogues we established [...] with all the Indigenous peoples of Mexico [...] To that we responded forming our *Juntas de Buen Gobierno* and saying: with the law or without the law we will govern ourselves, whether you want it or not (EZLN 2013, 23).

Roberto, from the Caracol IV in La Garrucha, and part of the MAREZ Ricardo Flores Magón, further explains what the autonomous government means for them in the everyday and how it is constructed:

> When we were already in the resistance we constituted our authorities, we organised to work together along our peoples, regions, municipalities and zones. We made collective works in the *milpa*, we grew beans, we cattled and grew coffee to strengthen our autonomy, to ease the works of the authorities in every centre and region, in the municipalities and the zones, so that we could exercise autonomy. Resistance does not mean that we will not work. Resistance is to work because it is done and built by the people; that means that resistance is our house, our roof, the tent that we will be as peoples and families, with our *compañeros y compañeras* that we work. [...] The task of the *Zapatista* autonomous government [...] is to bring our work in coordination with every instance of the autonomous government, as our municipal and regional authorities. We have to do the work and see how to bring advancement for our work in collectives, training in healthcare, education within our village and people to see the achievement and fruit of our work that we do in the resistance. (EZLN 2013, 38)

Also, as Valentina from the Caracol at Roberto Barrios states:

> The politics that our peoples and their autonomous governments focus on is the construction of autonomy, then our own thought and plan is to change the situation that our peoples suffer because of the bad government of the rich people, such as poverty, inequality, exploitation, injustice. We fight for having a life with dignity for all the children, young people, men, women and elders and that we all have the same opportunities and place, without any exclusion (EZLN 2013, 72).

These testimonies, collected from the memoirs of the *Escuelita Zapatista*, portray the spirit of *Zapatista* autonomy. In their words flourishes the experience of organisation for self-government, to build a communal horizon – 'a world where many worlds fit' – little by little. This means to build a plurivese while defending their territories from the military incursion, the co-optation by institutional politics and the influence of capitalist global value-chains. This form of government promotes a radical democracy based in co-responsibility and a justice system based on the communities' uses and costumes. Whether it impacts the capitalist system, overthrows (white heterocis-) patriarchy and breaks ties with the Western/Modern world, or not, is irrelevant. What matters at this stake is to be alive, to live in harmony both with human and non-human beings.

From another standpoint, *Caracoles* and *Zapatista* autonomy, as concrete forms of resistance, are seen as a response to the organisational needs of both strengthening and balancing the processes embedded in the *Zapatista*'s political practices, being aware of the inequalities among the communities and regions. *Caracoles* thus appear to also monumentalise the presence of the *Zapatista* movement, in the places most harassed by the Mexican authorities, the military forces and paramilitary groups. They make the application of the rights reclaimed in the San Andrés agreements feasible, as Indigenous Peoples, as well as organising the recovered territory and culminating the process of building legitimacy of the political actions aimed at self-government in the area since 1994 (Arevalo 2008).

Besides the political meaning of the *Caracoles*, as described above, it also shifts the action and modes of the organisation, setting boundaries and assigning roles in its structure: the EZLN, conformed by insurgent militias, limit themselves to assure physical security of the communities in the face of the possible paramilitary or military offensives; the JBG are in charge of the political struggle and the strategies for communication and connection between the communities and the civil society (*ibid.*). The governance of the recovered territories is in the hands of the support bases in the communities in resistance and the autonomous councils that constitute the MAREZ, and the JBG that are in charge of coordinating tasks and resources among the MAREZ; as such, *Zapatista* autonomous government operates in three levels of governance: from bottom-up, the communities, MAREZ and JBG.

In 2003, there were five communities. More recently, the EZLN announced the creation of another seven – making a total of twelve *Caracoles*. This was due to two main reasons. First, the organisational political work and example of their members to the places they inhabit. Second, traditionally state-aligned communities have felt the racism, contempt and voracity of the Mexican administration (led by President Andrés Manuel López Obrador since 2018) and have moved into hidden or open rebellion. The 12 *Caracoles* are currently composed by 43 autonomous municipalities (see: EZLN, 2019).

From another perspective, Mariana Mora (2008) argues that *Zapatista* autonomy fills in the void spaces left by the dismantling of the welfare state in Mexico. It is in the low capacity of governance, breach of agreements and failed promises that autonomy gains strength and is implemented. For her, *Zapatista* autonomy is able to burst and reverse hegemonic processes insofar the individuals and collectives exercise practices for implementation in the everyday, leading to the production of knowledge, senses of political doing, alliances with other actors and forms of self-understanding and acting in the world regarding recent and residual expressions of domination (Mora 2008, 308).

By *filling in the void*, I also understand that 'autonomy' is the emergence of self- and coordinated forms of resistance. On the one hand, it means resistance in the face of the need of the state as the default political organisation of the modern/capitalist/colonial system, contested through the very organisation of autonomous governance, in which a government serves without self-servicing for the people, and not for the foreign interests that the former model supposes. On the other hand, it means resistance in the lookout for anti-capitalist, anti-hegemonic, anti-patriarchal alternatives to establish social, economic and political relations from their own world views.

Meanwhile, the establishment of the *Caracoles* and *Mandar Obedeciendo* also represent a direction towards territorial peace, as it promotes autonomous expressions of development, in accordance to their political principles, ontologies, modes and rhythms. It is, at the same time, a proposal and the practice of building while walking towards an unknown horizon. It is a shout out claiming 'Enough!' transformed in movement and the possibility of creating co-existence and conviviality.

Zapatista autonomy as a form of governance in resistance – arguably –, also means that resistance is a condition of possibility for autonomy. Both, resistance and autonomy are interlinked. One sustains the other and together they provide sustenance for an alternative project of self-government. Autonomy, hence, becomes a political onto-epistemology through which collective action, a word that walks, transforms and creates. The autonomous government of *Zapatismo* would then politically orient the ethics and epistemologies of a way *other* of reaching agreement and self-organise as communities in resistance.

Lekil Kuxlejal, Autonomy and the Good Life:

Zapatista autonomy could also be defined in terms of *Lekil Kuxlejal*, as Jaime Schlittler (2012) understands it. It means 'the good life', or 'the blossoming of the three of life' for Tzeltal and Tsotsil communities in Chiapas. *Lekil Kuxlejal* enunciates, embodies and practices well-being, not only as material welfare, but as good life in relation to others, nature, and the environmental and spiritual realms one inhabits as part of a collective, part of the whole.

Autonomy, on the one hand, represents a political aspiration in motion towards a collective government from below, in which the peoples are the conductors of their tasks, duties and political and social modes; on the other, it represents a political economy *other*, that challenges the notion of development centred in economic growth for another based in well-being, from a conception of a good and abundant life, in harmony with nature, the spirit and the human collective.

The notion of *Lekil Kuxlejal* is not exclusive to the *Zapatista* communities in resistance; on the contrary, it is rooted in Mayan-Tzeltal and Tsotsil thought, shared by *Zapatista*s and non-*Zapatista*s alike. Juan López Intzin, a Tzeltal thinker, expresses, for instance, about the meaning of this idea in Tenejapa, in the Chiapas' heights:

> *Lekil kuxlejal*, whose base is *Ich'el ta muk'*, as an experience of the sacred and aspiration to an excelsior degree of kindness in abundance *Utsilal-Lekilal*, has both material and spiritual bases from our peoples. The recognition and respect for the greatness among living beings and with the supernatural entities will bring us peace and harmony in the heart and life in plenitude (*Lekil kuxlejal*), because, insofar we are co-responsible and reciprocal, our heart will laugh in joy as manifestation of what is full and dignifying.

> The material part in which both *Lekik kuxlejal* and *Ich'el ta muk'* anchor is related to the non-exclusion, to eradicating poverty, real recognition of others, sincere dialogue, the exercise of all rights in plenitude, real justice, truthful and not simulated, and equity for all.
>
> [...] It can be said that *Lekil kuxlejal* is not only a product of harmonic relations with nature, it is not a given fact, we have to collaborate together to achieve it [...] *Lekil kuxlejal* is not a gift that we will receive just by wanting it, it is not imposed by force, it is not the *Lekil kuxlejal* of those above, or of the banking centres or economic models, it is not an impossible dream, it is a constant edification in which men and women participate by recognising and taking into account their own greatness, their *Iche'l ta muk* (López 2013, 102-104; free translation, emphases in the original).

In this passage it is possible to see how *Lekil kuxlejal* is part of something greater than just an idea of Indigenous autonomy or development. It is part of a *cosmovision*, a *cosmopolitics* that goes beyond a communitarian horizon, the construction of the commonalities, conviviality and relationships with the different dimensions of life; it represents the hoping for a life in plenitude, peace, dignity and equity with all living beings and other human communities.

A *cosmovision* may be understood furthermore than just a look about/to the world that surrounds. It means to look at the world as a whole in relation to place and context in which human groups take action and are part of, and is made by the assumptions and convictions that allow humans to guide and orient themselves in such worldly space (Ferrer 1981). For *Zapatistas*, such *cosmovision* encompasses traditional Mayan forms of knowledge about their territory and the world they inhabit and a special outlook and interpretation about the situation of world affairs, felt as a multiplicity of forms of exploitation and injustice, produced through/by centuries of colonialism, capitalism and white patriarchy (Tunali 2020, 345). Perhaps it is better expressed in texts such as the *Sixth Declaration from the Lacandon Jungle* (EZLN 2005) or the series of seminars entitled *Critical Thought in the Face of the Capitalist Hydra* (EZLN 2016), in which they advert of the nature of capitalism, how they see the world and justify their rebellion.

Just as equal, the notion of *buen vivir* (the good life) is shared as a communitarian horizon in other places than Chiapas. It is a shared notion in the different 'geographies and calendars' of Indigenous and rebel movements; it is called *Sumak Kawsay* in Kicwhua and *Suma Qamaña* in Aymara, and all of them refer to life in harmony and plenitude, in their own terms. These lived concepts have been, for instance, consecrated in the constitutions of Ecuador and Bolivia, respectively, as they become plurinational states, and represent an achievement of the Indigenous struggles in Abya Yala, guiding new models of integrative development among the pluriverses. These concepts are often read as 'Indigenous socialism', political ecology or post-developmentalism; however, they are rather open questions to the interpretation of those who advocate for them, from their territories and ancestralities. Moreover, they represent an aspiration towards building the common ground under the premise of a good life with self-determination (Hidalgo-Capitán 2014).

When discussing development and post-developmentalism, Gustavo Esteva brings the following reflection from his experience along and accompaniment of the *Zapatista* communities in resistance:

> Post-development means, above all, to adopt a hospitable attitude towards the real plurality of the world. It means, as *Zapatistas* say, to put oneself in the construction of a world in which many worlds fit. [...] it is to be hospitably open to a pluriverse, in which cultural differences are not only recognised and accepted but also celebrated [...] In a very real sense, to go beyond development means to meet the good life, healing the planet and the social tissue from the harms that the developmental endeavour has caused (Esteva 2009; free translation)

In that sense, *Zapatista* autonomy also represents a way to promote development in the terms and common aspirations of and for the peoples, according to their needs and rhythms. In a way, autonomy represents the practice of that which theorists, such as Boaventura de Sousa Santos (2018; 2009), refer to as looking to do the unimaginable, looking for solutions to the problems caused by modernity from other knowledge standpoints.

On *buen vivir*, as a relational epistemology located in the global South, incarnated and practiced around the experiences of *sumak kawsay*, or well, in *Lekil kuxlejal*, Yolanda Parra (2013, 118; free translation) explains that:

> These postulates are enacted in everyday pedagogical practices that are performed in every moment of both the public and private life, a space to: teach and learn the rituality of the spoken word, food, music, planting, harvesting, service, dialogue and respect with all the forms of Life that inhabit the

territory where the communitarian life takes place as an expression of the true "*wealth*" of the People. That is to say, the foundations of the Good Life easily contain the requirements of that which the contemporary Western society has built at a high cost, such as the so-promoted *sustainable development*, the much-sponsored *intercultural education* or the famous *terrestrial identity*.

In other words, *Zapatista* autonomy sets in motion the *Lekil* (the good, the well-being) and animates the *Ich'el ta muk'* (respect, dignity).

Zapatistas Against the Capitalist Hydra: Locating the Struggle for Autonomy from the Local to the Global

For *Zapatistas*, autonomy is understood as a meta-theory in practice. As *subcomandante* Galeano puts it, in a speech of solidarity to the families of the missing students of Ayotzinapa:

> The system does not fear social explosions, as massive and bright as they may be. If a government were to fall, there's always another one waiting on the shelves as a replacement and as another imposition. What terrifies the system is the perseverance of rebellion and resistance from below.
>
> Below the calendar is different. It has another way of doing things. It has another story to tell. There is another pain and another rage.
>
> [...] We do not protest in order to defy the tyrant but to salute those who confront him from other geographies and other calendars. To defy him, we construct. To defy him, we create. To defy him, we imagine. To defy him, we grow and multiply. To defy him, we live. To defy him, we die. [...] What we *Zapatistas* have learned is that the answer is no, that the only thing offered from above is exploitation, dispossession, repression, discrimination. That is, all we can expect from above is pain. (SCI Galeano in EZLN 2016, 159–162).

By bringing this excerpt I want to call attention to the multiple directions, dimensions and scales in which *Zapatista* autonomy operates. Rather than proposing an *avant-garde* or unique model of resistance and rebellion for self-determination, they instigate other movements and collectives to organise and engage in practices of social reproduction while challenging social orders that produce forms of oppression and dispossession. For that, is used the figure of a 'wall to crack', representing the system that the communities oppose and resist to; as expressed in the words of *subcomandante Galeano* – a spokesperson, translator, interpreter and analyst of the *Zapatistas*, rather than a commander or chief.

This wall is not new, or appears only after 1994; it has been there for at least 500 years when European colonialism-capitalism-(heterocis)patriarchy invaded their lands and took the freedom to be themselves. What they theorise and practice, as a political methodology, is to resist its different manifestations, to crack it, to dismantle the system little by little, opening paths beyond what is known and seen. As such 'the purpose is not to defeat a supposed ideological opponent, but to respond to the question that all of us (*todos, todas, todoas*) will end up asking: What's next?' (ibid. 178; emphases in the original).

When stating that they oppose capitalism and its manifestations, another figure emerges, that of the *Hydra*, the mythological figure of many heads, one that they claim to know and have clarity about. Thus the assumptions they base their perception on are:

1. The current dominant system is capitalism [...]
2. This capitalist system is not dominant only in one aspect of social life, but rather has multiple heads, that is, many forms and ways of dominating in different and diverse social spaces. [...]
3. There is a disconcerting element in this Capitalist Hydra. If you understand the Hydra as a mythological animal you know that it has many heads and if you cut off one head, two more are born. One of these heads is like the heart of the Hydra, "the mother head" to give it a name. [...] It is the bloodiest and most cruel monster ever known in reality or fiction since humanity became divided into dominators and dominated. [...] there may be others who insist that is the state that is the mother head of the Capitalist Hydra and not the social relations of production, where some have capital and others have only their capacity to work (ibid., 179)

For *Zapatistas*, that is a manner of knowing themselves and learning to be (in) collectives, because it is always possible to lose the capacity for observation and surprise, to lose the whole by focusing on a part; it is thus necessary to be accompanied, to cover more focal points among all, to keep a peripheral look (ibid., 15–18).

Still, it is not enough to know themselves in the world, it is necessary to change themselves to change the world, to observe with other eyes and learn from the lessons from other geographies and calendars. As such, the politics of *Zapatista* autonomy represent itself a manner of collectively gathering knowledge, whether it is knowledge of politics, self-government, the manifestations of the *Hydra* in other places and times, or about the world, both the one that surrounds them and the world as a whole.

On the other hand, *Zapatistas* have claimed that to look further it is necessary to look inside. In that sense, a *Zapatista* methodology appears in their declarations and *communiqués:* analysing from the outside inwards, from the larger picture to the smaller, and then constructing from below. Hence, besides generating a critical and *heartened* understanding on the economic, political, ethical and epistemic system, represented through the figure of the Hydra, *Zapatistas* also comprehend that:

4. There is an element that is not explicit but which is fundamental: practice. What led us to begin this theoretical reflection [...] is the transformation of reality.
5. Although we begin from the assumption that the capitalist system is dominant, that is accompanied by the certainty that it is neither omnipresent nor immortal. Resistances exist, whether we know about them or not. The system does not impose its domination evenly and without disruptions. [...] we are not talking about something that could be, we are talking about something that we are already doing. [...]
6. 'Neither theory without practice nor practice without theory', we have said. In saying that we are not talking about a division of labor [...] critical thought carries within it this poison: if it's only thought, it doesn't manage to be critical. [...]
7. No lazy thought, no dogmatic thought, no deceitful thought [...] Critical thought has as its motor the act of questioning. Why this and not something else? Why this way and not another way? Why here and not in another place? As we *Zapatistas* say, one walks by asking questions'. (ibid., 180–181).

In yet another declaration, it is described this specific way to walk with collective thinking, integrating the whole and the part, the problem and the proposal, in a loop of feedback. It is, thus, a *snailed* thought, which, as explained above, parts from a larger situation downwards to the very heartened comprehension of the surroundings, the embodied and incarnated experience of the *Zapatistas* in regards to the whole; and then builds up from the experience and lessons of being in the world to affirm the need of a world *other*, to propose other possibilities to crack the wall and hew the Hydra:

> For hours, these beings of brown hearts have traced, with their ideas, a big snail. Starting at the international, their look and thought has followed inwards, passing sequentially through the national, the regional and the local, until they arrive to what they call "the *Votan*, the guardian and heart of the people", the *Zapatista* peoples. So, from the most external curve of the snail, words like "globalisation", "war of domination", "resistance", "economy", "ciudad", "countryside", "political situation", and others that are erased after the rigor question "Is the question clear?" After the road inwards, at the core of the snail, only a few acronyms are left: "EZLN". Afterwards there are proposals and drawings of, in thought and in the heart, windows and doors that only they see (among other things, because they do not exist). The uneven and disperse word begins to make a common and collective path. Someone asks '¿Is there agreement? "There is", responds stating the already collective voice. The snail is traced again, but now in reverse, from the inside out. The draft also follows the reverse path until it only remains, filling the old blackboard, a phrase that for many is delirium, but for these men and women it is a reason for struggle: "a world where many worlds fit." Later, a decision is made (SCI Marcos 2003).

At last, a key element of *Zapatista*' meta-theory is organisation. It allows an articulation of collective thinking and practice as an onto-epistemic-politico-ethical horizon: looking out the world inwards and then walking together from the small to the larger, from the personal to the global, in a conjoined struggle of all those below. In regards of organisation, *subcomandante* Moisés says:

> As *Zapatistas*, every time we get the chance, we tell people they should organise to resist and to struggle for what they need [...] We say that these are pieces of the little histories that have to play themselves out, that people have to learn for themselves that no one will solve their problems for them. We say that instead we will have to solve these problems ourselves, as organised collectives. It is the people who create solutions, not leaders or parties [...] We say that we shouldn't be afraid of having the people rule. It is the healthiest and more just way. It is people themselves who are going to make the changes that are truly necessary. [...] What interests us as *Zapatistas* is knowing how to resist and confront the many heads of the capitalist system that exploits us, represses us, disappears us, and steals from us.

> It is not just in one place or in one way that capitalism oppresses you [...] It's not to provide recipes for how to confront capitalism. Nor is it to impose our thinking on others. [...]
>
> We think that each of us has an obligation to think, to analyse, to reflect, to critique, to find our own pace, our own way, in our own time and places [...] Each person where they are must struggle to organise themselves (SCI Moisés in EZLN 2016, 287–297).

Then, it is with critical thinking, practice and organisation that *Zapatistas* show the way they build hope for themselves; little by little, breaking down walls and hydras that seem invincible; imagining, walking, questioning and doing a world in the pluriverse. It is interesting to notice how this figure of 'opening cracks to the wall' is related to Catherine Walsh (2018; 2008)'s decolonial cracks and insurgent epistemologies to analyse and track the challenges and changes in Latin American state politics in the last 20 years.

What is intended to show with all these excerpts is yet another interpretation of *Zapatista* autonomy, one that links several levels of analysis, from the personal to the global and vice-versa. Autonomy, in that sense means to put a localised and communal effort to defeat capitalism, at least in their territories, and a call to share struggles and experiences, to organise and to learn along other movements and rebellions. For instance, at the time this text is written (2021), *Zapatistas* have embarked in a rather unimaginable endeavour: They have travelled across the ocean and flown over to meet the *Europe of below*. They have travelled to share with collectives and social organisations that declare opposition in the core and origin of the colonial system, thank for their existence, tell them that resistance is worth the pain and struggle, see and analyse what is happening in other geographies, learn from their rebellions and bring hope of a *world without fear*. They began a tour (*La Gira Zapatista*, in Spanish) through Europe. This follows the call they have continuously made to create networks of resistance and rebellion all over, building with little efforts, according to each one's geography, possibility, mode and thought, but always looking forward to 'crack the wall and destroy the hydra' (see: EZLN, 2021).

Decolonising Knowledge, Politics and Power?

Throughout this chapter I portrayed three possible interpretations of *Zapatista* autonomy, a complex and holistic theory and practice that guides the struggle that the communities in resistance have practiced even since before theorising about it. Autonomy, as an incarnated political practice, transcends the theoretical-political discourse, and enacts a response to the challenges imposed by neo-liberal globalisation, and in this march, walks towards the construction of what they understand better for themselves.

In a sense, when *Zapatistas* reclaim autonomy as their meta-theoretical practice they go beyond reclaiming self-determination. This is an issue that the Mexican state still denies, even after the San Andrés Agreements to recognise Indigenous peoples' rights. Self-determination As Marc Woons (2014) argues, Indigenous self-determination is not something that has been lost or destroyed, but rather ignored through the logic and practices of colonialism. Meanwhile, Indigenous peoples are forced to adapt to assert their authority according to their modes and costumes, to feel-think with a land and a territory that provides a sense of community and shared identity (an ontological security perhaps, see: Mattos and Henao 2021) and make sense of the world and their place in it through the optics of difference.

This is to say that *Zapatistas* not only reclaim and insurgently assert self-determination over their Mayan culture and heritage in political terms in Chiapas, but also reclaim that for all the other peoples in Mexico and the World. They see themselves entangled in a larger frame of struggles; what affects them also affects others in different geographies, whether in other regions of Mexico or elsewhere. To assert their right to a territory, an authority and an organisation of both everyday life and political meaning, they declared rebellion and determined that there would never be a Mexico without them. For that, they covered their faces and rose up in arms against both the Mexican state and Capitalism. Then, they declared that their territories would be governed by their own authorities, embodied in the Good Government Councils and that through collective work and their own modes and costumes, calendars and rhythms they would give shape to a radical form of democracy; autonomous education, healthcare and justice systems; make their own economic development, and establish relations with other movements and collectives throughout the planet to make networks of resistance and rebellion.

In terms of decolonising power, politics and knowledge, the communities in their assemblies and everyday actions define more precisely the scope and range of whatever means good life for them. It is a way of responding to the colonial world by constructing the other worlds they aspire as a pluriverse, guided by a curiosity on how to solve modern problems from their ancestral and current knowledge. This is to say, they reclaim a future without the intromission of the system that oppresses them and many others.

More than decolonising theories, *Zapatistas* question, walk and do decolonial futures. Authors such as Walter Mignolo (2011), Catherine Walsh (2018) or Ramón Grosfoguel (2007) have already referred to practices that may be understood as decolonial, even when *Zapatistas* do not make mentions to that concept, from the revolutionary sense of their struggle/being/feeling/knowing/doing. Perhaps *Zapatistas* do not need a category to mean this, but have mentioned that their actions look forward to challenging and dismantling empire-like (capitalist) globalisation. They refer to their struggles as anti-racist, anti-patriarchal, and anti-capitalist.

Zapatista autonomy, thus, rearticulates the dynamics of power within their communities. It enacts and asserts self-determination and aims to reshape social relations from their localities to the global. The way to decolonise politics for them is to defend life above all things, constantly, in all its dimensions, at their own pace and mode. That is how, for instance, by establishing self-government, autonomy, and reclaiming their rights – regardless of state authorities – they are strengthening the community and building horizons of hope.

It could be said, to conclude, that autonomy is where the principle of pluricultural conviviality rests. It enacts an acknowledgement of other worlds and the *Zapatista* world amidst them, one that is constructed by walking with/towards *Lekil kuxlejal,* the good life, in plenitude and harmony; instead of a hegemonic, homogenising world of capitalist destruction.

References

Alonso, J. El Movimiento *Zapatista*, novedad que rompe las etiquetas". *Nómadas* 19: 48–57, 2003.

Arévalo, A. *De los Caracoles y el Mandar Obedeciendo*. 2008. Available at: https://mujeresylasextaorg.files.wordpress.com/2008/05/los-caracoles.pdf

Baschet, J. *¡Rebeldía, Resistencia y Autonomía! La experiencia Zapatista.* Ciudad de México: Ediciones Eón, 2018

Chiapas, Gobierno del Estado de. *Los Acuerdos de San Andrés.* Consejo Estatal para la Cultura y las Artes de Chiapas, 2003.

CNI. *Antología XX Aniversario.* Congreso Nacional Indígena, 2016.

Esteva, G. Más allá del desarrollo: la buena vida. *Revista América Latina en Movimiento* 445, 2009.

EZLN. *Communique from the EZLN's CCRI-CG And, We Broke the Siege,* 2019. Available at: http://enlacezapatista.ezln.org.mx/2019/08/20/communique-from-the-ezlns-ccri-cg-and-we-broke-the-siege/

EZLN. *Critical Thought in the Face of the Capitalist Hydra I.* Durham, NC: PaperBoat Press, 2016.

EZLN. *Primera Declaración de la Selva Lacandona.* 01/01/1994, 1 Available at: http://radioZapatista.org/?p=20280

EZLN. *Resistencia autónoma. Cuaderno de texto de primer grado del curso de La Libertad según las Zapatistas,* 2013. Available at: https://www.centrodemedioslibres.org/wpcontent/uploads/2017/08/Participacion-de-las-Mujeres-en-el-GobiernoAutonomo.pdf

EZLN. *Sexta Declaración de la Selva Lacandona.* 2005. Available at: http://enlaceZapatista.ezln.org.mx/sdsl-es/

EZLN. *The Journey for Life: To What End?* 2021. Available at: http://enlacezapatista.ezln.org.mx/2021/07/20/the-journey-for-life-to-what-end/

Ferrer, Urbano. "Filosofía y Cosmovisión". *Anuario Filosófico* 14 (2): 173–182, 1981.

Grosfoguel, R. Descolonizando los Universalismos Occidentales: El Pluri-Versalismo Transmoderno Decolonial desde Aimé Césaire hasta los Zapatistas". In: Castro-Gomez, S.; Grosfoguel, R. (eds.) *El giro decolonial: reflexiones para una diversidad epistémica más allá del capitalismo global.* Bogotá: Siglo del Hombre editores, 2007.

Gunderson, C. *The provocative cocktail: Intellectual origins of the Zapatista uprising, 1960–1994.* PhD Dissertation in Sociology. City University of New York, 2013.

Gutiérrez, R. & Navarro, M. Producir lo común para sostener y transformar la vida: algunas reflexiones desde la clave de la interdependencia. *Confluências* 21 (2): 298, 2019. https://doi.org/10.22409/conflu21i2.p645.

Gutiérrez, R.; Navarro, M.; Linsalata, L. *Repensar lo Político, Pensar lo Común. Claves para la discusión.* In: Modernidades Alternativas y nuevo sentido común: ¿hacia una modernidad no capitalista?. México: FCPyS / UNAM, 2017.

Henao, D. S. G. *Decolonizar la 'Seguridad' : Comunidades Zapatistas en Resistencia, entre la Guerra y la Lucha por la Autonomía Indígena"* PhD International Relations, PUC-Rio, 2019. Available at: https://doi.org/10.17771/PUCRio.acad.48791

HIDALGO-CAPITÁN, A. L. Seis debates abiertos sobre el sumak kawsay. *Íconos* 48: 25–40, 2014.

Leyva Solano, X.; ASCENCIO FRANCO, G. *Lacandonia al Filo del Agua.* México: CIESAS, 1996.

López J. Ich'el ta muk: la trama en la construcción mutua y equitativa del Lekil kuxlejal (vida plena-digna). In Méndez, G. *et al. Senti-pensar el género: perspectivas desde los pueblos originarios.* Red-IINPIM AC, México: 73–106, 2013.

Martínez Espinoza, M. I. "Autonomía de resistencia. Análisis y caracterización de la Autonomía en las Juntas de Buen Gobierno del Movimiento Zapatista". *Revista de Investigaciones Políticas y Sociológicas (RIPS)* 6 (1): 97–112, 2007.

Mattos, B.R.B; Henao, S. G. "Whose security/security for whom? Rethinking the Anthropocene through ontological security" In: Mobjörk, M; Lövbrand, E. *Anthropocene (In)securities: Reflections on Collective Survival 50 Years After the Stockholm Conference.* Oxford University Press – SIPRI, 2021,

Mignolo, W. *The Darker Side of Western Modernity: Global Futures, Decolonial Options* Durham, NC: Duke University Press, 2011: 213–251.

Mora, M. *Decolonizing Politics: Zapatista Indigenous Autonomy in an Era of Neoliberal Governance and Low Intensity Warfare.* PhD Dissertation in Social Anthropology, University of Texas at Austin. 2008.

Ornelas, R. "A autonomía como eixo da resistência zapatista. Do levante armado ao nascimento dos caracoles". In: Ceceña, Ana Esther (org.) *Hegemonias e emancipações no século XXI.* CLACSO, Consejo Latinoamericano de Ciencias Sociales, 2005.

Parra, Y. "La Otra Orilla: TerritorioCuerpoMemoriaPedagogía del Buen Vivir y ConocSentir de los Pueblos de Abya Yala". *Mitologías hoy* 8: 115–136, 2013.

Santos, B. S. *Epistemologias do sul*. Coimbra: Edições Almedina, 2009

Santos, B. S. Introducción a las Epistemologías del Sur". In: Meneses, M.P. & Bidaseca, Karina (coord.) *Epistemologías del Sur*. Buenos Aires: CLACSO/ Coímbra: CES, 2018.

Schlittler, J. *¿Lekil Kuxlejal como horizonte de lucha? Una reflexión colectiva sobre la autonomía en Chiapas*. MA Thesis in Social Anthropology, CIESAS-Sureste, México. 2012.

SCI MARCOS. *La treceava estrella, parte 1: Un Caracol*. Available at: https://komanilel.org/BIBLIOTECA_VIRTUAL/treceava_estela.pdf.

Tercios Compas. *¿Quién vive mejor? Spajel Kuxlejalil (comparando vidas)*. Autonomous Audiovisual Production, 2017. Available in CD-ROM.

Tunali, Tijen. "Voz, visibilidad y visión zapatistas: otra estética de la globalización". *Revista de Estudios Globales y Arte Contemporáneo* 7 (1): 343–78, 2020.

Walsh, Catherine E. "4 On Decolonial Dangers, Decolonial Cracks, and Decolonial Pedagogies Rising." Mignolo, W. & Catherine Walsh *On Decoloniality*. Duke University Press, 2018. 81–98.

Walsh, Catherine. "Interculturalidad, plurinacionalidad y decolonialidad: las insurgencias político-epistémicas de refundar el Estado". *Tabula rasa* 9: 131–152, 2008.

Woons, Marc. On the Meaning of Restoring Indigenous Self-Determination. *Restoring Indigenous Self-Determination: Theoretical and Practical Approaches*. Bristol, UK: E-International Relations, 2014.

12

Cultural and Artistic Expressions of Haitians on Mexicali, Baja California: The Road Toward Interculturalism.

KENIA MARÍA RAMÍREZ MEDA
& ADRIANA TERESA MORENO-GUTIÉRREZ

There are social dynamics where culture and the phenomenon of human mobility intertwine as non-passive interacting processes. This happens between individuals and groups that are native to the recipient societies and those who have decided to stay indefinitely – or for a set amount of time. Actions that arise from everyday situations that get enriched with the expressions and interactions that happen in the vivid space are slowly captured in the exchange processes that occur in the complex space between different subjects. In this process, the significations, constructions, exchanges, and dynamics between, toward and with the subjects of the recipient society become relevant.

In the city of Mexicali, Baja California, bordering to the north with the United States, migratory processes happen every day as part of its social dynamic and everyday nature, in which 'Mexicans, Americans, Chinese, Indian, and even Russian people cohabitate since the beginning of the 21st century' (Vizcarra y Peimbert 2021, 48). For this reason, the interactions between cultures produce an effect that goes beyond biculturalism, and multiculturalism manifests and expresses itself in migrant integration. It is worth mentioning that the border crossing between Mexicali and Calexico is one of the most active in California (Vizcarra y Peimbert 2021), so the human mobility dynamic is non-stop and interactive with an effect that creates and recreates the configuration of spaces and processes that materialize in cultural manifestations and expressions.

Artistic creation and its dissemination represent a tool for social integration, therefore, in this work the contributions and cultural and artistic expressions that these Haitian migrants make in the locality are evidenced in order to account for how these expressions contribute to an integration from an intercultural approach, and how these occur from a bidirectional scope when local public, private and social actors participate.

Interculturality in Migrant Cultural Integration.

In postmodernity (Beck 1998), social processes linked to globalization occur which enables the circulation, exchange and flow of messages, goods, people and, among these; culture. This interconnection is not limited to unique spaces or territorialities, but has an extended scope where different social groups, actors, groups, and individuals converge. The relationships that are gestated in the 'complex and multifaceted' space (Shmite and Nin 2006, 171) do not seem to be limited or rigid but rather appear to be quite the opposite, they are 'recreated amid the growing interaction between different cultures [...]' (Ávila 2004, 1) the foregoing, blurring the borders or territorialities that emerge from a conception of a physical or imaginary type, with culture appearing in this framework as an element of integration of migrants.

Cultural diversity occurs in contexts where people migrate and move in temporary or permanent way, those individuals who settle in cities or places and in the processes of social interaction, make their traditions, customs, thoughts, and their worldview known, inserting culture as a 'transversal axis' (Shmite and Nin 2006, 172), which will have multiple manifestations. People in a migration context who arrive at different entities, whether bordering or not, where they can remain temporarily or indefinitely, are dynamic-interacting providers (Hernández 2008). More than a mere spatial displacement, human mobility contributes to production and reproduction of social life in the economic, social and cultural spheres.

Ferrer et al. (2014) point out that since there is a 'strong identification with both societies or their cultures, it indicates an integration or biculturalism, in which the immigrant preserves the characteristics of their culture and participates or shares the culture of the majority group at the same time' (561). Beyond biculturalism, it is desirable to transcend multiculturalism to move towards interculturalism, due to the diverse and varied cultures that are shared between members of the community of origin and with those who are foreigners.

Multiculturalism is promoted by neoliberal and Eurocentric ideologies, where cultural contact generates rejection and intolerance, giving rise to racism and xenophobia (Zárate 2014). The term also refers to the dismemberment that participates in the pluralist community and produces subgroups that are themselves homogeneous and closed communities, whereas pluralism allows us to appreciate an open society enriched by multiple belongings (Sartori 2001). Thus, pluralism is distinguished and based on tolerance, consensus and the value of diversity, the latter being one of the main distinctions between the concepts of multiculturalism and pluralism.

Intercultural perspectives provide an explanatory framework in those societies in which there is a confluence of cultural groups without one exerting deculturation processes on the other, thus avoiding the loss or blurring of ethnocultural values. Interculturalism and decoloniality are approaches that complement each other and argue for the need to overcome the hegemonic and cultural dominance of dominant colonial societies.

For the historical case in Latin America, domination implied the dispossession and repression of the original identities of the diversity of social groups (Quijano 1998). Therefore, interculturality and a true intercultural dialogue make it possible to account for the situation of power and asymmetry in which they develop to avoid being co-opted and instrumentalized by the hegemonic power and the discourse of the dominant culture (Espinoza, Valencia, and Opazo 2019). It is important to note that interculturality is linked to the colonial domination that occurred between the mestizo and white Indigenous peoples. The concept was born in Latin America linked to Indigenous education (Ferrão Candau 2010) and is introduced as part of the demands towards the state to demand a change in society where relations are more egalitarian.

Interculturality is closely linked with bilingual education seeking to preserve customs, traditions, language and put an end to colonial domination (Quijano 1998), although interculturality itself is to accept the diversity of being as it is (Walsh 2003). The decolonial approach with emphasis on interculturality according to León (2015) leads to deconstructing the knowledge made from the modern world to reconstruct them from the symmetrical and recognizing dialogue of cultural diversity, for the author interculturality 'refers to cultural exchanges of multiple routes, in an equitable relationship of different peoples, people, knowledge and cultural practices' (20).

Similarly, cultural relations are necessary because they contribute to cultural development as long as they do not become relations of domination (Zárate 2014), although Tubino (2005) also points out that it is a strategy acquired by states as part of social cohesion. On the other hand, within cultural expressions, 'art fulfills several functions, it serves as a method of communication and transmission of knowledge, it is a tool to disseminate the culture of the place of origin of migrants as well as a communication channel through which it passes the exchange of thoughts, feelings, ideas, character, personal characteristics of the artist and people's aspirations' (Apreval, Cuza, and Fernández 2011, 2).

Migrant groups find in the artistic and cultural diffusion a channel to sensitize the population of the place that receives them about their history, customs, traditions, flavors, colors and beliefs. It has even been considered that artistic creation and its dissemination represents a tool for social integration. Thus, through art, according to Carrascosa (2010), the ability to assert immigrants in the host country can be developed, where artistic expression functions as a vehicle for training in life.

However, the cultural expression of immigrants in host or receiving communities implies 'subversion' (Quijano 1998, 233). This generates new meanings which are reflected and expressed in the culture from their own subjectivity and worldview.

The integration of migrants is a multidimensional process (Giménez 2006) that includes legal and cultural aspects. Culture and its dissemination is a tool little considered, generally the importance of regularization, employment, housing and other more tangible elements is pointed out, but little is said about cultural capital, which governments could take advantage of 'as a factor of integration cultural, values of coexistence and interaction can be promoted to exchange cultural aspects that would help to build a more inclusive society, more tolerant and more respectful of civil rights' (Rivas 2017, 110).

Migrant groups have the right to show and enjoy their culture, to maintain their cultural roots of origin and to use their native language in the host country both in personal activities and in the public sphere. This enjoyment of rights will be manifested in the dissemination of art and culture as stated by the Inter-American Commission on Human Rights of the Organization of American States in resolution 04/19, principle 39 called: Right to culture, which states that 'states should encourage and support the efforts made by migrants to preserve their cultural and ethnic identity through educational and cultural activities, including the preservation of their languages and knowledge related to their cultures' (Comisión Interamericana de Derechos Humanos 2019, 15).

Co-responsibility: the Actors of the Cultural Integration of the Migrants.

Integration not only happens through individual efforts but is a collective and two-way process that involves the migrants themselves but also the host society in general and, in particular, civil society groups, government institutions as well as businessmen. In different integration plans and / or documents of the countries it is indicated that integration involves the group of immigrants, the host society and institutions and organizations (Ministerio de Trabajo y Asuntos Sociales 2017). In this sense, it highlights the role of civil society that organizes social and cultural activities that include immigrants to promote cultural exchange and dialogue.

The role of civil society is remarkable, organizing social and cultural activities that include immigrants to promote cultural exchange and dialogue. At the international level, the Convention on the Protection and Promotion of the Diversity of Cultural Expressions is established as a legally binding agreement. It guarantees artists, professionals and other cultural actors, as well as citizens of the entire world, who can create, produce, disseminate and enjoy a wide range of cultural goods, services and activities, in addition to their own (Organización de las Naciones Unidas para la Educación, la Ciencia y la Cultura 2005).

Culture is a factor of sustainable development. There is a need to create an international regulatory framework that protects the rights of all peoples, individuals, groups and societies. It is necessary to establish relationships and integration of migrants from an approach that urges respect, tolerance and protection. No less important is the promotion of international cooperation where the different actors participate in the protection and promotion of the diversity of cultural expressions.

Conceptualizing Cultural Expressions.

Culture can be understood as a network of complex factors that include the modes of production, food, health, knowledge, beliefs, art, morals, law, customs and any other habits and capacities acquired by the man as a member of society (C. González 2012), On the other hand, culture comprises structures or schemes of meanings that have been socially established and based on these, people do a series of things, where mechanisms that control and guide such behaviors are involved (Geertz 1987). In turn, cultural expressions have a broad conceptualization in the sense that they represent a set of activities that manifest traditions of a specific time and place that can be both tangible and intangible. Therefore, culture refers to a set of practices and experiences linked to nationality, ethnicity, religion, ways of life, thought and the particular praxis of a human group (Zárate 2014).

Regarding decolonial studies, León refers to the need to rethink the conceptions of culture from dominated societies with the aim of not reproducing colonial forms of knowledge and interpreting it (León 2015). Culture can also be seen as cultural capital and that can exist under the forms a) incorporated state, under the provisions and duration of the organism; b) objectified state, which includes from pictures, books, cultural assets, instruments, theories and their criticisms, among others and; c) the institutionalized state, which takes a particular form of objectification (Bourdieu 1987).

In this regard, there are different types of cultural expressions, from those that can be considered as traditional, to modern and contemporary – and even those that adapt to new modernities. All of them are part of cultural expressions since they attend defined times, spaces and circumstances and express different situations that represent the contexts under which they were created. In this regard, the following forms of cultural expression are then indicated considering to (Román 2009):

a. Oral or verbal expressions.
b. Music.
c. Physical or bodily expressions.
d. Tangible expressions (works of art, paintings, mosaics, sculptures, pottery, basketry, architectural works, mosaics, etc).

Cultural Expressions: Haitian Artists

In the case of Haitian artists that have settled permanently in the city of Mexicali, the existence of a nurtured group of plastic artists, musicians, and cultural promoters has started to gain recognition. They have taken on disseminating part of the cultural expressions of their country through painting, music, dance, language, and literature. It has even been documented that those artistic activities are means of survival for Haitians that live in this city, from artists that offer their paintings at bazaars, streets, and parks, to music groups that offer their services for different social events. Such is the case of Roger Romain and Nixon Tervine, a pair of artists who sell their paintings and pictures in public spaces or K-Fel, a music group that provides entertainment at a social club at night.

In Mexicali, Baja California the cultural expressions of Haitian immigrants happen on different platforms and are supported by a variety of public, private and academic actors. They have contributed to the dissemination and positioning of these artists in the city. The promotion that the local media give to the cultural products generated by Haitian artists is important because it shows that the community is welcoming of the new artistic offering.

Methodology and Field Work

This research is based on a qualitative methodological strategy (Erickson 1985) which is made up of two elements; documentary analysis and field work that allowed to collect the experiences of Haitian artists in Mexicali, Baja California. According to the theoretical approach of interculturalism derived from the documentary review, its elements serve as a basis for determining the necessary indicators to consider that there is a cultural integration of migrants and a contribution to the generation of interculturality. To measure this, the documentary method is used through the review of printed media such as newspapers, magazines and gazettes. It is complemented by the review of audiovisual media such as broadcasts of television programs, radio and internet platforms.

For the field work the semi-structured interview was chosen, which is characterized by collecting various topics in a broad way during its development (E. González 2008; López-Roldán, y Fachelli 2015), the case selection method was a combination of intentional selection and snowball (Baltar y Gorjup 2012), where they were interviewed a total of 4 Haitian artists residing in the city of Mexicali and who have actively participated in the dissemination of art and culture in different disciplines.

Due to the Covid-19 pandemic, and the general recommendations for social distancing (Banerjee y Nayak 2020), the interviews were conducted remotely, online, in July 2021. They were transcribed and processed in the *Atlasti* software (Varguillas 2006) to obtain codes and relationships and to measure the indicators obtained from the literature review.

To determine if the cultural expressions of Haitian artists are a manifestation of interculturalism and cultural integration, the interviewees were questioned regarding four topics:

1. When you have presented your art in Mexicali (music, painting, writing) have you felt free to express yourself? Or has someone told you that you should do it in a certain way or have they limited you in some way?
2. Do you consider that you have had enough opportunities and spaces to present your art in Mexicali?
3. Who has supported you to present your art in Mexicali?
4. How have the people of Mexicali received your artistic presentations?

One example of this artistic offering is the different local events that have been organized to promote Haitian culture, for example, the painting exhibition 'Mixturado' as part of the 'Algo Por El Centro' festival carried out in September 2017. The exhibition was presented by painters – Romain and Nixon – who expressed that they sought to show their experiences in the different countries before reaching Mexicali. In the same way, the Institute for Cultural Research-Museum of the Autonomous University of Baja California, Mexicali campus, organized the 'Culture Festival' in October 2017 and included Haitian art and painting exhibitions, as well as Haitian music and food. Nixon stated that although he received opportunities to present his paintings in diverse spaces, they have not been enough given that these opportunities have come mostly from non-formal actors and to a lesser extent from government institutions. Only once did he get the attention of a government institution to get a chance to mount an exhibition in a gallery, but this did not materialize.

In November 2017, the first Haitian culture festival was organized in Mexicali by the Civil Society Organization Movimiento Haitiano en México, founded by Haitian immigrants to represent their interests in the city. The festival had the goal of showing Haitian cuisine, culture, and folklore to the Mexicali community. Around 200 people attended, which was considered a great success.

A considerable number of Haitian artists reside in Mexicali, among them 'Woldo' who is currently promoting his most recent album in the city. This album was recorded partially in Brazil, before he came to Mexico, and finished in Mexicali with support from some local sponsors. As an artist, Woldo affirms that he has total freedom to express himself through his music and songs that he composes in Portuguese, English, French, Creole and Spanish, as well as using his own traditions. However, he comments that he has not had enough opportunities to present his music, but he attributes it to the fact that he himself has not sought them out enough. He affirms that he has received a lot of support from the Mexicali community and the media, not financially but by supporting him to promote his videos and songs on social networks. He has not received government or business support in this regard.

In May 2017, a group of Haitian entrepreneurs established the first Haitian food restaurant in the history of Mexicali to showcase the culture and gastronomy of their country. They wanted the restaurant to serve also as a meeting point for the immigrant community, where they could have the chance to meet and connect, express their needs, help their compatriots, or even watch a soccer game. There are currently two Haitian restaurants in the city, and the people have well received both from Mexicali, and other immigrant groups in the city, such as Africans and Central Americans. This restaurant also provides 'a new element to the city of Mexicali and fulfills the need of Haitians to buy and prepare their own food' (Roa et al. 2017, 50). The restaurant managers confirm in the interview that normally Mexicans like Haitian food a lot, because the Mexican people always want to travel in novelty, they always appreciate cultural diversity. Many Mexicans come to the restaurant to savor and taste Haitian food and they really love it.

Even though the taste of the food is different from Mexican, Haitians do not modify their cooking methods to adapt to Mexican taste, because Mexicans themselves congratulate Haitians for their food when they come to eat at the restaurant, then they feel comfortable. He states that despite being a popular dish, there is no support for promoting Haitian food in Mexicali, neither from the government nor from the private sector.

During the International Book Fair 2018 of the Autonomous University of Baja California, Haitian writer Gama Luidor presented and sold his first book 'Francés', which intends to support French language learning by presenting every day, practical situations. The author comments in an interview that; when presenting his work of music, he has seen on people's faces an expression of curiosity for the fact that he plays different rhythms, people are attentive to listen, and he thinks that he has all the freedom to express himself. Also add that as a foreigner presenting works of art and culture, the community is always very enthusiastic, interested in listening to reading, etc. For me, the community is very open to new things in culture. Gama has received support to spread music and poetry from government authorities, yet he considers that the spaces to perform are still limited.

The book 'Sobrevivientes: Ciudadanos del Mundo' which narrates the journey of Haitian immigrants from Brazil to Tijuana and Mexicali in 2016, as well as their arrival and settlement in the city, was presented as part of the activities of the 'Group of Actors in Favor of the Integration of Haitian Immigrants in Baja California' in 2018 organized by the School of Political and Social Science of Autonomous University of Baja California.

Lastly, in 2019, the Art and Culture Institute of Mexicali organized a cultural soiree called 'Live Haitian Culture' with presentations by the Haitian music group 'K-fel', poetry by Gama Luidor, and a free cuisine exhibition open to the general public.

Aside from the different cultural expressions that have been addressed, it is worth mentioning that culture goes beyond expressions; it has allowed strengthening or establishing aspects that reflect the new ways and customs accepted by the Haitian community and have been identified as traditional. This is how many places that offer job opportunities have been framed as traditional places to find and develop certain productive activities – meaning that these spaces have been reconfigured and acquired particular significance for Haitians. Some examples are the wholesale food market in Mexicali and selling different products on the main roads and avenues of the city (Ramírez 2020).

The new spaces identified as traditional by Haitians provide additional benefits for certain job activities. In this sense, the link generated by work allows them to learn a language in an environment that links them to the traditions and customs of recipient societies but does not limit them. Language is one of the relevant aspects of the integration of immigrants since it is involved in different processes and in daily interactions.

One experience that confirms the previously stated is the case of Woodley Augustin. He arrived in the city of Mexicali and started working at a polyurethane factory. His employer provided a Spanish language course, and he says that he learned it in eight months, although it cost him eight hours of work every day. Currently, Woodley is a Sociology student at the Autonomous University of Baja California in Mexicali (El Migrante 2020).

Final Reflections

In the different spaces occupied by migrants to carry out their activities, their customs and traditions are printed, endowed and expressed, which provide meaning and symbolism in and towards a space, where exchange processes occur that take place in different directions towards and with the original individuals of the host society, with those who are not, but who have decided to remain and including those who have just arrived. Therefore, cultural expressions and representations can serve as a binding bridge that leads to the integration of migrants.

This chapter shows how the contributions and cultural and artistic expressions that Haitian migrants make in the locality of Mexicali, Baja California contribute to an integration from an intercultural approach, and how these occur from a bidirectional scope when local public, private and social actors participate.

However, for integration to really happen, it is necessary that there are no relations of domination to consolidate social cohesion. In the case studied in this work, the artists reflect a reality where they can express themselves freely, without impositions and even in their own language, where they can manifest their culture through the expression of music, poetry, writing and writing. painting and culinary art. Where, using elements of their culture, they have been received and accepted by the different actors involved in the appreciation, dissemination, and consumption of their products.

The cultural and artistic expressions of Haitian immigrants happen as a reflection of the road toward an integration process, which has a pending agenda that the main actors have still to address, for example, it is necessary to create more formal spaces where Haitian artists can present their cultural offerings, for government institutions to help promote their art, culture, and products so that this diffusion is made from formal platforms. Also, the actors involved; media, academia, government and private groups formulate joint strategies so that this diffusion has an even greater impact on the host society and reaches a wider public.

The way cultural integration has happened has been optimal by promoting Haitian art, culture, and food at different cultural events in the city promoted by the government, academia, civil society, and the media. We believe that these expressions help the socio-cultural integration of immigrants and that they are a tool to promote and help them become a part of the receiving society.

In this sense, we emphasize the importance of supporting and promoting Haitian art and culture dissemination initiatives by the government, business, academic, and media sectors, because the more the Haitian culture is known by the community, the integration process will be more fluid and dynamic.

Tables

Table 12.1. Characteristics of the Interviewees. Source: Own creation.

NAME	ACTIVITY	DATE OF INTERVIEW
Nixon Tervine	Painting	24/07/2021
Jean Pierre Benoits (Woldo)	Music	24/07/2021
Gama Luidor	Poetry and Music	25/07/2021
Cucetho Despeignes	Cooking	23/07/2021

Table 12.2. Cultural Dissemination Activities with Haitian Artist Participation in Mexicali, Baja California. Source: Own creation.

Type Of Actor	Name	Activity
Media	La Crónica newspaper (2017)	Promotion of Haitian artists on the front page.
	Televisa Channel 4 (2017)	Promotion of paintings made by Haitian artists.
	Radio Fórmula Mexicali (2018)	Promotion of paintings made by Haitian artists.
Civil Society Organization	Algo por el centro A.C. (2017)	Promotion of paintings made by Haitian artists.
	Civil Organization Movimiento Haitiano en México (2017)	"Haiti in Mexicali" Festival. Promotion of Haitian art, paintings, music, dancing, and gastronomy.
Educational/ academic	Autonomous University of Baja California (2017)	Culture Festival, Haitian art and painting exhibition, music, and cuisine.
	Autonomous University of Baja California (2018)	International Book Fair, promotion of the work of Haitian writers in Mexicali.
	Autonomous University of Baja California (2018)	Presentation of the book "Survivors" written by Pascal Ustin Dubuison, Haitian author.
Government	Art and Culture Institute of Mexicali (2019)	"Live Haitian Culture" Festival. Promotion of Haitian music, poetry, and cuisine.
Entrepreneurs	Haitian owner (2018 to date)	Haitian dish sale with promotion of cultural events and presentation of Haitian artists in Mexicali.

References

Apreval, Asela, María Cuza, y Laura Fernández. 2011. Las funciones sociales del arte desde la perspectiva del arte santiaguero: incidencia en la formación cultural del individuo. *Revista electrónica Contribuciones a las Ciencias Sociales*. https://www.eumed.net/rev/cccss/14/mhf.html

Ávila, Javier. 2004. Globalización y rituales religiosos andinos transnacionales. El culto al taytacha Qoyllur Ritti en Cusco, Lima y Nueva York. *Gazeta de Antropología*. https://doi.org/10.30827/Digibug.7262

Baltar, Fabiola, y María Tatiana Gorjup. 2012. Online mixted sampling: An application in hidden populations. *Intangible Capital* 8 (1): 123–49. https://doi.org/10.3926/ic.294

Banerjee, Tannista, y Arnab Nayak. 2020. U.S. County Level Analysis to Determine If Social Distancing Slowed the Spread of COVID-19. *Revista Panamericana de Salud Pública* 44 (julio): 1. https://doi.org/10.26633/RPSP.2020.90

Beck, Ulrich. 1998. *La sociedad el riesgo: Hacia una nueva modernidad*. Paidós Básica. Barcelona: Paidós.

Bourdieu, Pierre. 1987. Los tres estados del capital cultural. Traducido por Monique Landesmann. *Sociológica* 2 (5). http://www.sociologicamexico.azc.uam.mx/index.php/Sociologica/article/view/1043/1015

Carrascosa, María. 2010. Creación Artística, Inmigración y Género. 5: 14.

Comisión Interamericana de Derechos Humanos. 2019. Principios interamericanos sobre los derechos humanos de todas las personas migrantes, refugiadas, apátridad y las víctimas de la trata de personas. Organización de los Estados Americanos. https://reliefweb.int/sites/reliefweb.int/files/resources/Principios%20DDHH%20migrantes%20-%20ES.pdf

El Migrante. 2020. La comunidad haitiana en Mexicali, Baja California. https://internews.org/elmigrante

Erickson, Frederick. 1985. Qualitative Methods in Research on Teaching. Institute for Research on Teaching, College of Education, Michigan State University. https://files.eric.ed.gov/fulltext/ED263203.pdf

Espinoza, Alex, Juan Valencia, y Carolina Opazo. 2019. Interculturalidad y (de)colonialidad. Apuntes para un estado del arte. *Interciencia* 44 (2): 101–7.

Ferrão Candau, Vera Maria. 2010. Educación Intercultural En América Latina: Distintas Concepciones y Tensiones Actuales. *Estudios Pedagógicos (Valdivia)* 36 (2): 333–42. https://doi.org/10.4067/S0718-07052010000200019

Ferrer, Raquel, Jorge Palacio, Olga Hoyos, y Camilo Madariaga. 2014. Acculturation process and Immigrant's Adaptation: Individual characteristics and Social Networks. *Psicología desde el Caribe* 31 (3): 557-76. https://doi.org/10.14482/psdc.31.3.4766

Geertz, Clifford. 1987. *La interpretación de las culturas*. México: GEDISA.

Giménez, Carlos. 2006. *Qué es la inmigración: ¿Problema u oportunidad? ¿Cómo lograr la integración de los inmigrantes? ¿Multiculturalismo o interculturalidad?* Barcelona: RBA Libros.

González, Carlos. 2012. «Caracterización del concepto Cultura en la didáctica de las lenguas». *Cartaphilus. Revista de investigación y crítica estética* 10: 84–108. https://doi.org/10.6018/cartaphilus

González, Eva. 2008. Un proceso migratorio estudiantil (pre-migración, migración y post-migración): jóvenes marroquíes en la Universidad de Granada. *Revista Electrónica de Investigación Educativa* 10 (2): 13.

Hernández, A. 2008. De la dialéctica a la trialéctica del espacio: aproximaciones al pensamiento de Milton Santos y Edward Soja. En *Pensar y habitar la ciudad: Afectividad, memoria y significado en el espacio urbano contemporáneo*.

León, Franklin. 2015. Estudios culturales, decolonialidad e interculturalidad: lo particular y lo universal en tiempos de globalización. 7: 7.

López-Roldán, Pedro, y Sandra Fachelli. 2015. *Metodología de la Investigación Social Cuantitativa*. 1a ed. Barcelona: Universidad Autónoma de Barcelona.

Ministerio de Trabajo y Asuntos Sociales. 2017. Indicadores de integración migrante, propuesta para contribuir a la elaboración de un sistema de indicadores comunes de la integración. Dirección general de integración de los migrantes, España.

Organización de las Naciones Unidas para la Educación, la Ciencia y la Cultura. 2005. Convención sobre la protección y la promoción de la diversidad de las expresiones culturales. http://www.unesco.org/new/es/culture/themes/cultural-diversity/cultural-expressions/the-convention/convention-text

Quijano, Anibal. 1998. Colonialidad del poder, cultura y conocimiento en América Latina. *Ecuador Debate*, Descentralización: entre lo global y lo local, 44: 227–38.

Ramírez, Kenia. 2020. El camino hacia la integración de los migrantes haitianos en Mexicali. En *Multiculturalismo e integración: La migración haitiana en Baja California*. Baja California: Universidad Autónoma de Baja California.

Rivas, Ramón D. 2017. Migraciones, causas y nuevas identidades. *Revista de Museología «Kóot»*, n.º 7 (abril): 101–17. https://doi.org/10.5377/koot.v0i7.2985

Roa, Reryna, Ernesto Santillán, Dennise Islas, y Yara López. 2017. *Migración, Educación y Sociedad: Visiones y experiencias desde la frontera*. Colombia: REDIPE.

Román, Raquel. 2009. Las expresiones culturales tradicionales en las normas sobre derecho de autor. En *Textos de la nueva cultura de la propiedad intelectual*, UNAM, 141–61. México.

Sartori, Giovanni. 2001. *La sociedad multiétnica: pluralismo, multiculturalismo y extranjeros*. Madrid: Grupo Santillana de Ediciones.

Shmite, Stella Maris, y María Cristina Nin. 2006. Geografía cultural. Un recorrido teórico a través del diálogo de autores contemporáneos. *Huellas*, n.º 11: 168–94.

Varguillas, Carmen. 2006. El uso de atlas.Ti y la creatividad del investigador en el análisis cualitativo de contenido upel. Instituto pedagógico rural el mácaro. *Laurus Revista de Educación* 12: 73–87.

Vizcarra, Berenice, y Alejandro José Peimbert. 2021. «Infraestructura y sustentabilidad social ante la multiculturalidad en la frontera norte de México». *Contexto* 14 (22). https://doi.org/10.29105/contexto15.22-3

Walsh, Catherine. 2003. Las geopolíticas del conocimiento y colonialidad del poder. *Polis*. http://journals.openedition.org/polis/7138

Zárate, Adolfo. 2014. Interculturalidad y decolonialidad. *Tabula Rasa*, n.º 20: 91–107. https://doi.org/10.25058/20112742.172

Note on Indexing

Our books do not have indexes due to the prohibitive cost of assembling them. If you are reading this book in paperback and want to find a particular word or phrase you can do so by downloading a free PDF version of this book from the E-International Relations website. View the e-book in any standard PDF reader, enter your search terms in the search box, and then find what you are looking for. If you are using apps (or devices) to read our e-books, you should also find word search functionality in those.

You can download all of our books at: https://www.e-ir.info/publications/

www.ingramcontent.com/pod-product-compliance
Lightning Source LLC
Chambersburg PA
CBHW071611080526
44588CB00010B/1091